JOE GRIMALDI
HIS LIFE AND THEATRE

JOE GRIMALDI

HIS LIFE AND THEATRE

SECOND EDITION

Richard Findlater

CAMBRIDGE UNIVERSITY PRESS

CAMBRIDGE

LONDON · NEW YORK · MELBOURNE

Published by the Syndics of the Cambridge University Press
The Pitt Building, Trumpington Street, Cambridge CB2 1RP
Bentley House, 200 Euston Road, London NW1 2DB
32 East 57th Street, New York, NY 10022, USA
296 Beaconsfield Parade, Middle Park, Melbourne 3206, Australia

First published under the title *Grimaldi: King of Clowns* by MacGibbon & Kee 1955
Second edition first published by Cambridge University Press 1978

**Printed in Great Britain at the
University Press, Cambridge**

Library of Congress Cataloguing in Publication Data
Findlater, Richard, 1921 –
Joe Grimaldi, his life and theatre.
First published in 1955 under title: Grimaldi, king of clowns.
1. Grimaldi, Joseph, 1779–1837. 2. Clowns – Great Britain – Biography. I. Title.
GV1811.G7F56 1978   791.3'3'0924 [B] 78–7465
ISBN 0 521 22221 4 hard covers
ISBN 0 521 29407 X paperback

Contents

Illustrations

Colour plates
Between pages 140 and 141

One

Prelude

'HERE WE ARE AGAIN!' With a screech of laughter, the Clown jumps through the painted wall of time, turns a somersault head-first into the present, and comes down upon our stage with straddled legs and arms akimbo. 'How are you tomorrow?' he asks, and his oven-mouth splits into a rapturous grin which joins the red triangles on his whitened cheeks; the blue cockle quivers on his bald-pate wig as he screws his nose upon one side; and as he surveys his audience with round and rolling eyes, he shrieks again in an ecstasy of glee, ready for any roguery and sure of our approval. Thief, killer and everybody's darling, there he stands in his multi-coloured livery of frills and flaps and patches, his face marked with the warpaint of his trade, his body tensed for tumbles, jumps and falls. With toes turned in and hands thrust deep into the vast pockets of his baggy breeches, a cornucopia of stolen goods, he is the squat and unmistakable monarch of the English pantomime. His royal carriage is a child's cradle wheeled with cheeses, drawn by dogs; his sceptre is a poker; oysters, pies and sausages are his regalia; and around him his obedient Court — quicksilver Harlequin, dancing Columbine and doddering Pantaloon — wait for the Christmas chase to continue, in a world of lost laughter.

Here is Joey the Clown, the first of 10,000 Joeys who took their name from him; here is the genius of English fun, in the holiday splendour of his reign at Sadler's Wells and Covent Garden; here is Joseph Grimaldi, who during his lifetime (1778 to 1837) was generally acclaimed as the funniest and best-loved man in the British theatre. Look how he strides across the stage, 'some dozen paces to the mile',[1] then vaults and capers in the air, squeaking in a delirium of mischief. See with what joy serene he pockets a pig or steals a string of sausages; watch him nurse a saw-dust baby or serenade a chambermaid; listen to him sing, with changing voices, some rhyming nonsense that sets the theatre in a roar. Now he appears all topsy-turvy, with two odd eyebrows, a pair of left-and-right eyes, a wry nose, a crooked mouth, two left legs and a free and easy body without any bone in it and

9

apparently without any centre of gravity.[2] Setting himself to rights with one irresistible smirk, he begins to woo Columbine or to harry Harlequin. He performs one of his 'tricks of construction': making a man out of Covent Garden vegetables ('old Joe Frankenstein'); or sending up a Hussar officer by parodying his gear with coal scuttles, a ladies' muff, and household bits and pieces; or turning himself into a one-man band or Pantaloon into a comic hybrid monster. In ways that seem incomparably, infectiously funny, he guzzles, gets drunk, falls in love, is tortured, beats people up, mimics an opera singer, a ballerina, a juggler or a tragedian. Joe Grimaldi is himself, as one may see, not only a comic but a dancer, acrobat, singer, mime, swordsman, at home in farce, melodrama and spectacle as well as pantomime, accustomed to play ogres, animals, savages and spirits, as well as clowns. He is, moreover, not only a practical joker but a 'practical satirist', pillorying the fashions of the day. Not only can he set the house alight with his own laughter ('Who can relapse so utterly into giggling boyish joy?'), but he can make the audience cry as well. When he sits down on the stage and commiserates with an 'oyster crossed in love' the children laugh and then weep to see 'how his ridiculous and excessive sorrow makes its way palpably through all the grotesque paint'.[3] He can frighten them, too, with his own fear ('Who can be frightened like Grimaldi?') — as when he gives the dagger-scene from *Macbeth*, still in his clownish motley but dead serious, hushing the audience with the terror of his mime. Scarcely one Shakespearian word is heard in this sendup of 'straight' acting style; but it is never what Grimaldi *says* that matters. It is what he *does* and what he *is*. His whole body speaks, and even his knees 'become funny'. He is a walking grotesque, yet he seems 'extravagantly natural'. Half-rascal, halffool, he is criminal and innocent at once, an ancient of days and a London guttersnipe, immortal and bang up to the minute: the beloved enemy of law and order, family authority, class distinction and moral convention: a legendary name invoked as King of all the Clowns ...

From 1806 until 1823, when Grimaldi was forced into premature retirement by crippling illness, he won fame and affection as a national character in the shape of Joey. He featured in dozens of best-selling prints (some sixty are listed in the Harvard catalogue alone), and broadsheets of his most popular songs sold in their thousands, often with pictures of him in action. Offstage, Grimaldi was a quiet, friendly, nervous man, given to melancholia. Shortish, stocky, dark and sallow, with something of a boxer's build and with a dancer's strength in his legs, he appeared to some people to be as Italian as his name. To others there was 'something of the Jew' about him. In his lifetime there seemed 'always some mystery about Joe's birth. You could never get him to talk much about his family' (apart from his son). In fact this 'mortal Jupiter of practical joke — the Michael Angelo of buffoonery' (in J. P. Harley's words) was the bastard son of a clowning, syphilitic Italian ballet-master and a Cockney chorus girl over forty years his junior.

Grimaldi has become one of the apparently immortal names of international show business in the West. Yet his songs have long been forgotten; the harlequinade in which he starred seems as obsolete as the brougham or the crinoline; and his Clown is barely discernible in the third-grade Joeys of the circus. A year after his death H. D. Miles wrote in a biography, 'Grimaldi will in a few years be but a name; and our children's children must be content to take the tale of his merits on the credit of their ancestors. We believe in Garrick, whom we never saw, and those to come may believe in Grimaldi: for though in a low department of art, he was the most wonderful creature of his day, and far more unapproachable in his excellence than Kean and Kemble in theirs.'[4] Grimaldi's genius has, indeed, been taken on trust by posterity, but on far less evidence than that of Kean or Garrick. The best of their material endures in Collected Works: Joey's comedy burned away with his last laugh. The *Memoirs* published in 1838 give no more than perfunctory attention to his Clownship;[5] and no study of any kind appeared in book-form between Miles's plagiarised Life and the first edition of this portrait in 1955, apart from a brilliant chapter in Maurice Willson Disher's brilliant *Clowns and Pantomimes* (1925), to which I here acknowledge my own debt. The legend was so hazy that Grimaldi has often been misinterpreted as a circus clown, although he never — to our knowledge — appeared in the ring (as an adult performer, at least).[6]

When I set out to write this book in 1953, the questions I hoped to answer included: what was he like as a man? How was he so funny? What did he do? I looked first for evidence in books by the Clown's contemporaries, but this proved unexpectedly scarce.

In book after book concerned with the Regency stage his name is ignored, even by so detailed a chronicler as the Rev. John Genest. Scores of 'straight' players who were not much better than serviceable artists were more fully commemorated at the time than was a great buffoon like Grimaldi, because they were employed in a *respectable* branch of the theatre, while pantomime was despised as vulgar or childish nonsense by the majority of educated playgoers. 'It will hardly be expected that we should enter into a detail of these disgraceful mummeries which custom has sanctioned, but which custom is more honoured in the breach than in the observance. The dignity of criticism would be degraded by the inquiry, and we shall rather content ourselves with entering a decided, though unavailing protest, against what we consider as an insult to the common understanding of mankind.' This heartfelt, somewhat incoherent cry of indignation, uttered by a critic in the *Theatrical Inquisitor* in 1814, voices a common attitude among the writing classes during Grimaldi's lifetime, and it illuminates the difficulty of discovering facts about these 'disgraceful mummeries' and the lives of those engaged in them.

'A list of the pieces in which he appeared is valueless,' says the *Dictionary of National Biography*, 'and his adventures, though they furnish material for a volume, are to a great extent imaginary, or consist of accidents as are to be expected in his occupation.' This book is written in the belief that there is more to Grimaldi's life than such a catalogue of 'pieces' and accidents, and that his story — as a man and a Clown — needs to be retold. Yet the main authority for the events of his private life is the 'volume' to which the *Dictionary of National Biography* refers — the *Memoirs* of 1838, which has been indispensable in the preparation of this portrait (see Appendix C). The *Memoirs* are among the most disappointing reminiscences in our theatrical literature. They contain a selection of incidents from Grimaldi's original manuscript autobiography, abridged and 'improved' by two successive editors, and although a revised edition in 1846 exposed some of the book's grosser errors, no subsequent attempt was made to complete their correction or to enlarge the notes until my own edition published by MacGibbon & Kee in 1968. Here I have no space to consider in detail the contradictions and inaccuracies of the *Memoirs*, and I have omitted many of the anecdotes: this book is intended not as a replacement for the *Memoirs*, but as a companion portrait. With all that book's weaknesses it still suggests the picture of Grimaldi as he saw himself, however improbable or dull some of the adventures may seem, and — what is more to the point — it is all we have, in print, from the Clown, however indirectly. (The publication in 1969 of David Mayer's admirable *Harlequin in his Element: The English Pantomime, 1806–1836* has redressed the balance as far as Grimaldi's Clownship is concerned.)

The *Memoirs*, however, is not the only biographical material in existence. A hundred years ago, in a London sale catalogue, Grimaldi's autobiographical manuscript was put up for sale, with the invitation: 'It is now time for a new and true life of Grimaldi. Let it come out with all the garrulity and egoism of the original manuscript, and the public will gladly recognise the old familiar "Here we are again!" '[7] The purchaser did not accept the challenge, and the manuscript was never seen again in public. When I began my investigations into the life of Grimaldi a quarter-century ago I was assured that Joe's autobiography had been destroyed; but after persistent inquiries I found that it was in the possession of a British collector who preferred to keep secret both its existence and his own name. The ban on its publication or even consultation, still maintained in 1977, has meant that the 'new and true life' cannot yet be completely achieved, and it is impossible to test the claim of the 1878 auctioneer that 'The Clown was as true to his pen as he was to his calling.' Yet even if the manuscript were now brought out of its hiding-place — which, as this book goes to press, seems tantalizingly possible — the story would still require radical editing and detailed annotation, for it seems evident from our garbled version of the *Memoirs* that fact and fantasy were often indistinguishable in Grimaldi's mind. Much of his life must always remain — like the simplicity of his art — a mystery. Here I have attempted to provide a fuller picture of his private and public life than the reader will find in the *Memoirs*, set against the background of the times in which he lived and the trade in which he worked.

With the co-operation of the Cambridge University Press, I have — within the framework of the original edition in 1955 — substantially revised and rewritten many sections of the text, adding information that has come to my notice since the book was first published or that was then excluded for reasons of space. I have corrected errors of fact, changed interpretations and emphases, and extirpated some of the more grossly sentimental and rhetorical prose. I have also changed a number of the black-and-white illustrations, and the publishers have allowed me to add four colour plates.

The principal sources of material, outside the *Memoirs*, are the Percival Collection in the British Library; Grimaldiana in the Finsbury Library, and the libraries of the Garrick Club, the Shakespeare Institute in Stratford-upon-Avon, the Harvard Theatre Collection and the British Theatre Museum. I am also indebted to the archives of the Greater London Council; the Kay Robertson Collection; the Raymond Mander and Joe Mitchenson Collection; the British Library; the Minet Library, Lambeth; the Public Record Office; and the libraries of Birmingham, Bath, Canterbury, Chester, Edinburgh, Exeter, Finsbury, Glasgow, Liverpool, Manchester, Portsmouth, Weymouth and Woolwich. I am especially grateful to George Nash and his staff in the British Theatre Museum; Eileen Robinson of the Shakespeare Institute library; Kay Robertson; George Speaight; Dr David Mayer; and the late Laurence Thompson, who gave me some excellent advice on the first draft of this book. I should also like to express my thanks for their courtesy and assistance to the Secretary and Committee of the Garrick Club, who gave me permission to quote from the Grimaldiana in their keeping; to L. G. Dibdin and George Speaight, for allowing me to quote from the memoirs of Charles Dibdin the Younger, before their publication by the Society for Theatre Research; and to the following who have helped me in matters concerning Grimaldi during the past twenty-five years, though not all are here to see the result — Harry Beard, Gerald Forsyth, Alec Clunes, Sir St Vincent Troubridge, C. H. Donelan, W. MacQueen Pope, Barry Lupino, Leslie Staples, Frances Fleetwood, Thomas Walton, Martin Holmes, T. R. Fyvel, Reg Davis-Poynter, Reginald Rouse, Professor Nicola Mangini, Rose-Marie Moudous and Romany Watt, who as my wife patiently entertained Joe Grimaldi for more years than I care to remember.

A note on usage: I have used 'Joe' for Grimaldi and 'Joey' for the Clown he created; 'clown' is employed to describe comic pantomimists before the creation of Clown in 1800 and buffoons in general; and 'the *Memoirs*' refers to the *Memoirs of Joseph Grimaldi*, first published in 1838.

Two

The history of mirth is mainly Italian.—M. WILLSON
DISHER

A WEEK BEFORE THE CHRISTMAS SEASON began in the two great theatres of Georgian London, while the pantomime rehearsals were approaching their usual climax of disorder, an illegitimate son was born to the Pantaloon of Drury Lane by an erstwhile Columbine, his Cockney mistress. The child made his entrance on Friday, 18th December, somewhere in Stanhope Street, Clare Market — a slummy labyrinth of old frame houses where now the London School of Economics stands — and ten days later, when their show was again postponed (till 8th January), his parents took him down to the Strand to be baptized at the nearby church of St Clement Danes.[1] This was an aptly seasonal arrival for a boy who was to become the greatest star in the history of English pantomime.

The news of his birth, which soon spread around the capital's stage colony, provoked a good deal of mildly scandalized laughter and delighted gossip in the pubs and green-rooms. Bastardy was by no means uncommon in that age, but the humour of the occasion lay, for London's theatre-folk, in the timing of the birth and the characters of the parents. Rebecca Brooker, the mother, was a young, obscure dancer-singer in the Drury Lane company; but her lover, Signor Giuseppe Grimaldi, was something of a theatrical institution — an institution, moreover, which at 65 years of age was taking a new lease of life. Joe was the *second* illegitimate child born to him that December. A few days before Joe was delivered, another of the old man's mistresses, Ann Perry, gave birth to Henrietta Marguerite, who also took the name of Grimaldi. And the Signor was still married to a former dancer in the Drury Lane chorus, who had borne him four daughters in the past decade. It was as good as a pantomime, said the actors over their ale or brandy, to see how 'old Grim' received the ribald congratulations of his colleagues and to hear him swearing, in his notoriously broken English, that he would put the 'little ting' on the stage as soon as he could walk. (By his third Christmas Joe was, indeed, at work.)[2]

Within a few weeks of the birth Rebecca Brooker was back in the *corps de ballet*, and her baby made his first acquaintance with the London theatre in the dressing-rooms and green-rooms of Drury Lane. To his mother, a butcher's daughter born in Holborn,[3] the Theatre Royal was a second home, for she had worked here, off and on, since her childhood, when Mr Brooker rented her to David Garrick as an occasional fairy; and the Signor had been in almost continuous employment at Drury Lane since his arrival in England twenty years earlier, most of the time as a ballet-master, a role which combined the duties of dancer, pantomimist and part-time choreographer. Young Joe's parents were an ill-matched couple, not only in age and nationality but also in temperament and status, and their relationship seems to have been stormy and irregular.[4] Yet Rebecca bore the old man two or more children, and Joe owed some of his success to this backstage misalliance. On the one side, a short, dark-haired, sallow-skinned London girl, with a sharp tongue and a talent for comic dancing: on the other, a beady-eyed, grey-haired Italian, a born intriguer and a natural comic, superstitious, eccentric and cruel, 45 years her senior. From his mother Joe inherited, one may suppose, the native common sense and humour of a line of City tradesmen and shopkeepers; on his father's side he stemmed from a cosmopolitan family of dancers, acrobats and mimes, with a tradition of all-round theatrical skill. In Joe the Brooker and Grimaldi strains combined to create a living caricature of John Bullishness, whose native comedy was expressed by a most un-English capacity for mime.

There were other debts. The relative lack of comfort and security in Joe's early home life, his father's way of running at least three families at once, and the harshness of his paternal task-master were probably necessary stages in the education of a Clown. Audiences of Regency London may well have been grateful that Grimaldi's childhood was marred by bullying, poverty and (above all) loneliness. Has *any* great clown ever enjoyed a happy childhood? It was to his father, too, that Joe owed his first job, and the Signor's professional influence sustained him in the early days of his apprenticeship to laughter. Yet the Signor may also have helped to end Joe's career prematurely, for the Grimaldi inheritance appears to have included syphilis.

16

HENCE, LOATHED MELANCHOLY — this was the auspicious, Miltonic motto above the stage on which Joe Grimaldi began his career as a public entertainer.[5] The day was Easter Monday, 1781, and the place was a 'summer theatre' in the fields of Islington which for many years had been the semi-rural rendezvous of Londoners in search of holiday amusement. It was at Sadler's Wells, beside the New River, that the future King of Clowns faced an audience for the first time. He was twenty-eight months old.

Sadler's Wells Theatre, where Joe Grimaldi worked for the rest of his professional life, stood on the site of a pleasure garden opened in 1684, when a medicinal spring was discovered in the grounds of the original Mr Sadler, a surveyor of the highways. To amuse the customers who came to drink the waters, Sadler engaged acrobats and tumblers (who performed in the open air), a dulcimer-player, and a band. This enterprising showman built a wooden Musick House, to which a stage was later added, and the timber playhouse was still doing a thriving trade when Joe's father came to the Wells as a ballet-master; but during the Signor's brief régime it was pulled down by a local builder, Mr Rosoman, who replaced it in 1765 with a stone theatre, built in seven weeks at a cost of £4,225. When Rosoman, whose name is still commemorated in a local street, retired in 1772 with a large fortune, the management was taken over by Thomas King and two more or less sleeping-partners, Arnold and Serjeant; and it was Tom King, the original Sir Peter Teazle and the Signor's executor, who gave Joe Grimaldi his first job.

In Rosoman's day you could buy a seat at the Wells for three-pence, and the programme — repeated four or five times a day — included hornpipes, ballad-singing, tumbling, and 'a kind of pantomime ballet':

> There was drolls, hornpipe dancing and showing of postures,
> With frying black puddings, and opening of oysters:
> With salt-boxes, solos, and gallery folks squawling;
> The taphouse guests roaring, and mouth-pieces bawling.

For the audience it was Liberty Hall: Charles Macklin recalled, at the end of the century, that 'we smoked, and drank porter and rum and water as much as we could pay for, and every man had

17

his doxy that liked it, and so forth', and that it was 'a good deal the baiting-place of thieves and highwaymen.'[6] But by the time of young Grimaldi's advent, the noise had diminished, the prices had increased, and the thieves and highwaymen were no longer conspicuous — inside the theatre, at least. In the words of a ballad of 1775:

> *Since tasteless tea 'gan to prevail*
> *With rural 'Squire, instead of ale,*
> *And lank hair lengthened to a tail.*

> *The barn grew larger much, and higher,*
> *Assum'd a proud, ambitious spire,*
> *Fit for the Doctor, or the 'Squire . . .*

In point of comfort, there was little difference in 1781 between Sadler's Wells and Drury Lane, the theatres which served as Grimaldi's nursery and university. At the Wells, as at the Lane, you paid eighteenpence for a place to sit upon a hard, wooden bench in the pit; and on a popular night you had to do battle for this place, for until seat reservations were introduced a generation later unarmed combat was a recognized means of entrance. Aggression was, indeed, endemic among eighteenth-century playgoers, who were often ready to demonstrate their inalienable rights of disapproval by tearing down the curtains, breaking up the benches, and bombarding the stage. Throughout the evening the theatre was fully lit, for there was no darkening of the auditorium, and Grimaldi, standing on the stage, could see many faces quite clearly instead of the pale blur which represents the audience for the modern actor. He was, moreover, nearer to some playgoers at the Wells or the Lane than his successors at either theatre today, for the stage still projected a little way beyond the proscenium arch into the audience and there were stage boxes on each side. Sadler's Wells was the more intimate of the two theatres — an important distinction in the history of pantomime — and the audiences at Islington were on the whole noisier, rougher and less sophisticated than those at Covent Garden and Drury Lane: at this time the Wells playgoer was entitled, for another sixpence, to a pint of wine — Port, Mountain, Lisbon or Punch — a privilege which may have kindled his traditional appetite for 'Jack

Pudding's antic fun'. During the performances the customers not only drank but ate on a large scale: 'in the pit there is a shelf running along the back of the seats on which the occupants order bottles of wine, glasses, ham, cold chops and pasties to be placed ...', wrote a German traveller in 1786. Their appetite matched the clown's.

Although, since Rosoman built the theatre, the suburbs had edged a little way out into the fields, Sadler's Wells was still distinguished in Grimaldi's childhood by a pastoral setting. 'The district is very lovely,' noted Sophie von la Roche in 1786, writing of the nearby Spa, 'large meadows alive with herds of excellent cows; lakes with trees in front of the house itself and numerous avenues with delightful tables and benches for visitors, under trees hung with tiny lamps. In the open temple lower-class lasses, sailors and other young people were dancing.' Yet although thousands of Londoners made the expedition to Sadler's Wells every summer, playgoing by the New River had its dangers. Gang crime flourished in those days before the Peelers, and many customers returning from the Wells were attacked and robbed along the New Road or across Spa Fields, the stretch of common-land which for generations had been a playground for duck-hunting, prize-fighting, bull-baiting and other democratic sports. Theatre managers were obliged to offer armed protection, and on contemporary playbills it was announced that: 'A Patrole of Horse and Foot are stationed, from Sadler's Wells Gate, along the New Road to Tottenham-Court Turnpike: likewise the City Road to Moorfields; also to St John Street; and across the Spa Fields to Rosoman Row, from the hours of Eight to Eleven.'

Such precautions were not, however, needed during the winter months, when the theatre closed down. Sadler's Wells opened its doors every Easter Monday, and usually shut them in the second week of October, for winter theatricals were the prerogative of the royal 'patent' theatres (Drury Lane and Covent Garden) which enjoyed a monopoly of the 'legitimate' drama. At the Wells all dialogue was doomed to have a musical accompaniment, however perfunctory; no competition was allowed with the prose repertory of the 'patents'; and the theatre presented pantomimes, ballets and burlettas, 'feats of strength and agility' as they were known on the bills, juggling, tumbling, and tight-rope walking, singers, dancers and animal trainers — in a word, 'variety'. This was the world in which Joe Grimaldi spent most of his working life, among the age-old international confraternity of the fairs.

* * *

On the night of Easter Monday, 1781, the brightly-lit theatre was crowded with noisy Cockneys who had just returned from the great annual spree of the Epping Hunt, and were ready — in holiday mood — to give a good send-off to the new season. It was a long programme, for audiences then were gluttons for entertainment and would sit on wooden benches in a hot, smoky atmosphere for six hours or more, to get their money's worth from the management. It was also a typical programme, unremarkable to posterity except for the names of Master and Miss Grimaldi among the dancers.

The star of the evening was 'the inimitable Mr Saunders', a slack-wire artist who stood on his head on a drinking-glass, balanced a French horn on his lips and sounded a 'minuet' without using his hands; and, what is more, performed 'a continual Summerset on the Wire, while Fireworks are playing from different parts of his Body'. (He was at Islington twenty years before, in the Signor's day). The Wells also introduced 'Rope-Dancing by the most capital performers in the known world (lately arrived) viz. Signor Placido, and the Little Devil' (artists who later befriended young Grimaldi); and 'a new Serio-Comic, Prophetic, Political, Musical Piece, consisting of Recitatives, Songs, Choruses, Dancing, etc., The Medley, or a Masque in Masquerade', whose setting — 'a very striking part of Mr Cox's Museum '— was billed as one of its main attractions. And, of course, there was a pantomime — no Easter Monday bill would have been complete without one — called, in true traditional style, *The Wizard of the Silver Rocks: or, Harlequin's Release*.

What did the young Grimaldis feel that night, as they danced out upon the stage in their carefully rehearsed routines, watched from the wings by their grim old father? For weeks he had coached them in the simple steps required, beating them when they made mistakes, sending them off to bed with bread and water, until they were as perfect as he could expect. For the Signor, a bad performance would be a black mark on his professional reputation. His eldest daughter Mary, who was about 18 years old, was a shield between his anger and the tiny, uncomprehending boy, who moved among the veterans of the Wells — Tom Lowe, the singer, and Peter Garman, the tumbler — like a scared but nimble puppet; but it is to be hoped that the children did not stumble as they moved through the measures of the dance, and that the pantomime went off without a hitch. Perhaps when, at midnight, the young Grimaldis set off for home, their father had some words of praise for the Easter Monday ordeal; or perhaps he beat them, on principle; yet the memory of that first appearance — of the shouting crowds in front and the tumbling, singing, dancing giants around him — remained in Joe's mind as his initiation into the real business of life. Whatever the *quality* of his first appearance, it had no bearing upon young Joe's future: his career was to be on the stage from that day forward. This was the way in which the old man had learned his craft, in the fairs and market-places of France and Italy, and it was obviously the road — so he decided — which his baby son must follow. It was not unusual in those days for parents to launch their children upon the stage at what may seem to us a shockingly early age; in the 'variety' theatre, especially, boys and girls began their training in tumbling, dancing and acrobatics almost as soon as they were out of the cradle, and these infants were earning their keep at an age when modern children are at a nursery school. The young Grimaldis grew up with the sons and daughters of other Sadler's Wells performers, finding their practical education behind the floats (as the footlights were known): Joe followed in the footsteps of his half-sisters, and two years later his brother John followed *him*. Soon after Joe's début at the Wells, the Signor introduced him to Drury Lane, and in these theatres his son spent the greater part of the next twenty-five years.[9]

The boy was not deprived of orthodox schooling, but it was taken distractedly and in snatches. For some years he attended a boarding school at Putney, when the pantomime finished at Drury Lane, and remained there until the Sadler's Wells season opened at Easter. Mr Ford's academy was favoured by other theatrical fathers, including Thomas Harris, the chief proprietor of Covent Garden, but Joe's attendance there was sometimes no more than two months in the year.[10] As he wrote a fairly good hand and a comparatively literate letter, he must have had a grounding in the meagre curriculum of the times, but whatever he learned, in whatever school, it was the education of the green-room, the stage and the streets that meant more to the future clown. From his father he learned how to use a sword in stage combats, how to time his jokes, how to perform the acrobatic feats and dance routines which were the stock-in-trade of Continental *forains*; and this part of his education is suggested in a song of 1803:

I'm not the first Clown, who when merry made reels,
Or wanting a head, that has ta'en to his heels,
Kit in hand, step by step, to advance!
Like a turkey well taught on a warm iron plate,
Was compell'd to cut capers before I cut meat,
And picked up my crumbs by a dance!
The word of command thus they gave me, poor Elf!

Handle your feet,
Dress your feet,
Step out your feet;
Mark time with feet,
Step short with feet,
And change your feet,

To 'go to the devil and shake yourself'!

It was by the aid of such early instruction that Joe Grimaldi became a celebrated comic dancer, who burlesqued the Fonteyns and Beriosovas of his day; and his mother, who made a small reputation as a character dancer, helped to train him in the fundamentals.

Joe also took lessons in skinwork, as an imitation bear or monkey. There is an often-quoted story in the *Memoirs* about his supposed first season at the Wells in 1782, when 'he played a monkey and had to accompany the clown [his father] throughout the piece. In one of the scenes, the clown used to lead him by a chain attached to his waist, and with this chain he would swing him round and round, at arm's length, with the utmost velocity. One evening, when this feat was in the act of performance, the chain broke and he was hurled a considerable distance into the pit, fortunately without sustaining the slightest injury; for he was flung by a miracle into the very arms of an old gentleman who was sitting gazing at the stage with intense interest'.[11]

Monkey tricks were a traditional line of business for theatre children until the twentieth century, and a particular tradition of the Islington stage before it became a home for ballet, opera and drama. Some eighty years before Joe's début, the press noticed in 1701, as one of the Sadler's Wells attractions, 'a strange sort of monster that does everything like a monkey. He has given such wonderful content to the butchers of Clare Market that the house is every day as full as the Bear Gardens, and draws the city wives and prentices out of London much more than a man hanged in chains.' Right up to the middle of the Victorian age the man-monkey was a popular draw at minor theatres — Gouffé, a half-imbecile pot-boy who shinned up and down walls in furs, was perhaps the most notorious exponent of this crude speciality. In young Grimaldi's time, and for a century to come, animal impersonation was often a child's apprenticeship to the stage, when pantomimes, ballets and burlesques were stocked with a veritable bestiary of anthropomorphic roles. Skinwork provided a more or less pleasant initiation into the mysteries of the family profession, when no trade union secretary or Government department intervened in the regulation of juvenile labour: disguised as a monkey or a dog, a boy might acquire the rudiments of a theatrical education, while his sister was more often conscripted as a denizen of fairyland. Joe Grimaldi frequently appeared as an animal in his infancy. At the age of five he played Cat in a skin so badly made that he fell down a stage-trap, broke his collarbone and missed the rest of the Drury Lane season.

Among the other, somewhat less dangerous roles open to a small boy at Sadler's Wells and Drury Lane were sprites and demons in pantomimes and spectacles, and Joe was also needed to 'fill up' in the processions and crowd scenes of big-scale productions, when scores of supers were employed. During the Christmas season, indeed, most of the three Grimaldi families must at times have been employed in the 1780s on the stage of Drury Lane — father as clown, at least one mother in the chorus, and the children masquerading as animals and fairies.

Backstage lessons aside, London was an education in itself for a lively, active boy. It was a rapidly changing, challenging city in which Joe grew up, a city of dark and light extremes, of picturesque charm and vicious squalor, of grinding poverty and ostentatious wealth. In its narrow, winding streets, lit fitfully by dim oil lamps and the flares of passing linkboys, mob violence quickly turned to murder. Watches were badges of social status then; tea and sugar were luxuries which only the well-to-do could afford; and people without a well bought their water from dealers in the street. Yet it was a city in which the country habit was still strong. Green fields began at Chelsea, Hackney and Islington when Joe was born; there were meadows at Marylebone and orchards along Millbank; and from Drury Lane or Covent Garden he could walk into open country within fifteen minutes. This was a pastoral London, and a London of proletarian misery: it was also, for half his life, a London at war. In the year of his birth the American colonies were in revolt; France was fighting England all over the world; and, according to the *Annual Register*, 'a situation more singular and perilous could scarcely be traced in history,' for Britain was 'abandoned by all mankind'. Grimaldi grew up with the French Revolution and the Napoleonic Wars. Yet of such events there was little sign in the theatrical quarter of London, where young Joe spent his childhood. The world of the stage was preoccupied, as ever, with its own singular and sometimes perilous trades.

Clare Market was then, and for many years afterwards, a traditional centre of the London butchers but, like most of the streets in the neighbourhood of Drury Lane and Covent Garden, Stanhope Street housed a few stage folk in its old tenements. In those days actors lived near their work, and the best work was to be found at the east end of the Strand in the rival 'patent' theatres. Most of the playhouses' artists and technicians lived within a half-mile radius, and in the middle of this theatre colony were the taverns which acted as social clubs, employment exchanges and clearing houses. Joe did not remain long in Stanhope Street, which may well have been a temporary lodging of his mother, but it was in this quarter of the city that he spent his first ten impressionable years, and from here he drifted through the dazzling, dirty splendour of the London streets.

Joe listened to the cries of street vendors, many of them in distinctive liveries — the bellows-mender, the bandbox man, the cats'-meat woman, the sellers of shrimps and rosemary, of gingerbread and pippins, of cherries and sealing wax. He watched the old apple-women, roasting hot codlins on their fires; the country wenches in black taffeta hats and gowns, swinging their bright

24

milk cans as they walked through the West End; the little black-faced boys shouldering their soot-bags and crying 'Chimney sweep! Chimney sweep!' as they ran along at their masters' sides. The voices rang out all day in the squares and streets, long before breakfast and long after tea: the dustmen, ringing their bells and shouting 'Dust-o!', the newsmen, with their horns, crying 'Great and Glorious News' or 'Bloody News' — there was usually some of *that* in stock; the muffin men and the ballad-mongers. Joe walked along Oxford Street at eleven o'clock at night, when the shops were still open and the pavements crowded, and he peeped through the windows into the family scenes of the living-rooms behind. He visited the wild beasts at the Tower of London (London's Georgian Zoo); he saw the mail coaches clattering off from Holborn to the north and from Piccadilly to the west; and he laughed with the crowds in Spa Fields at the old rural game of grinning through a horse collar, 'the frightfullest grinner to be the winner'. In Bond Street and Piccadilly the dandies paraded in their splendour; peers and politicians sat in their boxes at the Lane, and elbowed their way into the green rooms; and on his way to Sadler's Wells, during the summer season, Joe passed through foul and filthy slums, where the bucks and the fops never came and where the criminal armies of the capital made their home. What a city for a growing boy! He absorbed its multifarious life with the passionate curiosity of a mimic, and acted it out again for his own delight in the dressing-rooms.

All this was free, but if he had a few shillings to spare young Grimaldi — in 1786 — could take his pick of the town's more respectable pleasures. There was Rackstrow's Museum, near Temple Bar, where for two shillings he could see 'a large collection of curiosities finely preserved in spirits; amongst which are miscarriages, from the size of a pin's head to a perfect state; the surprising skeleton of a whale, seventy-three feet long'; and — the star attraction — 'that curious figure of a woman six months gone with child, representing, by red liquors flowing through glass tubes imitating arteries and veins, the circulation of the blood, actions of the heart and lungs, and showing how the child is nourished in the womb'. In Cockspur Street, from one till six, there was the Celebrated Musical Child 'no more than four years old', and the Lyceum offered the delights of a Wax-work Cabinet. In the Exhibition Rooms over Exeter Change Grimaldi

25

might have seen the *Eidophusikon* of that celebrated designer De Loutherbourg, who had once quarrelled bitterly with the Signor,[12] and who withdrew from Drury Lane in order to devote himself to this miniature precursor of the cinema ('Various Imitations of Natural Phenomena, represented by Moving Pictures').

The dominant fact in Joe Grimaldi's childhood was his father. No Moving Pictures, street fights or backstage wonders could compete with the daily dramas of his home. Life with the Signor was, it seems, an education in itself. But before continuing the Grimaldi story, this seems a suitable point at which to outline the nature of that bizarre entertainment in which both father and son excelled: the pantomime.

*   *   *

By the time the elder Grimaldi arrived in London, pantomimes were a staple ingredient of British theatrical diet, not only at Christmas but throughout the metropolitan year. (It was not until the mid-Victorian era that they were limited to Christmas holiday showing.) Although they were, like those of the following two centuries, the most consistently profitable *genre* in a persistently chancy trade, they bore little resemblance to the fading Christmas institution of the same name today: a burlesque fairy-tale roughly shaped into a vehicle for TV comedians, 'personalities' and speciality acts, with song, dance and scenery aspiring to the condition of spectacle, and a patchily resurgent tradition of rhyming couplets, animal impersonation and token sex-reversal. This was the holiday hotch-potch Max Beerbohm meant when he wrote about 'the one art-form that has been invented in England, an art-form specially adapted to English genius.' The pantomime of Signor Grimaldi's day was, like that of our own, a theatrical ragbag, but it had an unmistakably Continental stamp: it was derived from Parisian versions of the Italian Comedy, or *Commèdia dell' Arte*, and its gallery of characters, who had become international types by the end of the seventeenth century. These favourites of the fairs included a number of rascally servants such as Arlecchino, Pulcinello and Pedrolino, better known in England for the last 280 years at least as Harlequin, Punch and Pierrot; an amorous serving girl, Colombina, who in her English avatar as

Columbine progressively acquired both virtue and social status (though she never achieved parity in billing with the men); and Pantalone, a miserly and randy old merchant (loose breeches were dubbed 'pantaloons' in his honour), who became among other thing a kind of symbolic scapegoat for those who hated the authority of parents, politicians and the state, of the old, the rich and the aristocratic. Early in the eighteenth century in London Harlequin took the lead from Mezzetin, Scaramouch and other popular *Commèdia* figures, largely because of the personal ascendancy of John Rich, who was not only one of the most powerful men in British show business, as manager of Covent Garden theatre, but was also (as Lun) the star Harlequin of his own pantomimes for some thirty years.

Rich's pantomimes, and those of his competitors, usually included — like today's 'monstrous medlies' (as they were called by Colley Cibber some 240 years ago) — dancing, singing, spectacle, stage trickwork and comic knockabout with, sometimes, performing animals and 'variety' acts. Gradually a loose pattern settled into popular favour and theatrical 'tradition' (a verbal sanction that may date back 300 years — or, rather more frequently, a decade). The show took its name from an 'opening', borrowing from classical mythology or (later on) a fashionable novel, travel-book or some topical sensation. In these few scenes the characters wore huge carnival masks (known as 'big heads') and loose costumes over their true dress, the harlequinade livery. When they were 'transformed' by some supernatural agent into Harlequin, Clown, Pantaloon, Columbine, etc., they stripped off their top costumes and a comic chase began. Harlequin danced in pursuit of Columbine, was opposed by Pantaloon and his servant, but finally — with the aid of his magic sword or bat — defeated his enemies and won the girl. Almost the only fixed element in this harlequinade was the 'dark scene' towards the end of the chase, when Harlequin somehow lost his bat and his Columbine in some underlit grotto, wood or Gothic ruin. Then the representative of Good who had worked the change from the 'opening' came to the rescue, and contrived a spectacular climax or 'splendid scene' — the forerunner of today's 'walkdown' — when all were reconciled.

This was the kind of pantomime in which Joe Grimaldi was to make his name, as the character who had started life as Pantaloon's servant some 300 years earlier. The harlequinade lasted some sixty to ninety minutes as an 'afterpiece', preceded at Christmas by a tragedy such as *The London Merchant: or, The History of George Barnwell*. It survived the younger Grimaldi by little more than a quarter-century. By mid-Victorian times the 'opening' filled almost the whole evening. The harlequinade shrank to one token scene, and disappeared early in this century.

But now it is time to return to Joe Grimaldi and his intimidating father . . .

Three

*For the first time in my life I beheld a CLOWN, and for
the first time also felt something stir within me that was not
just mere childhood excitement. That something said to me:
I WILL. I will become what that man is there upon the
platform.*—GROCK (Life's a Laugh)

'WHENCE CAN ARISE the pleasure of seeing children suspended in
the air, or tossed about, at the utmost hazard of their lives, to
gratify the avarice of unnatural parents?'[1] That was the question
posed by Robert Paulet, a horrified visitor to Sadler's Wells in
1773, some years before Joe Grimaldi made his bow at the tender
age of twenty-eight months. Yet it would be rash to condemn
Signor Grimaldi, on these grounds, as an 'unnatural parent'; he
was, on the contrary, behaving with a conventional respect for
private enterprise and public taste. The customers took for granted
the appearance of performing infants as prodigies of the 'legitimate' stage or as human 'props' in a variety bill, and any attempt
to deprive them of such a traditional amusement would un-
doubtedly have provoked a riot. It was, after all, an age of brutal
entertainment. Public executions still provided a popular way of
passing an hour or two: they were, said the grim Mr Paulet,
'accounted the next diversions to Sadler's Wells; and, by use,
men can see a monkey dangling from a wire, or a fellow creature
expiring at the gallows, with equal unconcern'.[2] This was an age
when some of the noblest names in England gathered around the
cockpits near St James's Park to see two birds slash each other to
death, or watched bulldogs tearing a baited bull to pieces, or
gambled fortunes on marathon bare-knuckle contests in the open
air. Men were suspended in chains at Tyburn and Newgate as
moral incentives to the labouring poor; starving subjects of the
King were transported for stealing bread; and unpopular offenders
were sometimes stoned to death in the stocks and the pillory. It is
against this background that we should consider the early start in
life of Master Joe Grimaldi.

Was it so hard a beginning? The children of the poor — those
who survived — were sold as climbing boys to chimney sweeps,
a job which had its almost inevitable sentence of death or dis-

figurement; they went to sea as ship's boys and powder-monkeys in the floating slums which made up so much of the Royal Navy in pre-Trafalgar days; they slaved in their thousands in the mines and mills of the new industrial England. In the cotton towns of Lancashire children worked a ninety-hour week, from five in the morning until six at night; and in the Northern coal mines little girls of ten, naked on all fours, dragged trucks along the underground tunnels. The children of the rich, escaping such character-forming experience, endured penal tortures as a part of *their* education. If Joe had gone to Rugby, he might have been flogged out of his bed in the early hours of the morning; he would have been required to work from six to nine every morning on an empty stomach; he would have been ill-fed, overworked, and bullied. By comparison, the working life of a young acrobat or dancer was often pleasant and profitable, although it usually began and ended some years earlier than the life of a public-school boy.

Grimaldi's childhood, however, seems to have been harsh in comparison with that of other theatrical minors, for the Signor was a man of unusual severity and the gap between father and son was unusually wide. Although Joe described him in after years as 'a severe but excellent parent', one is tempted to agree with a biographer that 'the phrase does honour to his filial feeling, though it cannot blind the judgment of others'; and the stories in the *Memoirs* confirm one's impression of the cruelty involved in the education of a lively child by a tyrannical, melancholic old man in his seventies. The Signor applied to Joe and his brothers and sisters the same notorious discipline which he meted out to his other pupils — by putting them, for example, in 'a kind of stocks' or in a cage which was hoisted up to the flies — and this was maintained for the young Grimaldis both in and out of working hours. Thus, although the old man encouraged his son to play monkey-tricks as a part of his trade-to-be, he punished him for practising them offstage. At Drury Lane and Sadler's Wells, young Joe entertained the company backstage with his antics, improvising buffoonery and imitating the actors, but if his father caught him he would thrash the boy, lift him by his hair, put him in a corner, and order him not to move. As soon as the Signor was out of sight, Joe's lamentations would stop short, and 'with many of those winks and grins which afterwards became so popular, he

30

would recommence his pantomime with greater vigour than ever; indeed, nothing could ever stop him but the cry of "Joe! Joe! here's your father!" upon which the boy would dart back into the old corner, and begin crying again as if he had never left off. This became quite a regular amusement in course of time, and whether the father was coming or not, the caution used to be given for the mere pleasure of seeing "Joe" run back to his corner; this "Joe" very soon discovered, and often confounding the warning with the joke, received more severe beatings than before...'

Signor Grimaldi, moreover, had a taste for macabre practical joking, which he carried zestfully into his private life. On one occasion, according to the *Memoirs*, he played the time-honoured jest of pretending that he had died, in order to discover the true filial sentiments of Joe and John. His sons were brought to his 'deathbed' in a darkened room with due ceremony by the Signor's Negro servant. Joe saw through the grisly hoax, and without any hesitation threw himself upon the floor in a paroxysm of grief. This, he realized from long acclimatization to his father's stratagems and self-pity, was the part he was required to play. But his brother, less experienced in the ways of the world, saw nothing in the Signor's 'death' but a blessed liberation — and showed his feelings by skipping about the room, singing and snapping his fingers, in a very ecstasy of delight. This candour was too much for Signor Grimaldi. With a cry of rage he jumped off his bier and thrashed John out of his illusion of freedom, while Joe ran away to hide in the coal cellar: here he was discovered hours later and restored to the arms of his neurotic father, who was now satisfied for the time being that at least one son really loved him. A true story? Whatever its trimmings in the *Memoirs*, this anecdote throws a revealing light on the childhood of a clown. It is all the more revealing if Joe made it up.

Thomas Goodwin, son of Covent Garden's music librarian, recorded a variant of this tale: 'My father...always told the story that he [the elder Grimaldi] had *disappeared*, and the report generally became current that he had fallen from the cliff at Margate, and had perished in the breakers. Three or four days later, however, when his family ought to have been in their deepest sorrow, he suddenly made his appearance among them, and finding them apparently very comfortable under their affliction proceeded to give them a severe scolding, and some of them a sound beating for their lack of feeling on the mournful occasion.'[3]

At least one premature announcement of the Signor's death in a different manner reached the press. In August 1785 it was reported from Brighton that 'Mr Grimaldi this morning died suddenly just after eating a hearty breakfast; he was found sitting upright in his chair.' A few days later the *Morning Post* carried a correction that he 'ate himself dead' at Brighton and was 'brought to life at Fulham the same day — three or four times a year he eats himself into a second sleep, and he appears as dead.'

Another insight into the Signor's character is given by the story in the *Memoirs* of how he looked after Joe's pocket-money. At both Sadler's Wells and Drury Lane Joe became something of a backstage favourite. Tom King sometimes gave him a guinea (equivalent to about a tenner today) to buy a 'rocking horse' or some other toy. The Earl of Derby — then a frequent visitor backstage at Drury Lane, because the actress Elizabeth Farren was his mistress — often gave Joe half a crown. All these benefactions, however, were expropriated by the Signor and locked up in a box with Joe's name inscribed thereon. 'Mind, Joe,' he would say, 'ven I die, dat is your fortune.' On one special Sunday outing when Joe went to visit his grandfather Zachariah Brooker, the Signor bestowed a guinea on him from the 'fortune box', to demonstrate to the other side of the family that he was a gentleman. Joe gave the guinea away to a 'female of distressed appearance' whom he saw *en route*, and confessed to his crime when he returned home. The Signor then promised to beat him. According to the *Memoirs* one of his eccentricities was that 'whatever he promised he performed; and that when, as in this case, he promised to thrash the boy, he would very coolly let the matter stand over for months, but never forget it in the end. This was ingenious, inasmuch as it doubled, or trebled, or quadrupled the punishment, giving the unhappy little victim all the additional pain of antici-pating it for a long time, with the certainty of enduring it in the end.' Four or five months later, indeed, the Signor suddenly summoned Joe and 'gave him a caning which he remembered to the last day of his life' — because he had given away the guinea.

* * *

Although he may have heard a good deal of boasting gossip from his father about the family, there is no firm evidence of Joe's pedigree.[4] The older Grimaldi has been identified with other Grimaldis in European show business on no stronger evidence than the name, which has inspired some enthusiasts to claim for the Clown a blood-relationship with the Princes of Monaco. The confusions and contradictions are matched by those in Joe's own story, and it is characteristic that he did not even know his correct age — throughout his life he believed that he was born in 1779, a date perpetuated in several books and collections. Yet there is little doubt that Joe's father belonged to an international dynasty well-known in the theatres of France and Italy, and on occasion he returned to the cross-Channel world where he spent the first forty years of his life.

His first job in London was, it seems, at the King's Theatre in the Haymarket — as a ballet-master? — but it was at Drury Lane on 12th October 1758, that his first appearance on the English stage was announced on the playbills. This was a year of theatrical upheavals, for Harry Woodward, the great Harlequin and panto-mime producer, left Garrick to go into management in Dublin with Barry and Macklin; and with these three leading actors went players from both the patent theatres, leaving many gaps in the rival companies. It was, perhaps, in an effort to make up for Woodward's departure that Garrick engaged Grimaldi, with other new recruits, in the pantomime department of Drury Lane; and the Signor was one of the first in a long line of Continental dancers — most of them Italian — who worked at Drury Lane in the next fifty years. The Giorgis came in 1760, Tassoni in 1765, the Sieur Dagueville and Signora Vidini in 1769, Signor Como and Signora Crespi in 1773, Signora Hidou in 1774, the Riccis in 1777, and the Zucchellis in 1778; and all the while, it seems, Grimaldi ruled the roost. His own appearances as a dancer were intermittent, but he continued to compose ballets, to train dancers, and to perform in pantomime.

It was in a pantomime dance, 'The Millers', that he made his début at Drury Lane, and a contemporary criticism in *The London Chronicle* provides a clue to the pedigree of the Clown created by his son:

Grimaldi is a man of great strength and agility: he indeed treads the air. If he has any fault, he is too comical; and from some feats of his performing, which I have been a witness to ... those spectators will see him ... with most pleasure, who are least solicitous whether he breaks his neck, or not. ...

This critic noted a change of taste which helped to confirm Grimaldi in popular favour when he wrote: 'The French in this kind of merit for many years carried all before them; but of late the Italians seem to have the start of them; and it must be allowed, the latter are much better actors which, in the comic dance that now almost everywhere prevails, is infinitely more requisite than those graceful postures and movements on which the French dancers for the most part pique themselves; but in this case a vast deal depends on the Maître de Ballet; and whoever composed "The Millers" has, I think, shown himself a man of genius. ...' The 'man of genius' was Signor Grimaldi, and he subsequently became — on the strength of this successful appearance, perhaps — the ballet-master of Drury Lane, a post which he retained until his death.

It is a sign of his curious, special status at Drury Lane that he was cast in Garrick's Shakespeare Festival of 1769 to 'walk' Falstaff in the great procession: in fact, to be drawn on in a 'car'. This event, like so many on Garrick's doomed programme, never took place at Stratford; but Drury Lane's great actor-manager must have had particular trust in the Signor's powers to consider allowing him to pass through Stratford as a character who inspired one of the most popular passages in Garrick's own 'Ode to Shakespeare':

> With sword and shield he, puffing, strides;
>   The joyous revel-rout
>   Receive him with a shout,
> And modest Nature holds her sides.
> No single pow'r the deed had done,
>   But great and small,
> Wit, Fancy, Humour, Whim and Jest,
> The huge misshapen heap impress'd,
>   And lo — Sir John!
> A compound of 'em all
>   A comic world in ONE.

Grimaldi also appears to have been responsible for arranging the 'antique' country dances for the Festival: among these was 'Falstaff's Minuet.' (When the procession was staged at Drury Lane in *The Jubilee* during the following season, it was not the Signor but James Love who appeared as Sir John.)

As a dancer the elder Grimaldi was conspicuously athletic, right into his sixties.

> Among his other qualities he excelled in *jumping*, not to any extraordinary height, but in imitation of animals. We once saw him in a pantomime where, in the character of a savage, he had to descend a pile of rocks in quest of a sleeping shepherdess, and he bounded from rock to rock in such a close imitation of nature, that it appeared more the agility of a roebuck than a man.

That comment comes with the authority of the *Sporting Magazine*, in October 1811. Dancing and choreography, however, satisfied only one side of his talents, and the buffoonery that seemed 'too comical' in occasional dances found fuller scope and apt expression in the English pantomime. Garrick knew to the full the value of this theatrical department, not only financially but aesthetically (his own acting was influenced by Carlin, Lun and other Harlequins).

There is some confusion about the older Grimaldi's role in the eighteenth-century harlequinade and his influence upon the creation of Joey the Clown. The Victorian journalist Andrew Halliday said, in a piece later reprinted in *Comical Fellows* (1866), that 'it was Grimaldi the elder who paved the way for raising Clown to the first place in the pantomime.' Apparently influenced by this judgment, Maurice Willson Disher declared that he was 'the founder — and, in several cases, tutor — of the new school of pantomime', and it is certain that many entertainers emerging at the end of the century owed their training to 'old Grim', not the least of them being his son Joe. But there is no evidence of the way in which the Signor trained this 'new school', or of the extent to which Joe's innovations were influenced by his father, re-collected in tranquillity; and although the elder Grimaldi is usually described as a clown — Frederick Reynolds refers to him as 'the celebrated clown',[6] and Henry Angelo says he was 'for many years the favourite clown'[7] — he was best known in the Drury Lane harlequinades for his performance of Pantaloon, while during his short career at Sadler's Wells from 1763 to 1768 there is no record of his appearance in any other role. Indeed, it was not until Joe's birth that his father appeared as a clown in panto-mime, and his career in that part lasted for only a few years. Signor Grimaldi played it for the first time at the age of 69 — on 11th May 1779 for a benefit performance at the Lane. The pantomime was *The Elopement*, a popular piece in the repertory, and the cast was one of those scratch companies often assembled for the last benefit nights of the London season. He cannot have enjoyed a very enthusiastic reception, for though he played the role again when *The Elopement* was revived, he resumed his Pantaloonery in the other stock pieces. It was not apparently until 1784 that the Signor created a new clown role, but then, at the age of 71, he achieved a minor triumph, in *Harlequin Junior, or, The Magic Cestus*, where he attracted attention by comic transformations, a brand of humour in which his son later excelled. He appeared twice more as clown at Drury Lane, and as clown and Pierrot at the Haymarket (1786), but he died before he could develop his new line of business.

This record scarcely seems enough to justify the descriptions of Grimaldi the elder as the true begetter of Joey the Clown, but one reason for posterity's confusion is a degree of vagueness in theatrical terminology and classification. When later critics wrote of Delpini, Follet, Dubois or the elder Grimaldi as 'leading clowns', they did not mean that these artists appeared in the character of Clown as we understand it or even as the clown of pantomime before it was transformed by the younger Grimaldi. The word was used as a synonym for a buffoon, and was applied to a pantomimic comedian whether he was playing Pierrot, Pantaloon, Scaramouch or Clodpate.

Whatever influence Signor Grimaldi may have exerted upon the development of English pantomime, it was chiefly as a ballet-master, a Pantaloon, and a father. How funny *was* Joe's father? George Lupino declared — in a privately printed lecture on pantomime — that he was 'the first to make the sad pierrot into a comic one and was known as the rough and tumble pierrot'. According to James Boaden, writing in 1825, 'in broad humour he fully equalled his son, who has given such infinite delight to the present generation'.[8] Yet this is, at the least, open to question, for it was not in 'broad' humour that his son's especial genius lay, and unlike his father Joe was seldom charged with indecency.

The Signor sometimes went too far for English taste: his dance of 'The Quakers' was so strongly opposed by the Society of Friends that its repetition was prohibited by the magistrates.[9] The elder Grimaldi's humour belonged to a cruder, more boisterous tradition of the fair-booths, fired by his own taste for cruel practical joking and his preoccupation with mortality. The verdict of a later critic gives, perhaps, a more accurate picture than Boaden's sweeping eulogy: 'He was a low humorist; and, in those days of practical joking thought a very clever fellow; but his inability to make himself clearly understood by the million enabled Follet, Delpini, etc to get a hold upon public favour, and he ceased to attract.'[10] Signor Grimaldi was, after all, a foreign fool: more foreign than his fellow-Italian Delpini. Offstage, Grimaldi's voluble, polyglot English — accompanied by vivid gesture and mime — was thought to be so comic that people would call on him especially for the pleasure of hearing and watching him talk.

Little was known of the elder Grimaldi's private life until ten years ago, with the publication of the author's edition of his son's *Memoirs*. Rumours were current in his lifetime that during his earlier years on the Continent he had a female partner so like him in appearance, agility and strength that she was suspected of being his sister or his daughter. The implication of incest was accompanied, in this story, by the charge that he was sent to prison for indecency, and that shortly after his release he came to England — leaving his wife behind, never to see her again.[11] The half-truth in the tale seems to be that in the 1740s a dancer called Grimaldi and his sister appeared with some success at the Opéra Comique in Paris, and this man may well have been Joe's father; but the many rumours of a sinister past illustrate the nature of the reputation which old Grimaldi enjoyed in the London of the 1780s. This short, saturnine foreigner was a bully, an eccentric, a card and a libertine: Joe's mother was not the last in his long amorous progress.

The Signor's private life may best be glimpsed in a petition for divorce brought in November 1779, before Joe was a year old, by his father's legal wife.[12] This document, which came to light after the first edition of this biography, is preserved in the archives of the Greater London Council; but there is, unfortunately, no evidence of what happened to the petition. It reveals that Mary Blagdon, a dancer in the Drury Lane company, married the elder

37

Grimaldi in 1762, when she was 16 and he was 46, at St Paul's Covent Garden. During the next five years they had four daughters — Mary (b. 1763), Isabella Louisa (b. 1764), Margaret Charlotte (b. 1765) and Catherine (b. 1767). 'Very soon' after the marriage Grimaldi began to behave cruelly to his wife. He was, she alleged, 'a person of a very morose, surly, cruel and savage temper and of a wicked and lustful disposition.' A few days after the birth of their first child he suddenly attacked his wife as she lay in bed, beating her unmercifully, 'without other provocation than that the child was a daughter'. Later that year he suddenly threw knives, forks and plates at her, cutting and bruising her so badly on several occasions that she was unable to dance at the theatre — which made him fly into further rages.

According to Mary Grimaldi, the Signor 'spent the greater part of his time in the company of men of bad character and abandoned women...frequented notorious brothels or bawdy houses and frequently stayed at such houses until four or five in the morning', when he returned to tell her in detail about his sexual adventures. In the Sadler's Wells seasons of 1761 and 1765 he publicly carried on affairs with three sisters, the Wilkinsons, of whom one at least (later Mrs Mountain) was his apprentice. They featured as dancers and rope-walkers at the Islington theatre. It was probably Caroline Wilkinson who gave him syphilis in 1767. Grimaldi insisted on having intercourse with his wife, although she was pregnant, and she caught the disease in a virulent form.

About 1770 he set up house separately in Chelsea, leaving Mary without any money. On one occasion he battered her so badly that she was blind for ten days. At another period he kept her locked in the bedroom for six weeks, forbade anyone to speak or correspond with her, and set his mother Catherine to guard the room with a brace of loaded pistols that the old lady carried around with her all the time. It is scarcely surprising that in 1775 Mary Grimaldi ran away from the Signor's tyranny to live with her widowed mother. About that time he began his affair with Rebecca Brooker; and he also carried on a liaison with Ann Perry, who was living with him as Mrs Grimaldi when the legal wife brought her petition in 1779.

The Signor's penchant for young girls was well enough known for it to be suggested in a print, 'Grim-All-Day at Breakfast' (now in the Burney Collection of Theatrical Portraits). This was published in the month of the Signor's death, March 1788. Maurice Willson Disher identified the girl in the print as Rebecca Brooker: on no stronger evidence, it would seem, than the assumption that the *Memoirs'* picture of Joe's family life was true. But this unknown girl — who seems taller and fairer than her lover, shown making his morning toast — might well be Ann Perry. Rebecca Brooker is said to have been short and dark.

Giuseppe Grimaldi was not only a dancer, clown, balletmaster, dancing-teacher and (for a time) theatre manager: he was also (according to an obituary) a conjuror, a physician and a dentist. No firm evidence of his conjuring or medical activities has survived; but the story of his dentistry (once discredited as family fantasizing) can be substantiated. He is said to have arrived in England as a royal dentist in the retinue of Queen Charlotte, losing his job because of the disrespectful manner in which he approached the royal mouths. On one occasion, when sent for by the King, he thrust his thumb and finger into his master's mouth and without further ado forced the loose tooth out: this was the end of his employment at court, though he continued to practise on his pupils in his new profession of dancing-master. Dentistry, indeed, gave the Signor scope for practical joking, and he is said to have substituted a horse's tooth for the molar of one credulous patient, persuading him of its prodigious rarity as a human tooth. But the Grimaldi *Memoirs* deny that the Signor was ever dismissed from Court — 'an accusation which his son always took very much to heart, and which the continual patronage of the King and Queen, bestowed upon him publicly, on all possible occasions, sufficiently proves to be unfounded': in fact, Joe declared, his father *resigned* from Court in order to give lessons in dancing and fencing, and to pursue his old profession in the theatre.

This story has been dismissed in recent years as one of the inventions and fantasies of the *Memoirs*. Grimaldi, it is pointed out, arrived in England before Queen Charlotte, and the currency of the tale is explained by the Signor's notoriety as a 'character' in London theatrical circles, where stories about his eccentricities, real or imagined, thickened into a stage tradition. One could believe anything of 'old Grim', even that he was dentist to the Queen, and he took pleasure in reinforcing the rumours and embroidering the tales. That is a rational explanation, for there seems to be no doubt that the Signor did help to create his own legend in his lifetime, but it is — on this occasion — unfair to the old dancing-master. There *was* a dentist called Grimaldi in London during the 1760s, who lived at 19 Martlett Court, Bow Street, an address which, though not among those recorded for the Signor, is in the Drury Lane district where he lived for some twenty years. Moreover, he appeared at the new Liverpool theatre in 1760, and while there 'the Signor resided at Mrs Davis's in the old church-yard, where he advertized his skill "to draw teeth, or stumps, without giving the least uneasiness in the operation". He also offered to wait on those who wanted dental advice, or assistance'.[13] More conclusive, however, is the fact of his will, in which he instructed that everything he owned at his death should be sold, and that all the money due to him for benefit tickets, notes and 'for the teeth' should be invested in the public funds or otherwise put out to the best advantage on behalf of four of his children. A confirmation of his medical abilities may be found in his recipe for an embrocation which is said to have performed a great many cures, especially on the members of his masochistic profession. His son, who often used it with success for bruises and sprains, gave the recipe to a doctor near the Wells called Chamberlaine, who prescribed it for many years under the label of 'Grimaldi's Embrocation.'[14] It is a tradition in the Lupino family that 'old Grim' was also a scene-painter and a watchmaker, and that his house was filled with scores of clocks.

Among the stories of 'old Grim' which were current in the London of Sheridan and Fox, many were unfit to print: 'we would multiply their number', one chronicler notes, with dis-appointing modesty, 'but, unfortunately the humour of the ancient Grimaldi was of the Smollett school, and delicacy forbids detail.' His offstage sense of humour is illustrated, however, by 'his persuading a fellow performer to have a face painted upon a peculiar part of his frame, and to go privately and exhibit it to Garrick' — what Davy had to put up with! — and his delight in practical joking was notorious, as the following anecdote suggests:

Rich, the manager of Covent Garden Theatre, who was ever ready to catch at any thing that was novel, or of pantomimic tendency, listened with rapture to Grimaldi, who proposed an extraordinary new dance: such a singular dance that would astonish and fill the house every night, but it could not be got up without some previous expense, as it was an invention entirely of his own contrivance. There must be no rehearsal, all must be secret before the grand display in, and the exhibition on, the first night. Rich directly advanced a sum to Grimaldi, and waited the result with impatience. The *maître de ballet* took care to keep up his expectations, so far letting him into the secret that it was to be a dance on horse-shoes, that it would surpass anything ever seen, and was much superior to all the dancing that was ever seen in pumps. The newspapers were all puffed for a wonderful performance that was to take place on a certain evening. The house was crowded, all noise and impatience — no Grimaldi — no excuse, until at last an apology was made. The grand promoter of this wonderful unprecedented dance had been absent above six hours, having danced away on four horse-shoes to Dover, and taken French leave.[15]

The story of Grimaldi's behaviour in the Gordon Riots of 1780, when young Joe was barely two years old, is one of the most famous anecdotes in the canon. During the riots Londoners chalked up 'No Popery' on their doors, to save their houses from the violence of the anti-Catholic mob. According to Henry Angelo,

> at the time, he resided in a front room on the second floor, in Holborn, on the same side of the way near Red-lion-square, when the mob passing by the house, and Grimaldi being a foreigner, they thought he must be a papist; on hearing that he lived there, they all stopped, and there was a general shouting. A cry of 'No Popery!' was raised, and they were just going to assail the house, when Grimaldi, who had been listening all the time, and knew their motives, put his head out of the window, from the second floor; making comical grimaces, he called out, 'Genteelmen, in dis hose dere be no religion at all.' Laughing at their mistake, they proceeded on, first giving him three huzzas, though his house, unlike all the others, had not written on the door 'No Popery'.[16]

Although some of these anecdotes may be apocryphal, they illustrate the reputation which old Grimaldi enjoyed among his contemporaries and the parental influence he exerted upon his son; and there is little doubt of the existence of his chronic and obsessive melancholia, with which many stories are concerned.

According to the *Memoirs*, the Signor was 'a most morbidly sensitive and melancholy being, and entertained a horror of death almost indescribable. He was in the habit of wandering about churchyards and burying-places, for hours together, and would speculate on the diseases of which the persons, whose remains occupied the graves he walked among, had died, figure their death-beds, and wonder how many of them had been buried alive in a fit or a trance: a possibility which he shuddered to think of, and which haunted him both through life and at its close.' This fear of being buried alive was fanned by the conversation of an old Lambeth bookseller, with whom the Signor used to walk around St George's Fields, 'detailing and discussing all the superstitious legends of Germany and Great Britain'; and this erudite crony lent him a work called *The Uncertainty of the Signs of Death*, which had so powerful an effect upon Grimaldi that he made a special provision in his will to guarantee his own mortality.[17] His eldest daughter Mary Williamson was, he said, 'to see me put into my coffin and the day that I am buried to sever my head from my body, the only favour I request, and then to follow me to the place of my burial' — a place which he had often pointed out to her in the course of his mortuary walks. This macabre request was carried out, when the time came, with filial piety: Mary sent for a surgeon, who cut off her father's head, 'she touching the instrument at the time.'[18]

Was young Joe, then nine years old, nearby at this grisly scene? By that time the boy must have been acclimatized to the facts of death, as presented in the haunted conversation of his father. How often had he walked with the grim old man round London churchyards, at St Paul's and St Clement Danes, listening to his soliloquies upon the graves? Joe Miller's tombstone, in Portugal Street, was one of Signor Grimaldi's favourite cues for melancholy, offering him as it did a platform for self-pity. He enjoyed, of course, an audience. How often had Joe heard the old man begging his family, one by one, to ensure that he was not buried alive, reading aloud from *The Uncertainty of the Signs of Death*, or repeating, time and again, his superstitious fears? Joe's father was afraid of death in general, and in particular of the fourteenth day of the month. 'At its appearance,' according to the *Memoirs*, 'he was always nervous, disquieted and anxious; directly it had passed, he was another man again, and invariably exclaimed, in his broken English, "Ah! now I am safe for anoder month." If this circumstance were unaccompanied by any singular coincidence it would be scarcely worth mentioning; but it is remarkable that he actually died on the 14th day of March; and that he was born, christened and married on the 14th of the month.' The persistence of this story is illustrated in another version by the pantomimist Jacob Decastro, whose reminiscences were published some fourteen years before the *Memoirs*. 'Mr Grimaldi, senior, had a dream, terrific in its nature, and one that made such an impression on his mind, that nothing could efface it. It was a strange one to be sure and he used to relate it thus — That the Devil one night appeared to him in it, and told him, that on the first Friday in some month, he would come for him. He therefore, the first Friday evening in every month, entertained company, who sat up with him, thinking thereby (as some people say) to cheat the Devil. But it is very remarkable, that he did die on a Friday, and the first in the month, which in some measure, verified his dream.'[19] It was on such merry tales as these that the Pantaloon of Drury Lane brought up the future Clown. (He died on a Friday — the 14th.)

Melancholy reflections upon mortality were, perhaps, more dramatically frequent in an age where the expectancy of life in peacetime was so much shorter and where religious tenets still influenced popular notions of the hereafter. But the Signor's night thoughts were so obsessive that he expressed them upon the stage in many of his ballets and pantomimes. Celebrated for his 'expiring faces',[20] he is reputed to have invented the skeleton scene, which was for many years a popular ingredient of many pantomimes, and which represented a Clown writing a letter in a lonely room, 'the whole purpose of the situation being to enable the Clown, by means of dumbshow, to give a forcible delineation of intense terror':[21] in at least one version, he died of fright. (When this scene was included in a pantomime revival of 1866, its semi-tragic character was strongly resented by the audience; yet its popularity may be seen by its persistence, in a debased version, in the older automatic tableaux of our seaside piers.)

In 1782, when Joe was three years old, his father was involved in a theatrical venture from which he hoped to win new wealth and influence, and which throws some light upon his character. Astley's Ampitheatre was then a sensational success, and Charles Dibdin the elder planned to build a rival enterprise in partnership with a trick-rider Charles Hughes. Dibdin put up the scheme, found the backers, and was assured of a third of the profits, with £150 a year in addition; and an open-air arena was built on St George's Fields, by the Lambeth marshes, at a cost of £15,000. After many vicissitudes, and under many names, it was to play an important part in the history of the English theatre.[22]

Hughes was in charge of the equestrian department, for horses were, as at Astley's, to be the main attraction, and Grimaldi, who was engaged as ballet-master, was also put in charge of a company of sixty children, some twenty of whom were bound apprentice to him for a fixed period of years.[23] A schoolmaster and schoolmistress were, with unusual generosity, engaged to look after those children who did not live with their parents, and it was announced on the bills that 'Feats of horsemanship will be relieved by the efforts of a number of children educated in the Academy, who will perform their exercises in music, dancing, oratory, etc.' The Royal Circus and Equestrian Philharmonic Academy, as it was modestly called, opened on 7th November 1782 and perhaps the young Grimaldis took part in the grand children's ballet of 'Admetus and Alceste' or the burlesque pantomime.[24] It was a notable success, and the new establishment seemed to be set for a prosperous season. But the proprietors had failed to obtain a respectable burletta licence: within a month the Surrey magistrates closed it down, calling in the military and reading the Riot Act from the stage. When it reopened in the following March both Grimaldi and Dibdin had gone. What had happened?

Dibdin's story of the backstage intrigues at the Circus is clearly one-sided, and allowances must be made for his violent prejudices against foreigners in general, and against Signor Joseph Grimaldi in particular. Yet, even so, his testimony gives us an insight into the character of Joe's eccentric father.[25] The Signor, said Dibdin, 'performed his duty, perhaps, better than any other could have done', but the commendations which he earned for his efficiency fired his ambition. Behind Dibdin's back, he 'wormed himself' into the proprietors' favour; he ignored Dibdin's authority and made mischief against him at the Circus; and he finally succeeded in secretly buying a half-share in the theatre. Yet all the time, Dibdin says indignantly,

he had made a parade of declaring, that he conceived himself

44

under the highest obligations to me, that I had given him his bread at the Circus, and he would rather die, than do anything that could militate against my interest.

In fact, 'the grovelling Italian would have pawned himself to that devil that, in his last moments, he said was waiting for him, to have accomplished my destruction.' Moreover, the parents of Grimaldi's apprentices were 'eternally presenting' Dibdin with petitions against the Signor's treatment of their children. 'Criminal accusations were preferred, addressed to religious lords; the magistrates interfered, and a complete investigation into the morals and conduct of the place was ordered,' but, to Dibdin's everlasting regret, without result. The Signor's insidious diplomacy ensured that 'most unpardonable faults' were glossed over in training his young pupils, who included two future luminaries of the lighter stage — the Austrian girl Thérèse de Camp, later Mrs Charles Kemble, and the Jewish-Italian Maria Romanzini, who won fame as a ballad-singer under the name of Mrs Bland. Yet the 'practised Italian' did not remain long to enjoy the sweets of power: there was clearly more to his 'nauseous history' than gossip, and the enmity pervading Dibdin's charge that he was 'thankless in his nature; envious in his heart; honour is with him a joke; religion a mockery'. One reflection of the Signor's reputation is given in these lines by a contemporary lampoonist 'Anthony Pasquin' (John Williams), from a poem called, simply, 'Grimaldi' (though the name was at first concealed by asterisks).

> *What monster is this, who alarms the beholders,*
> *With folly and infamy perch'd on his shoulders,*
> *Whom hallowed religion is conspiring to save*
> *Ere sin and disease goad the wretch to his grave?*
> *'Tis Grimaldi! Alas, Nature starts at the name,*
> *And trembles with horror, and reddens with shame.*
> *In the hate of his principles all are agreeing*
> *And the fruit of his loins curse the cause of their being*
> *With a pestilent curse he infects these sad times*
> *A vile abstract of hell and Italia's crimes.*[26]

Pasquin added a note to the poem when it was republished: 'the detested caitiff personified in this description, read his portrait, reflected and expired'; but this seems to have been yet another premature obituary. (Pasquin himself is described in the *Dictionary of National Biography* as an 'unprincipled and mercenary wretch'.)

On a somewhat more prosaic note, David Garrick described Grimaldi — in a letter to his brother George in 1771[27] — as 'the worst behaved man in the whole company and should have had a horse whip', a 'tartar' and an 'impudent fellow' who dunned him for money outstanding from the Jubilee two years earlier. ('I never was more provoked and astonished in my life.') Signor Giuseppe Grimaldi clearly had the power not only to horrify but also to infuriate people: he had an exceptional talent for making enemies, as well as for teaching dancing, extracting teeth, seducing young girls and making people laugh. Yet not long after this outraged letter Garrick sent the Signor on a mission to Paris: a letter from Jean Monnet (in the Forster Collection preserved in the Victoria and Albert Museum library) thanks Garrick for giving him the pleasure of seeing, once again, 'le sublime et divin Grimaldy' — who talked to him in three languages that he could scarcely have understood had it not been for the expressiveness of Grimaldi's gesture and pantomime. It may well have been Monnet, Garrick's friend and representative in Paris for some thirty years, who had first recommended the Signor to Garrick, as he had introduced many other artists.

* * *

How rich was the Signor? According to the *Memoirs,* he lived in some state. In 1783 he employed three or four female servants and a Negro footman; and when he died his funded property — so his son claimed — exceeded £15,000. If this were so, the ballet-master of Drury Lane must have done exceptionally well. Certainly as a teacher of dancing he enjoyed the custom of some illustrious clients, if his son is to be believed. 'In those days of minuets and cotillions private dancing was a much more laborious and serious affair than it is at present', Dickens wrote in the *Memoirs,* 'and the younger branches of the nobility and gentry kept Mr Grimaldi in pretty constant occupation.' At the Theatrical Fund dinner in 1824 the Duke of York said to Joe Grimaldi, 'I remember your father well. He was a funny man, and taught me and some of my sisters to dance.'[28] But the Signor could scarcely have accumulated £15,000 from his theatrical pay. At the time of his death in 1788 he was earning 16s. 8d. a day at the Lane, when at work, with as much as £115 from a half-benefit every other year, and incidental earnings from provincial and minor theatres. A family budget published in the *London Advertiser* in 1786 estimates that a man needed £400 a year to keep a wife, four children and two maids; and we do not know whether the Signor contributed to the upkeep of his own daughters, or to Rebecca Brooker's expenses. His relative prosperity, as well as his eccentricity, may seem to be indicated by the story told in the *Memoirs* that 'he purchased a small quantity of ground at Lambeth once, part of which was laid out as a garden. He entered into possession of it in the very depth of a most inclement winter, but he was so impatient to ascertain how this garden would look in full bloom that, finding it quite impossible to wait till the coming of spring and summer...he had it at once decorated with an immense quantity of artificial flowers...' Yet it seems more than likely that the picture of a prosperous childhood in a settled home painted in the *Memoirs* is one of Joe's nostalgic fictions, conjured up in the relative poverty of his own retirement. The Signor's frequent changes of address — at least ten in twelve years — may well be a reflection of financial as well as sexual problems; and although he left a will in which his property was to be sold and invested in the funds on trust for Mary, Joe, John and William, there is no evidence for the estimate of £15,000.

* * *

'In my early years,' Joe Grimaldi used to say in his retirement, 'my father gave me a broad sword and a guinea, and sent me into the world to seek as best I might.' When the old Pantaloon died of dropsy in 1788 it can have made no substantial difference to the working life of his nine-year-old son. Joe was already a veteran.

Four

The folly of clowns should always be the bouquet of long and slowly gathered wisdom.—JAMES AGATE

'IT IS EVER BETTER,' wrote George III to Lord North on the topic of his errant elder son, 'that Persons should feel their situations will by degree improve, and particularly Young Persons.' The Young Persons who watched the burial of Signor Grimaldi one windy March day in 1788, in the graveyard of an Islington chapel, had no such certainty of improvement.[1] Life had been hard while the old Pantaloon was alive, but it was harder still after his death; for although the absence of weekly thrashings and soliloquies upon the grave may have brightened the homes of his families, the absence of his subsidy (however erratic) and his backstage influence caused a sharp reduction in their standard of living. At Drury Lane Richard Brinsley Sheridan rose to the occasion by raising young Joe's pay (in 1789 it was £1 5s a week), and by allowing his mother to work at Sadler's Wells while Drury Lane was open[2]; but the proprietors of the Wells are said to have cut Joe's pay from 15s. to 3s. a week, at which level it remained for the next three years. In later years Joe felt a strong sense of grievance at this way of marking the Signor's death, but the management's action is understandable. They owed nothing to old Grimaldi's memory; Joe, who had outgrown the imps and animals, had not yet reached the age of general utility; they were giving employment to his mother in the chorus; and, what is more, they could not *afford* to be generous. At that time the Wells was in difficulties and there were rumours that it might be turned into a Methodist chapel: shares in the theatre were sold, it is said, for as little as £60 for an eighth interest.

What had happened, then, to the Signor's £15,000, the four servants, and the town house? The young Grimaldis were, alas, cheated of their heritage! That, at least, was Joe's story. The estate was managed by only one executor, Joseph Hopwood, a lace manufacturer in Long Acre, for Tom King refused to act in that capacity (because, perhaps, of his usual and various financial embarrassments). Hopwood went bankrupt within a year, fled the country, and was never heard of again: nor was the fortune of the

48

Grimaldi heirs. It is a dramatic excuse for underprivilege, yet it should be noted that Mr Hopwood was back in London in 1791 (according to the directories).

Mr Hopwood was rapidly followed abroad, it seems, by John Grimaldi. Joe's younger brother, released from the Signor's iron rule, showed his independence by refusing a regular engagement at either the Wells or the Lane, 'for he thought and dreamt of nothing but going to sea, and evinced the utmost detestation of the stage'.[3] Although he sometimes earned a shilling by appearing at Drury Lane as a reluctant dog or goblin, his aversion to the career for which his father had trained him was so manifest that the acting manager of the Wells, Richard Wroughton, incredibly found him a berth on an East Indiaman and paid some £50 for his outfit. Within two days John was on board the ship but, on finding that he had to wait ten days before it sailed, he swam from the East Indiaman to a naval vessel which was just setting sail, signed up as a cabin-boy under an assumed name and left behind him all the clothes that Wroughton had so generously bought. He was not yet ten.[4] John was never seen again — except on one mysterious evening some fifteen years later, when he suddenly turned up at Drury Lane for a joyful reunion with Joe and then inexplicably vanished without trace, for ever, in the space of an hour.

There were still, it seems, three Grimaldi children in the theatre, for at Drury Lane that Christmas of 1789 — the year the French Revolution broke out and the Opera House burned down — 'the three young Grimaldis' were billed as supernumerary children in the pantomime of *Harlequin's Frolick*. If John had gone to sea, these were Joe, William and Catherine, for Mary had married ten years earlier — her husband, Lascelles Williamson, was a pantomimist trained by the Signor.[5] But this is apparently the last recorded reference in the bills to Grimaldi's brothers and sisters, and in the *Memoirs* none of their names is mentioned, for in later life he seems to have recognized only the existence of his brother John, and to have kept secret the fact that there were at least two other Grimaldi ménages near Drury Lane besides his mother's. She moved about this time to Great Wild Street, not far from Joe's birthplace in Clare Market.

Schooldays at Putney were over for the boys, although the master, Mr Ford, was prepared to adopt Joe as his son and continue his education, a generous offer refused by Mrs Brooker, to whom the boy's wages were indispensable in making ends meet, for during the Lane season he already earned more than she did. Although the Signor's death brought Joe closer to his mother, however, it also confirmed his dedication to the theatre; there was now no tyranny at home for this nine-year-old boy, but there was little comfort, either; it was at the Wells and the Lane that the child spent most of his time, for the rooms in Great Wild Street were empty most of the day and night. Backstage he could always find companions and an audience, even if, as yet, he was scarcely noticed on the boards. Loneliness and insecurity helped to fashion the mask of Joey the Clown.

* * *

Growing up in a theatre at the end of the eighteenth century presented an enterprising child with many opportunities now denied — for better or worse — to the 'babes' and 'tappers' of our own well-regulated stage. In the dressing-rooms and green-rooms he or she was soon introduced to the easy-going morality of the backstage world, and Joe, like all his friends at the Wells and the Lane, had a precocious acquaintance with the seamy side of life and its assorted vices. At Islington, in particular, offstage manners were rough and ready, and the language of both ladies and gentlemen in a crisis might well silence an entire TV programme today. Drunkenness on stage was, perhaps, less common than at the Lane — a glass too many in Shakespeare was embarrassing, but a skinful on the 'trapwork' could prove lethal. Yet heavy drinking was habitual among pantomimists, whose acrobatic exertions in the hurly-burly of the harlequinade were relieved by barley-water during, and by gin or brandy after, the performance. Since his first appearance, at the age of two, Joe Grimaldi had seen many actors, of both the 'legitimate' and variety stages, ruined by drink and overwork — in how many theatrical obituaries of the time one reads that 'his career was cut short by intemperance'! — and even among the children of the pantomime, recruited at Christmas time from the slums of Covent Garden, the gin-habit had taken hold. A few pennyworth of spirit, shared in the chilly dressing-rooms, kept off the cold in the long winter nights between bouts of exercise on the stage. Grimaldi himself, who was ranked in a somewhat superior hierarchy, learned the hard way about the Demon Drink; and although he was always a convivial drinker, he acquired the reputation in later life of relative temperance in his habits.

Tippling, intriguing and whoring were, no doubt, at least as popular among the theatrical profession then as now; and Joe soon became familiar with backstage vendettas and conspiracies. From his own contemporaries currying favour with the stage-manager, to the leading ladies of Drury Lane plotting and counter-plotting against each other's reputations (public and private), Grimaldi could see his own ambition for advancement reflected in a world of cut-throat competition. He began with an initial advantage — his father's influence — but this might well have become a handicap, had he not been able to justify it by his own industry and talent; and he acquired enough worldly wisdom, at an early age, to recognize the enormous social gulf that cut off theatre-folk from the 'respectable' world, and the lesser but still often unbridgeable abyss between artists of the legitimate drama and those of the 'variety' stage. Everyone knew his place in the caste system: right at the bottom were the pantomimists and dancers, regarded by many managers and performers as regrettable necessities rather than as artists in their own right.

There were, however, some consolations for members of this theatrical underworld. In the ranks of the 'legitimate', promotion below the top level was still governed by seniority and influence (couch-casting, as it is known today, was inevitably a minor factor); and players still enjoyed private rights in special roles, bequeathed to junior colleagues at their retirement, dismissal or death. In the pantomime departments of the patent theatres, however, ambition was less hamstrung by precedent and tradition, and there were greater opportunities for rapid, unstratified success. Not only was retirement earlier and mortality higher, but, more significantly, the harlequinade played a decisive role in theatrical economics. Then, as now, a theatre's balance sheet often depended on a pantomime's success or failure, and under the patent system some harlequinade artists had a bigger market than straight actors, who had less opportunity at the minor theatres. Young Joe Grimaldi, with a foot in both worlds, was later able to take his choice between respectable security, in the drama of the spoken word, and a more humiliating — but more prosperous — career in the kingdom of slapstick, dancing and melodrama.

Backstage life, moreover, provided many other compensations for a growing boy, ready to 'learn by doing'. At Sadler's Wells Joe had the freedom of the theatre, and outside the discipline of work he enjoyed a liberty of action unknown to less fortunate children of the poor or rich alike, shut up in their factories and schools. When he was tired of pottering behind the scenes, young Grimaldi could play with his friends on Spa Fields or — within a few minutes — he could be in the country, chasing butterflies or picking fruit in summertime, making snowmen or sliding in the winter months, when the Wells was closed. Yet the theatre was Joe's principal hobby, and even when not officially on duty he would work with the carpenters, building the sets and framing the stage-traps which played so big a part in the entertainments of the day, in allowing the arrival and departure of ghosts, demons, and other theatrical institutions. Sometimes he would help the scene-painters to carry out the designs of Thomas Greenwood, the rhyming artist who was for so long the Telbin or Messel of the Wells; preparing the brushes, mixing the size, watching the genesis of Chinese palaces, Highland glens, and Surrey taverns, he learned the plain facts of illusion. Joe was a willing helper, too, in the wardrobe, where he revelled in dressing up and disguising; when time was slack he would often slip into the room of Mrs Lewis, mistress of the robes, for some lessons in the art of make-up, and as he peered earnestly into her mirror, dabbing at his face with hare's foot and rouge, he would try to reproduce the features of his latest butt or favourite, grimacing away in a manner which Mrs Lewis — and many more people at the Wells — found irresistibly comic. Another indispensable part of Joe's education and entertainment was provided in the property-room, where he helped to make pantomime tricks and comic 'changes'. This mechanical humour had been a feature of the harlequinade since its introduction to public favour by John Rich at the beginning of the century, and Rich had borrowed it from the Franco-Italian comedy of the Paris fairs. Harlequin might change a monkey into a man, or a house into a prison, by tapping the floor or the scene with his bat or wand, whereupon the stage hands released catches which held the top of a hinged 'flat' in position. As it fell, the man or prison painted on the top half of the reverse side fell — with a smart crack — into place. Sometimes the trick-piece consisted of a number of separate flaps, spring-hinged together to make one object, which on release flew outwards into a new arrangement of painted reality. The craftsmen at the Wells taught Joe how to design and make such simple stage devices, whose contrivance and improvement became his lifelong hobby.

In every department of the theatre the young Grimaldi learned not only by watching but also by listening, furnishing his mind with the gossip and manners of the audience and the backstage staff. Watching from the wings, or in the gallery, he studied the art of timing — the secret of all comedy — seeing how a laugh was missed by a hair's breadth or doubled by a second's pause; he learned, by experience, what an audience at the Wells considered funny and what made it erupt in riotous, righteous protest, though its moral susceptibility was never completely predictable. This was not, of course, so much a deliberate course in theatrical art as an instinctive, continuous process of assimilation: Joe Grimaldi lived in the theatre and for the theatre throughout his boyhood and his adolescence. And he had time to talk of other things with such institutions of the Wells as Wren, the fat eccentric who sold refreshments in the gallery and whose cry 'Come, Ladies, give your mind to drinking' used to ring out all over the theatre in the intervals; and Wheeler, the lanky old porter, who had been a footman with a talent for sprinting and had many choice stories about the great households of the rich.[6]

Joe had friends of his own age, however, in the lower ranks of both Drury Lane and Sadler's Wells. With Richard Lawrence, Bob Fairbrother and Jack Bologna, all sons of performers who arrived at the Wells in 1786–7, Joe struck up a close and lasting friendship; and among the younger children at the Lane was 'the little French fairy' Miss De Camp, who had been a pupil of Joe's father at the Royal Circus. Many of his new friends were to win fame and fortune in later life, but perhaps the most important to Joe was Jack Bologna (1781–1846), an Italian boy, three years his junior, who settled in England with his family at the age of five and became one of the most celebrated Harlequins in the history of pantomime.

Pietro Bologna, his father, brought a troupe of tumblers to England in 1786, under the name of 'The Italian Company', which toured through the provinces with some success. At

Doncaster they were engaged by Tate Wilkinson, who was so impressed by their work that he recommended them to Wroughton at the Wells; and there Pietro soon appeared as clown to the rope (the compère and buffoon who kept the show going when the rope-dancer was not in motion and whose comic failure to do the tricks magnified his master's skill), while his family — a wife, two sons (Jack and Louis), and a daughter (Barbara) — performed 'Extraordinary Exhibitions of Postures and Feats of Strength'. Wilkinson, who described them in his memoirs as 'well-behaved, honest people', said that the Bolognas' act was 'on the whole, the best conceived and the most worthy attention of anything of the kind I ever beheld', and that Pietro himself was 'the best, as to doing wonders, of any person I ever saw; he really did more than a man, for he went through performances incredible and masterly'.[7] His enthusiasm was justified at the Wells, where the Bolognas made an immediate success, Pietro winning particularly favourable notices. One critic described him as 'a handsome Italian, who swung on the slack wire with amazing grace and ease, and was the most whimsical and laugh-compelling clown we ever saw. He plays on two flutes, a first and second part, through his nostrils, and on two drums, in a very *nouvelle* style.' The importance of the Bologna family in Joe Grimaldi's life is that they were, for him, an incarnation of his own family tradition — the nomadic, cosmopolitan tradition of the fairs — and, to some extent, he adopted them as a substitute for his own broken home. Although the 'clown' of Pietro Bologna was not the Clown of Joe's devising, young Grimaldi enlarged his 'laugh-compelling' education with the help of this Italian troupe, and took useful lessons in 'doing wonders' and 'posture making'.

Grimaldi's early working life was influenced more directly by another foreign artist who arrived at the Wells in the year of the Signor's death. John Baptist Dubois (1762–1818) was a French tumbler and dancer who since 1780, at least, had earned his living in the English circus ring. In 1787 he was working in a short-lived East End circus — Jones's Equestrian Amphitheatre in Whitechapel — as clown to the horsemanship (the grandiloquent name has disappeared, but the function survives, in the world of circus today), when the business closed down before its metamorphosis into Methodism; so Dubois deserted the circus for the theatre, and came to Sadler's Wells. Here he made so great a success in clowning, without the horses, that he was engaged by Drury Lane for the Christmas pantomime of 1789, *Harlequin's Frolick*, and from that year until 1806 he was London's leading clown. Dramatic talent of a more sober kind was discovered in the Frenchman, who was, one of his admirers recorded, 'particularly happy in portraying a dark, malicious and ambitious part', while 'his performance of Orson ... displays a thorough insight into human nature, debased. He mixed the tricks and sagacity of the monkey with the gleams of matured reason, so judiciously, that an enlightened audience would have been delighted.' Yet virtue became him, too: in 1803, when this tribute was written, its author claimed that Dubois 'bears away the palm from all without exception, to whom speech is denied'.[8]

He was primarily, however, a man of the circus, an acrobat, juggler and tumbler, straight out of the fairground world in which pantomime had its roots; and he was known less for his Orson than for an act in which he spun thirteen funnel-shaped caps, hooked them up one by one with his feet, and then caught them all on his head; while another of his special feats — sometimes performed between the acts of more solemn fare at Drury Lane — was to dance the traditional 'egg hornpipe' in wooden clogs.

A dozen or more eggs were placed at certain distances marked upon the stage, the dancer taking his stead was blindfolded, and a hornpipe being played in the orchestra, he went through all the paces and figures of the dance, passing backwards and forwards between the eggs without touching one of them.[9]

The reason for Dubois's place in the history of pantomime, however, is not so much a versatility less astonishing in that age of all-rounders, but rather his enterprising spirit of innovation and his influence upon Joe Grimaldi. Young Joe grew up in Dubois's heyday: for twelve years, at the Wells and the Lane, he watched the Frenchman's routine from the wings and 'out front', saw him conducting rehearsals for the harlequinade and talking shop at the local tavern, the Myddelton's Head.[10] Although in later years Grimaldi denied that he was a pupil of Dubois, who ran his own school of children, from which he recruited a touring act, it is clear that his mind was steeped in the Frenchman's buffoonery. It was from Dubois, perhaps, that he learned to develop his own talent for Orsons; and encouraged by the Frenchman, who is said to have introduced colour into the long white clothes of the traditional Pierrot[11], he dared to experiment more radically in the dress and make-up of his own English Clown. But Joe, in his maturity, was to oust Dubois from his place at both Sadler's Wells and Drury Lane, a circumstance which not surprisingly made him less willing to acknowledge his debt to the older man.

Dubois and Grimaldi had mutual friends in the Richers, the Little Devil, and La Belle Espagnole — more exotics who helped, in their time, to draw the crowds to Sadler's Wells. The older Richer was a tight-rope walker who had worked at the Wells, on and off, for many years, and Dubois was once the clown in his act at Astley's and other places. In the usual way of nepotism, Richer introduced his wife, son and daughter to the Islington theatre, and Joe Grimaldi grew up with the family, though young Jack Richer, who later excelled his father as Joe outdid the Signor, was some years older and made his name while Grimaldi was still in complete obscurity. It was Young Richer, it seems, who by 1793 — twenty years after his father's début at the Wells — was attracting unusually modish audiences to Islington, so that, in the words of one newspaper puff, 'a train of coronets is altogether as familiar to the eye in the Wells Yard as at St James's Square', and a poetical publicist observed that

> ... there, at present, Fashion keeps her Court:
> Both Belles and Beaux do to the haunt resort;
> And crowded Boxes nightly there do ring
> With 'Richer! Charming Richer is the thing!'

Charming Richer, who achieved European fame in his lifetime, was, according to J.P.Malcolm, 'one of the handsomest and best-made men in England. His skill therefore in dancing is aided by the most elegant motions, and his steps are infinitely more pleasing on the narrow diameter of a three-inch rope than nine tenths of our professed dancers are on the stage. The wonderful leaps he takes, nearly his own height, terrify those who see him for the first time.'[12] From Hazlitt he earned this tribute:

He was matchless in his art, and added to his extraordinary skill exquisite ease, and unaffected natural grace.[13]

Following in their fathers' footsteps, the sons of Sadler's Wells went on to win a greater fame, with the aid of their inherited talent and their own innate skill. Yet another graduate of this strange school, who later challenged Grimaldi in his own field, was the son of The Little Devil and La Belle Espagnole, two more Continental troupers who arrived in England in the 1780's. Pol or Paulo Redigé (The Little Devil) was the son of a tumbler, Jean Redigé, who ran a kind of theatre on the Boulevard du Temple; his juggling sister made a Parisian reputation as 'la petite Saxonne'; and he himself, after making his début at Saint Germain in 1779, came to the Wells in 1781 with honours already won in France and Ireland. Redigé arrived in partnership with another Parisian, Alexandre Placide Bussart, professionally known in England as Signor Placido — ancestor of a family celebrated in the annals of the American stage — and the two men made their first appearance on the same Easter Monday that the infant Grimaldi took his bow. (Placido played Harlequin in Paris, and wrote a number of pantomimes: Redigé was a Pierrot.)[14] La Belle Espagnole, or Signora Spagniola, was Redigé's mistress and later, it seems, his wife; she first appeared at the Wells in 1784, billed for her fandango with castanets, but was better known for her rope-walking, and for an act in which she danced with two swords tied to her feet, and two eggs under them, while she carried two baskets upon a board! Nonetheless she had time to befriend young Grimaldi, who remembered with grateful affection the kindness which the Redigés had shown him in his childhood, before the Bolognas arrived on the scene; and his gratitude mellowed his feelings towards their talented son, Paulo, who came next to Grimaldi in the clowns of his generation.

Another of his closest cronies was Bob Fairbrother, who seems to have made his début at the Wells in that fateful year of 1788. Expert in swordsmanship, Fairbrother never made much of a name on the stage, though he worked for many years at Sadler's Wells and Drury Lane, but he later held some ambiguous post as a confidential servant or secretary to Sheridan and, with greater claim to our attention, became the father of a famous theatrical dynasty. Among his more celebrated progeny was his grand-daughter Louisa, a Columbine who became the morganatic wife of the Duke of Cambridge. According to the *Memoirs*, Grimaldi may take some credit for the family tree, for it was through him that Fairbrother met his wife, the daughter of Joe's landlady, Mrs Bailey. After their marriage Mrs Bailey took her son-in-law into business as a furrier, and he gave Joe occasional employment in the shop; some years later, Fairbrother apparently became an undertaker, and it is possible that the future Clown might have found some experience in that trade, too. He also worked for a time in the butcher's shop of his grandfather, Zachariah Brooker, in Holborn, learning the mysteries of those sausages in whose theft he later become so comically adept upon the stage. Such experience among fur and flesh may have been a welcome change after the narrow backstage world; but even more welcome was the money. Although Joe earned a living wage in Drury Lane, his summer season at the Wells was a struggle to make ends meet. After a flying start as an infant prodigy, under the protection of his father, his name had vanished from the bills.[15]

Five

*Ever since I can remember, all kinds of inanimate objects
have had a way of looking at me reproachfully and
whispering to me in unguarded moments: 'We've been
waiting for you ... at last you've come ... take us now,
and turn us into something different ... we've been so
bored, waiting.'*—GROCK

THE DRURY LANE THEATRE in which Joe Grimaldi grew up has
scant connection, beyond the site, with the massive contemporary shelter of American musical comedies. Although it
had been twice remodelled, in 1762 and 1780, it was still substantially the same historic building in which Betterton himself
had acted — an intimate, apron-stage theatre, built by Wren,
made glorious by Garrick, looming high above the warren of
slummy streets that housed so many of its dependants. Since 1674
it had served as a temple of English acting and, perforce, as a home
of pantomimes; but now, in Grimaldi's boyhood, the great theatre
was in a state of dangerous disrepair. To the audience this was less
conspicuous than to the actors, for while the auditorium had been
enlarged and redecorated the conditions backstage were rather
worse than in the days of Sir Christopher, except for the stars.
The anonymous legion of supers, adult and infantine, were
crammed into seventeenth-century cellars, and to them, as to the
stage technicians, the theatre's historic associations may have
seemed less noticeable than its venerable plumbing. Grimaldi,
who was first introduced to the backstage world as a babe in
arms, knew the old Drury Lane in every grimy nook and cranny;
the dark and smelly corridors, the peeling walls of overcrowded
dressing-rooms, the nest of departments, each with its own
particular odour of paint or patchouli — these were his home in
wintertime, much more than the lonely rooms in Great Wild
Street. How well he knew the stage, across which he marched so
often in mute processional relief or danced in concert with his
boyhood friends — a wide, steep floor of dirty, ancient boards,
cut by traps and grooves and slides, splintered and stained and full
of snares for any unwary children. This Drury Lane was peopled
by giants and witches, who might sometimes give you a word

of praise or send you flying with a box on the ears; and though from the evidence of backstage gossip Grimaldi knew that these giants were all-too-mortal (some were dangerous to boys and girls alike), their presence and authority inside the theatre were awesome to stage urchins such as Joe.

Life backstage at the Lane was, indeed, very different from the bustling democracy of Sadler's Wells. 'It being a royal theatre,' one actor complained, 'from the manager to the *prompter's deputy deputy*, all speak in the *plural* number.' Stage discipline was severe, even for the most temperamental stars. When Mrs Crouch once refused to appear in the costume selected for her, John Philip Kemble fined her the statutory forfeit of five guineas, after a battle royal in the green-room; and on another occasion he refused to allow Mrs Jordan's brother, George Bland, behind the scenes, and fined the stage-door-keeper five shillings for letting him in, with the result that Mrs Jordan, always eager for an excuse, declined to act that night. Yet Mrs Crouch and Mrs Jordan were, in a manner of speaking, the Evelyn Laye and Gertrude Lawrence of their day. The list of forfeits was long and detailed: you had to pay two-and-sixpence if you stood on the stage during a rehearsal in which you were not taking part; you forfeited nine nights' salary for refusing a role assigned to you by the manager; you forfeited a night's salary if you fluffed your lines in performance and a week's pay if you failed to attend at night. More summary and violent punishments were meted out to juvenile delinquents.

In the year of Signor Grimaldi's death a new regime had been inaugurated at Drury Lane, when Tom King, after enduring a war of nerves waged against him by Sheridan, the chief proprietor, was succeeded in the stage management by John Philip Kemble, with whose family young Grimaldi's destiny was henceforward to be closely linked. Kemble regretted that he was obliged to take over in that season, for, as he recorded in his diary:[1]

> The Theatre laboured under great Disadvantages from fre-
> quent Indisposition of the Performers, from the uncommon
> severity of the winter, from the Concern all People took in his
> Majesty's Indisposition, and from their loyal Joy for his
> Recovery.

That was the winter in which George III first went mad, and a seven-week frost gripped the South of England: the Thames was frozen over below London Bridge, and was covered with 'booths, puppet-shows and wild beasts', sights which could not have been missed by Joe Grimaldi or any other able-bodied small boy in the metropolis. (The King recovered soon after the thaw set in.) Yet every season, as Kemble soon discovered, had its own difficulties — not least those 'Indispositions' which were part of the Thespian strategy of the time. Mrs Jordan was a particularly intransigent player in her 'temperamental' phases, and on 27th December Kemble noted: 'I spent above two hours in coaxing her to act. NB she was as well as ever she was in her life, and stayed when she had done her part to see the whole pantomime.' At a later date, after longer experience at the Lane, Kemble observed: 'Always keep well with the leading performers, particularly with the women, though they be ever so unreasonably troublesome — by humouring half a dozen you uncontrollably command three score.' Yet it was not always easy for Black Jack, as he was sometimes called in the green-rooms, to put this 'humouring' precept into practice where the rivalries of a Jordan and a Crouch were concerned. There were also, of course, the Indispositions brought on by drink: Kemble, like other managers, had to deal with actors who hit the bottle so hard that they failed to put in an appearance at the theatre, or, even worse, concealed their chronic intoxication until they were in mid-scene before the audience. The tragedian John Henderson used to drink sixteen glasses of gin every morning without noticeable effect at night, but he died at 38. Cooke and Kean were later exemplars of great acting combined, spasmodically and self-destructively, with spectacular boozing.

As Grimaldi himself discovered in later life, in the smaller establishment of the Wells, the problems of stage management were luridly onerous, far more so than in today's commercial or subsidized theatres. There were no long runs then; all playhouses worked the repertory system, maintaining not a mere half-dozen pieces in the programme but a large stock of productions of many kinds, including musical farces, spectacles, pantomimes and ballets. In Grimaldi's time all the jobs now shared by a dozen specialists were united in the person of the stage manager, who held office from the proprietors as impresario, administrator, producer and often a leading actor in the company. John Philip Kemble commanded a vast, self-supporting enterprise on a scale unknown on

61

the modern stage, at least until the advent of the National Theatre. All the costumes were made on the spot by a large staff of tailors and dressmakers; all the scenery was prepared in the paint-room; the master-carpenter and machinist had big departments of their own; the theatre had its own music copyists, police and firemen; and the front-of-house personnel included ten money-takers, ten check-takers, porters, watchmen and lamplighters. The acting strength of the company, some five times as large as the average today, was augmented on spectacular occasions by as many as a hundred supers. Company members might remain on a theatre's payroll for twenty years, and they often brought with them — as Signor Grimaldi had done — sons, daughters and other dependants. The orchestra leader composed much of the music; the prompter was often expected to write pieces; and the manager, too, sometimes added the role of dramatist to his other chores.

In our own national theatres the difficulties of combining aesthetic and administrative leadership in one all-purpose male have seemed, at times, insuperable. How, then, did Kemble cope — without subsidy of any kind? And to the usual problems of 'royal' management was added Sheridan. In most ways, it seems, Kemble was a better manager than Tom King, as well as being one of the most illustrious actors and directors in the history of the English stage; but Sheridan's authority was supreme, and his notoriously feckless conduct imposed unnecessary burdens upon Kemble. Urgent decisions were indefinitely postponed; serious claims were ignored while passing whims were indulged; he was extravagant, indecisive and interfering. Moreover, the theatre was usually in debt to its own players. Drury Lane's finances were in a condition of permanent crisis, and the treasury was often empty on the day the ghost should have walked. If, as the *Memoirs* say, Sheridan sometimes intervened on Joe Grimaldi's behalf and kept an eye on his career for the sake of the old Signor, such mediation is unlikely to have endeared the boy to the long-suffering manager.

Kemble, moreover, although condescending to recognize the harsh necessity of pantomime — his prescription for one in 1789 was 'It must be very *short*, very LAUGHABLE, and VERY CHEAP'[2] — had a nature framed for higher, graver things; and although he could on occasion even condescend towards the pantomimists themselves, such occasions were infrequent at the Theatres Royal. Kemble stood on his dignity: it had cost him years of struggle.

* * *

When the Drury Lane and Sadler's Wells seasons coincided, as they usually did between April and June and in September to October, Joe Grimaldi was often obliged to work a double shift; and after rehearsals and odd jobs all day at one theatre or the other, he acted until midnight. One evening when he was delayed at Sadler's Wells, he ran hand-in-hand with Bob Fairbrother to the stage door of Drury Lane in eight minutes, helter-skelter through the lanes and alleys of Holborn and Clerkenwell; and on another occasion, when the Drury Lane company was playing at the Haymarket, the young men covered the distance from Sadler's Wells in fourteen minutes, a considerably shorter time than a modern taxi might achieve. Joe's only call that night at the Haymarket was to walk on in a procession in *Cymon*, and once that had passed across the stage a few times he ran back alone to the Wells in thirteen minutes, arriving just in time for the pantomime.[3] Cymon himself was played by the composer Michael Kelly, who was drawn on to the stage in a chariot pulled by two fine horses, while at his feet lay a large-eyed boy of four in the character of Cupid — Master Carey, better known in later years as Edmund Kean.

Joe was working at the Haymarket that season because the historic old theatre in Drury Lane had been pulled down at last, in 1791. Three years later — on 21st April 1794 — the new Drury Lane was opened, with room for over 3600 people, nearly twice the capacity of the old building. The Grand National Theatre of Sheridan's dreams was, indeed, the biggest ever seen in England, and it was also the most expensive, so expensive that the exterior was never completed. The financial troubles of the Lane grew more turbulently absurd in this grandiose, echoing monument, for it proved to be too big for anything but spectacle, and even pantomime dwindled in its wide open spaces; in spite of the improvement in comfort and efficiency, Grimaldi and his friends must have often regretted the disappearance of the old theatre which, for all its imperfections, was built to human scale. In the year that the new Drury Lane was opened, Robert Baddeley, the last English actor to wear the royal stage livery of scarlet and gold to which, as King's Servants, the players of Covent Garden and the Lane were entitled, was taken ill while dressing for Moses, the part which he had created in *The School for Scandal*; and his death at such a time seems to mark the passing of one era in theatre history and the opening of another — an era of huge theatres in which authors were eclipsed by the scenery. It was the golden age of pantomime. It was also an age of war.

When the French Revolution broke out in 1789, the minor theatres reflected the burning enthusiasm for the people's cause that Wordsworth expressed in his famous lines:

> *Bliss was it in that dawn to be alive,*
> *But to be young was very heaven!*

Sadler's Wells marked the event by staging *Gallic Freedom: or, Vive la Liberté*, which depicted 'the various agitations of that glorious struggle which gave birth to National Freedom', and the storming of the Bastille inspired many stage managers and machinists whose notion of what it was all about was vague but fervent. By 1794, however, Joe Grimaldi, now 15, was playing villainous Sans Culottes and dastardly French prisoners of war, and when Joe's old friend Signor Placido performed his tight-rope act with a French flag as his balance he was obliged to give a public apology after rough handling by the indignant audience. Apart from such changes in the repertory, the outbreak of war — declared on 1st February 1793 — made little difference to Grimaldi or to any of the foreigners who were then so popular on the English stage. The patriotic zeal of playgoers had not yet reached the pitch where foreign-sounding names were taken as evidence of sin and treason, and although some artists substituted a discreet 'Mr' for 'Monsieur' on the bills they continued to work with no greater inconvenience than occasional jeers at their broken English. Yet although it was still possible for artists and ideas to travel between countries engaged in a world war, the English theatre was inevitably cut off from its traditional source of light entertainers — the Paris fairs — and from this wartime period of insulation emerged an anglicized generation.

Joe Grimaldi was already firmly naturalized, thanks to his Cockney mother: he knew no country but England, and throughout his life he never crossed the Channel to visit the family's happy hunting-ground. Dublin and Edinburgh were the farthest limits of his travels, and unlike Charming Richer he was quite unknown in the capitals of Europe during his lifetime. Joe, indeed, was a Londoner bred and born, and so was the Clown which he created in his manhood. No military service interrupted his career, and press gangs passed him by; no ENSA parties tempted him to entertain the troops abroad, though soldiers and sailors later flocked to see him on the stage at home; and, apart from finding that his pay shrunk in value because of the rising cost of living, Joe would not have known that there was 'a war on'. Yet the war contributed to his success: for not only did it restrict competition from abroad, but it brought new prosperity to the theatres — a boom in show business that, recurring in later crusades for this and that, has been a compensation to more vulnerable artists and employers.

During the early years of war with France, Joe Grimaldi, when not employed at Sadler's Wells or Drury Lane, was often catching butterflies. In that lost London, where hay was still sold in the Haymarket, an energetic boy had not far to walk to find green fields; and from many summer expeditions across heath and meadows now buried under miles of brick and mortar the young Grimaldi built up a collection of some 4000 butterflies, carefully mounted in cases made with the connivance of the theatre carpenters. At a Drury Lane rehearsal one summer morning in 1794, Mrs Jordan, inquisitive about the contents of one of these boxes so affectionately carried by the young actor, expressed her admiration of his skill so graciously that Joe resolved she should have a box of Dartford Blues to herself. For Dorothy Jordan, in 1794, was still the woman who had captured the hearts of William Hazlitt and Sir Joshua Reynolds, and who was Joe Grimaldi to resist her charm, even if there was a royal lover in the background? (She had been for three years the mistress of the Duke of Clarence, the future William IV, to whom she bore a large, devoted family.) That summer, when rehearsals permitted, Joe walked the fifteen miles to Dartford at night after performances at the Wells were over, and walked back again the next afternoon with Mrs Jordan's butterflies, if he was lucky. By the time the new season began at Drury Lane in September, he had filled two boxes with first-class specimens; and, choosing his moment of glory with care, he presented them to Mrs Jordan, after she had finished rehearsing Rosalind. Braving the ribaldry of the older men and the wrath of the prompter, Joe handed over his precious boxes to the reigning goddess with an explanation which stammered away into silence; but Mrs Jordan won his allegiance for ever by confiding to him the following day that the Duke of Clarence thought Grimaldi's butterflies were as good as, if not better than, any Dartford Blues he had ever seen.

About this time Joe and his mother moved from the rooms in Great Wild Street to the fringe of Georgian London's green belt, the new suburb of Pentonville, where they shared a house in Penton Place with Mr and Mrs William Lewis of the Wells. Here Joe was gradually beginning to be recognized by the press and the profession as a boy of promise, a recognition made easier by his famous name. By 1792, when he was 13, he already rated a share in a benefit night, a sign that he had achieved some status in the company, and on that occasion he drew the attention of a discerning critic, who observed that 'The comic abilities of this youth are very great — we wish him his deserved success.' Yet for some years at the Wells Joe was cast not in comic roles but in character parts (at the Lane he was still one of the crowd) although cheerfulness would keep breaking in. In 1794 he played such relatively large parts as the dwarf in *Valentine and Orson*. But it was not until 1796, when Joe was 17, that he set his foot on the ladder that led to fame.[4]

In 1796 — the year when Jenner demonstrated the use of vaccination, Lewis's *The Monk* was published, and an invading French armada was defeated by the weather — there were two changes in the management of London theatres which had a notable effect upon the fortunes of Joe Grimaldi. After eight arduous years, Kemble left Sheridan and Drury Lane, where he was succeeded by Richard Wroughton; and Wroughton's successor at the Wells was Tom Pitt, later known as Tom Dibdin (1771–1841), one of the prolific and gifted illegitimate sons of the celebrated song-writer, Charles Dibdin. Both Tom and his brother Charles (1768–1833), as the authors of hundreds of songs, burlettas and pantomimes, were intimately connected with Grimaldi's later triumphs, and did a good deal to launch his career of clowning: for Joe, the arrival of the Dibdins in the London theatre seems to have been providential. And at the Lane, as

Wroughton knew something of Joe's quality he was somewhat less remote than Kemble.

When the Wells season opened on Easter Monday, 1796, Grimaldi appeared in a new Dibdin pantomime *The Talisman: or, Harlequin Made Happy*, and having made the most of his opportunities as the Hag Morad, an evil witch who travelled nefariously around the globe in a Necromantic Box, he was cast in several other small parts with some success. Until now he had made only one appearance on a Drury Lane bill, when he took over the tiny role of a Second Page for one performance of *Lodoiska*, but at his benefit in October 1796 it was announced that there would be 'an humble attempt at the Clown by Master Grimaldi'; and at Christmas he secured the part of Pero (Pierrot) in a revival of *Robinson Crusoe*. Thus Grimaldi was in the Drury Lane limelight for the first time, although he was earning less money at 18 than at 9, when his father died.

As Grimaldi was completing his training at the Wells, another young man, whose talents were of a somewhat different order, came to Islington at nights to broaden his Cambridge education. It was a *common* place, to be sure, with 'mean upholstery', but in later years this visitor confessed that 'half-rural Sadler's Wells' was 'richly graced with honours of her own'; and that

> Taking my seat, I saw (nor blush to add,
> With ample recompense) giants and dwarfs,
> Clowns, conjurors, posture-masters, harlequins,
> Amid the uproar of the rabblement,
> Perform their feats...
> ...the laugh, the grin, grimace,
> The Antics striving to outstrip each other,
> Were all received, the least of them not lost,
> With an unmeasured welcome.

It is sad that having watched Grimaldi, the Bolognas and Jack Richer at work William Wordsworth should have described them in *The Prelude* without mentioning their names.

Six

Fools, they are the only nation
Worth men's envy or admiration;
Free from care or sorrow-taking,
Selves and others merry making . . .

BEN JONSON

THE YEAR OF 1796, when Joe Grimaldi won his first small success
at the Wells, was important not only in his stage career but also
in his private life: the two, indeed, were closely intertwined, for
at the age of 17 he fell in love — with the boss's daughter. There
may have been other girls before Maria Hughes; but backstage
flirtations and green-room crushes were now overshadowed by
his first romance, a romance which had a decisive influence upon
his future as an actor and a man.

Maria Hughes was the eldest daughter of the principal proprietor of the Wells, Richard Hughes, who bought a quarter-
share in the theatre in 1791, after a successful career in provincial
management, and increased his power and his holding as the years
went by.[1] Apprenticed in Birmingham to a button-painter, he
began his stage life in a 'spouting club', that is to say, in a counterpart of the modern amateur dramatic society (with two distinctions
— it was generally associated with heavy drinking in convivial
surroundings, and its members respected the professional stage).
Hankering after the freedom of the actor's life, Hughes joined the
celebrated touring company of Roger Kemble as a scene-painter,
handyman and general utility man, and travelled all over England
with the strollers, taking his share of their hardships. Sleeping on
straw, living on raw vegetables dug up in the fields, touting for
patronage, chivied by magistrates and parsons, playing in barns
for a handful of yokels' pennies — this was too often the lot of
the strolling player, and although Kemble's company was a
nursery of genius, many actors never escaped from the provincial
treadmill into management. Hughes, however, succeeded —
and romance was his salvation. During the 1770s, he arrived, 'on
the hoof', at the theatre in Plymouth Dock, and there he fell in
love with the manager's daughter, Lucy Williams, who became
his wife. Hughes soon took control of the theatre, gave up acting,

and began his career as a manager. The Plymouth Dock playhouse was not an elegant building — even twenty years later it is described as 'more like a country barn furnished up for theatrical representations' and 'one of the most inconvenient in England' — but in the garrison and dockyards there was a large potential audience, and Hughes knew how to bring them in. Within a few years, he began to extend his interests. In 1787 he bought the Exeter theatre, and gradually acquired control of those in Weymouth, Truro, Guernsey, Penzance, Dartmouth and other small towns, but it was his arrival at Sadler's Wells which set the seal on his career. He brought in as a fellow-proprietor an old comrade in the Kemble troupe, William Siddons (who married Roger's daughter, the great Sarah), and installed his own large family in the house which then formed part of the theatre building.

Hughes was not a popular figure at Sadler's Wells: he was chilly and reserved in manner, compared to the easy-going Tom King, and he had a reputation for avarice, though these are vices frequently detected in employers by their staff. He also insisted upon a relatively high moral tone:

> he will suffer no actor, nor actress, to appear upon the boards in an improper dress, nor allow those liberties which country performers are too apt to take.

But he worked hard, he had a good head for business, he knew every aspect of the trade from long and bitter experience, and he was not above giving a hand in the painting-room or the carpenter's shop when occasion required. This powerful, wealthy man, a phenomenon of the expanding theatre of those days, was Grimaldi's prospective father-in-law.

The shadowy Mrs Brooker was, it seems, the unconscious match-maker between Joe and Maria.[2] After a morning rehearsal at the Wells she would often remain at the theatre until the evening performance, taking a light meal in the women's dressing-room and passing the time with needlework and gossip; and here, on many afternoons, she was joined by Maria Hughes and some of her sisters, who walked over from the proprietor's house. Maria, according to the *Memoirs*, was 'a young lady of considerable accomplishments, who had always been much attached to Grimaldi's mother, and who embraced every opportunity of being in her society': no other description survives, except in formal tributes to her character. Another frequent visitor to this dressing-room hen party was Joe, who arrived at five o'clock to take tea and stayed among the wigs, gowns and gew-gaws until the women came to change for the evening performance.

It seems likely that Maria's deep affection for Mrs Brooker's company was not unconnected with her interest in Mrs Brooker's son, and that Joe's appetite for feminine gossip was whetted by the presence of the proprietor's daughter; but, be that as it may, an intimacy soon began to ripen between the two young people, although for some time it remained undeclared. Joe, always diffident and nervous in his private life, was conscious not only of his inexperience (Maria was some years older) but also of his social inferiority; Maria, though granted an unusual degree of liberty, was none the less circumscribed by conventions of girlish conduct, and Mrs Brooker was apparently unaware of any change in the emotional climate at her tea-parties, although she *was* surprised to see her son so often out of working hours. Matters came to a head, however, on the day after Grimaldi made a success as the Hag Morad, at the beginning of the season in 1796. When he arrived for tea, after pacing up and down beside the New River under the poplars, he came prepared: if Miss Hughes paid him a compliment upon his performance, he would return it in a way which would indicate his feelings. He had spent hours rehearsing exactly how he would convey this message in a few subtle, well-chosen words, but when the moment came — when Maria, over the tea-cups, said that he played Morad so well that she was certain no one could have done it as well — Joe was so tongue-tied that he could make no answer at all. He blushed, made an awkward bow, and, to his mother's amazement, retreated from the room, just as the women of the company began to arrive. Their habitual banter about the luridness of his love life plunged Joe into a frenzy of embarrassment, and for some weeks after this incident he absented himself from the felicity of afternoon tea with Mrs Brooker; for he had no conclusive reason to suppose that Maria had any interest in him, and, with all the anxious suspicion of first love, he suspected that she might be in league with the other girls to ridicule his clumsiness and shyness in feminine society. So the success of the Hag Morad was over-shadowed by the misery of unrequited love, with all the customary symptoms: 'he ate little, drank little, slept less, lost his spirits.'

One night that summer, however, Grimaldi went to the ward-robe for a change of costume; and there, instead of Mrs Lewis, he found the demure Maria. With no sign of emotional concern, the young lady asked him why he had not been to tea for so many days, and Joe, scarlet with embarrassment, mumbled the excuse that he had not been well.

'Not well,' said the young lady. And she said it so kindly that all poor Joe's emotion returned; and being really ill and weak, and very sensitive withal, he made an effort or two to look cheerful, and burst into tears.

The young lady looked at him for a moment or two quite surprised, and then said, in a tone of earnest commiseration, 'I see that you are not well, and that you are very much changed: what is the matter with you? Pray tell me.'

At this inquiry, the young man, who seems to have inherited all the sensitiveness of his father's character without its worst points, threw himself into a chair, and cried like a child, vainly endeavouring to stammer out a few words, which were wholly unintelligible. Miss Hughes gently endeavoured to soothe him, and that moment, Mrs Lewis, suddenly entering the room, surprised them in this very sentimental situation; upon which Grimaldi, thinking he must have made himself very ridiculous, jumped up and ran away.

The next day, however, Joe confided in Mrs Lewis, who had quickly drawn her own conclusions — no difficult deduction — and who offered to act as the go-between. At her suggestion, for she already had a shrewd idea of Maria's feelings, Joe wrote a letter to his beloved in which he declared his passion, and Mrs Lewis delivered it the following day. That night, two days after the meeting in the wardrobe, Joe was on the stage when Maria appeared in Mr Hughes's box. He had been in an agony of suspense all day to know how she would receive his letter — perhaps she would laugh at his spelling! — and now he felt that his destiny was in the balance. It was almost unbearable to look at her, but when he raised his head Grimaldi saw, in all that rowdy, rollicking, audience, only one pair of eyes, the eyes of Maria as she smiled to him from the box, the eyes that said 'Yes, of course.' On the stage which for fifteen years had been his workshop and playground Joe saw the signal of happiness in a new life.

He never heard that he did not finish the scene in which he was

engaged at the moment, and he always supposed, in consequence, that he did so: but how, or in what manner, he never
could imagine, not having the slightest recollection of anything
that passed.

He had a clear recollection, however, of what happened later in
the evening, when a heavy platform collapsed and knocked him
to the ground.[3] Joe was carried home to Penton Place with 'a
severe contusion of the shoulder', but his pain was relieved by the
Signor's embrocation, and the memory of Miss Hughes's eyes;
and next morning, as he lay resting at home, Maria came to express
her sympathy, and to show that his love was returned. The
coincidence of pain and pleasure is, as the *Memoirs* emphasize, a
recurrent pattern in his life:

> throughout the whole of Grimaldi's existence . . . there always
> seemed some odd connexion between his good and bad fortune;
> no great pleasure appeared to come to him unaccompanied by
> some accident or mischance: he mentions the fact more than
> once, and lays great stress upon it.

*   *   *

Maria insisted upon telling Mrs Hughes immediately, but after
long persuasion from her suitor she did not reveal the news to her
father. A romance between a young actor and his manager's
daughter was not uncommon, as Richard Hughes and William
Siddons themselves could testify, and it often proved to be a
stepping-stone to fame and fortune. Yet when Joe Grimaldi met
Maria he was still a junior member of the company and his
earnings amounted to less than £3 a week in the best months of
the year: apart from objecting to his age, there were sound
reasons why Hughes should have opposed the match, and to Joe
it appeared that any premature publicity might lead to his dismissal from the Wells. Mrs Hughes, however, made no determined effort to separate the couple, and allowed Maria to continue
her visits to Mrs Brooker's tea-parties and to spend part of Sunday
with Joe — under the eye of one of her numerous brothers and
sisters — in the hope, perhaps, that the attachment might fade and
that her daughter might find a better match. So Joe now spent
less time chasing butterflies, practising somersaults or hanging
round the green-rooms of Drury Lane and Sadler's Wells, and

whenever the opportunity came his way he would set off with Maria, and another Hughes as chaperone, to visit a pleasure-garden or a waxwork show; and in the summer the young lovers would dawdle along the country lanes beyond the Wells, picking flowers in the hedges, building castles in the air. It was a long courtship and, perforce, a temperate one; and as the months went by Joe's status gradually improved, while Mrs Hughes, at least, grew resigned to Maria's marriage. It is hard to believe that the girl's father was not well aware, in so small a world, of the romance between young Grimaldi and his daughter, but he preferred to delay his recognition of the fact and allowed them to maintain some show of secrecy.

In 1798 Joe reached his stage majority, and was described for the first time on the Sadler's Wells bills as 'Mr' and not 'Master' Grimaldi; his star was slowly rising, and he was ranked as one of the principal characters of the Islington pantomimes, though not as yet in the role he was soon to make so famous; and by 1799, when he was earning £4 a week at the Wells, he decided that it was time to ask Maria's father for his consent to their marriage: they had waited long enough. Although there were people at the Wells who had tried to break up the affair by malicious gossip meant for the proprietor's ear, Richard Hughes raised no objection to the match and, indeed, welcomed Grimaldi as a son-in-law and a friend. To Maria this may have been less startling a capitulation than it seemed to Joe, who had exaggerated notions of the social differences between himself and his future wife and who was innocent enough to suppose that Mr Hughes had been completely ignorant of the three-year courtship.

Before the marriage took place, Joe rented a house in Penton Street, part of the tiny suburb of Pentonville, built twenty years before among the fields of Islington, and then enjoying the cachet of a Hampstead or a Chelsea today. It was separated from the Wells by a long stretch of meadowland and scrub, and at the end of his road the White Conduit House, a famous pleasure resort in decline, was a sign of the district's reputation as a beauty spot; for the Belvedere Tavern, which still stands at the corner of Penton Street, had some claim to its name when Joe Grimaldi took number 37 at the end of the eighteenth century. From here, as the two lovers walked back to Sadler's Wells, they looked out across a pastoral landscape of market gardens, common land, meadows and a few suburban villas; and the little villages of St Pancras, Kentish Town and Somers Town straggled in picturesque clusters where now the great railway stations and goods yards lie smokily among a waste of chimneys. Joe was going up in the world and, as his enemies at the Wells did not fail to point out, he was doing himself a bit of good by marrying into the boss's family; but his enemies were few in number at either theatre, for the lively, irrepressible little boy had grown up into a kindly, nervous, amiable young man, still doing his monkey tricks and mimicry, still setting the scene-men or the dancers in a roar by his ridiculous grimacing and involuntary clowning, but never cruel or coarse or inconsiderate. Grimaldi was always proud of his reputation for being a gentleman: that, in private life, was the ideal by which Joey the Clown attempted to shape his conduct; and Penton Street was a very respectable place to which a gentleman might bring his wife.[4]

It was with the full consent of all concerned that Joe and Maria were finally married on 11th May 1799, at St George's Hanover Square, with their go-between Mrs Lewis, from the Sadler's Wells wardrobe, as one of the witnesses. This was the Whitsuntide weekend, and after the performance ended at the Wells that night Mr and Mrs Grimaldi went home to the little house in Penton Street as man and wife. On that first Sunday together, the future seemed rich with promise: a new life stretched before them in the springtime colours of the landscape at their feet. With Maria at his side Joe felt that he was stepping into a sunlit security which had seemed beyond his dreams. But life had many surprises still in store for the future King of Clowns: the harlequinade had a long way to go, and the Columbine was doomed.

Seven

*My boy, if you want to be a successful clown, first you must
be an acrobat, then a trapeze artist and a tumbler; in fact
you must be able to do everything, and then you can think
about being a clown.*—SIGNOR TRUZI, A CIRCUS PROPRIE-
TOR, QUOTED BY COCO THE CLOWN

FOR THE THIRD CHRISTMAS RUNNING, there was no pantomime at
Drury Lane in 1799: harlequinades were losing public favour and
were ousted at holiday time by such blood-and-thunder melodramas as *Blue Beard*, *The Castle Spectre*, and *Feudal Times*. These
spectacular thrillers exploited the new appetite for 'tales of terror'
which had been titillated by the successful novels of Mrs Radcliffe
and 'Monk' Lewis and encouraged, perhaps, by the violence of the
times. Bleeding nuns, avenging ghosts and rumbustiously un-
English tyrants usurped, for a season, the place of Harlequins and
Columbines of peacetime fare, and the backstage staff at the
London theatres applied themselves to the Middle Ages, conjuring
up dungeons, drawbridges and armour, arranging the Conflagrations and Explosions imported from the enemy's theatres in Paris.
It was a thin time for pantomimists who could not adapt themselves to the new medievalism or make themselves useful outside
the harlequinade.

Joe Grimaldi, however, suffered no such handicap. In this 1799
season at Drury Lane he appeared for the first time in a succession
of 'legitimate' parts, as a member of the acting company; and
although he was cast in obscure, borderline roles of the kind
reserved for low comedians, he thus achieved a new status in the
theatre and qualified for membership of the Theatrical Fund, from
whose charity mere dancers and buffoons were commonly
excluded. Grimaldi was one of the few pantomimists of the period
admitted to the Fund, for most of his contemporaries, it was
generally agreed, should be seen and not heard, and had no talent
for 'straight' comic acting; the Delpinis and Dubois, though
excellent in dumbshow, had meagre English and poor memories.[1]
Although Grimaldi himself was a 'bad study' — he found it
difficult to learn even the sketchy speaking parts of the harlequinades or the simple words of his comic songs — he was

recognized to be, in his way, an admirable actor.[2] This season gave him scant opportunity to show his peculiar talents — as a Country-man in Sheridan's *A Trip to Scarborough* (the bowdlerized *Relapse*) or a maid in *Rule a Wife and Have a Wife* — but to the new Mrs Grimaldi it represented another stage in Joe's progress towards a respectable niche in society, and a degree of security which was heartening to an inexperienced girl. Once an actor was enrolled on the register of Drury Lane or Covent Garden, he had a fair chance, other things being equal, of being fully employed for a period of some twenty years or more. Maria was exultant: she had always known that Joe would make good — and without her father's help.

Grimaldi's best role in that Drury Lane season was in the spectacle of *Lodoiska*, a Parisian hit naturalized by John Philip Kemble in 1794, whose 'flaming walls and delightful music' made it one of the most popular entertainments of the day. Long after its initial success it remained in the repertory, as perennial as *The Gondoliers*, say, in our own unstable theatre. It was as Camazin, a Tartar chief, that Joe 'obtained some celebrity' in this tuppence-coloured flummery — not for comic relief, but for acrobatic swordsmanship. In the famous final scene, when the castle was in flames, he fought to the last upon a parapet, dashed through the fire with appropriate desperation, and then leaped over a high balustrade on to the stage. Here he had fresh enemies to overcome, and he continued to fight them crawling along the ground, con-torted in the agony of his imaginary burns — a crawling fight which, it is said, was taken by Kean as a model for the final combat in *Richard III*. Grimaldi was known as a stage swordsman long before he was known as a clown, and for years after his success in motley he kept his reputation for the production of mock fights. The audience of today, accustomed only to the careful choreo-graphy of Shakespearian duels, may find it hard to envisage the times when 'a combat of eight' was billed as a star attraction, and a woman such as Mrs Wybrow could achieve stardom by her prowess with the sword; but in those days physical action had not yet been exiled from the stage, and the exploits of a Douglas Fairbanks or an Errol Flynn were normal supplements to the poetic drama.

It was in *Lodoiska* that Michael Kelly, the Novello of his day, had an opportunity to show his devotion to the star of the show,

Mrs Crouch, who also happened to be his mistress. In the last act, when the castle was in flames and Camazin had finished his fight, Mrs Crouch was regularly rescued from the fire by Mr Kelly; but one night, the actor-composer recalled in his memoirs,

> just as I was quitting the platform a carpenter prematurely took out one of his supports: down I fell, and at the same moment the fiery tower, in which was Mrs Crouch, sank down into a blaze, with a violent crash; she uttered a scream of terror. Providentially I was not hurt by the fall, and, catching her in my arms, scarcely knowing what I was doing, I carried her to the front of the stage, a considerable distance from the place where we fell.

The applause from the audience for this improvement in realism was sustained, for playgoers were well acquainted with the off-stage relation of the stars, and thereafter Mr Kelly always carried Mrs Crouch to the front of the stage, to enjoy a similar reception.[4] That collapsible tower in *Lodoiska* 'seems to have been the model of all the fortresses subsequently stormed',[5] and after 1794 Real Conflagrations and Last Minute Rescues helped to subsidize the staider drama of the classic repertory: 'a *blow-up* at the end of a piece was formerly a metaphor and signified its perdition; it is now a reality, and ensures its success.'[6] Thus the stage career of Joe Grimaldi was punctuated with musical catastrophes of fire and water, and at the Wells he was almost as renowned for sinister skulduggery in melodrama as for comic roguery in pantomime.

Night after night, in that winter of 1799, Maria Grimaldi sat in the audience at Drury Lane, watching her young husband upon the stage. How versatile he was, dancing with his mother in a comic ballet, dressing up as a girl, (but that was really rather vulgar!), cutting and slashing through the flames of *Lodoiska!* How kind of Mr Sheridan to put her on the free list! When the show was over, Joe and Maria would drive straight home to Penton Street, discussing the night's entertainment and Grimaldi's own performance in loving particular; in those halcyon days of early marriage he was rarely seen in his old haunts around Drury Lane, and he kept Maria away from the backstage world, yet nothing was allowed to interfere with his career, a career which the young couple planned, in endless conversations, with the infinite, self-centred optimism of the happily, newly married. After they had celebrated their first Christmas that year, there was more good news for the Grimaldis, although Maria received it with less enthusiasm than her husband. Talent had already won Joe a place at the Wells, and influence confirmed it; during the courtship Richard Hughes asked Charles Dibdin to help the young man if he could do so without damage to the theatre, and after the marriage promotion was expected and deserved. For some time Dibdin had watched Grimaldi at rehearsals or in the Wells yard, entertaining the other artists with his buffoonery — usually when Maria was not in the neighbourhood — and sending them into fits of laughter, surfeited though they were with seasons of traditional clowning. Dubois now seldom raised a laugh offstage, for he had repeated all his jokes a hundred times and his antics were as familiar to the company as the well-worn bars of music that gave a legal warrant to every entertainment; but Joe Grimaldi, it seemed, could not help being funny, and his comrades could not help laughing. Would he still be funny on the stage? It was a risk which Dibdin decided to take, and he resolved to use Grimaldi in an experiment he had planned for the summer season of 1800, an experiment which, he hoped, would breathe new life into the harlequinade. The Easter pantomime at the Wells was to have *two* clowns, and one of them was to be Grimaldi: what is more, they were to be clowns of unusual dress and appearance, for, as Dibdin soon discovered, his new recruit had some novel ideas on the reform of pantomime buffoonery, and as the chief proprietor's son-in-law he was given the opportunity to put them into practice. (See Chapter 14).

There was a great bustle in the Grimaldi home as the time drew near for the opening of the Wells. For weeks beforehand, during February and March, the pantomime took shape in the theatre's painting-room, carpenter's shop, and wardrobe; rehearsals on the stage — while Maria watched from her father's box, shivering despite the special fire — were sometimes interrupted by quarrels with Dubois, who jibbed at the competition of his young rival, and were often followed by private conferences in Penton Street; and on their journeys back from Drury Lane, jolting over the cobbles, Joe told a sleepy Maria his new ideas — they changed from week to week — for a bit of comic business or an innovation in his make-up. Mrs Lewis was often called in to advise Joe on his wigs and 'changes', and when work permitted she and Mrs Brooker would join Maria in the parlour of the Penton Street house for gossip over a sewing-party, while the clown's dress came to life under their busy fingers.

At last the great day arrived, 14th April 1800. Sadler's Wells had, as usual, to meet keen competition from the other minor theatres, which opened their doors on the same day. At the Royal Circus, Montgomery was the clown again (he 'stands unrivalled', said *The Times*), and Byrne ('the first English Dancer we have') presented a new ballet; and at the Amphitheatre *The Daemon's Tribunal* was acted by a company which *The Times* described as 'one of the best and most numerous that ever belonged to any summer Theatre whatever', adding that Laurent, the clown, was 'a prodigy of Nature'. In spite of such dazzling rival attractions, however, the Wells was packed with a holiday crowd on the night of Easter Monday, the same kind of crowd that had watched Grimaldi's début with his sister nineteen years before. It was a characteristically mixed bill. The programme opened with a 'musical bagatelle', *Old Fools: or Love's Stratagem*; then Richer gave his rope-walking act, while Dubois clowned below; there was a new pastoral ballet, *Filial Love: or The Double Marriage*, and an historical ballet of action, *Boadicea: or The British Amazon* (the Queen of the Iceni was frequently exploited as a patriotic symbol during the wars with France). But the star attraction of the evening was the long-awaited pantomime of *Peter Wilkins: or The Flying World*, which like most of the bill was written by the tireless Dibdin. This appears to have been the first stage version of Robert Paltock's once celebrated fantasy of flying, 'a work of uncommon beauty' (Coleridge) published in 1751, but to the audience at Sadler's Wells it presented several more obvious innovations; not only were there two Harlequins, but also two Clowns — Gobble, the Eating Clown (Dubois) and Guzzle, the Drinking Clown (Grimaldi) — both of whom wore costumes 'more extravagant than it had been the custom for such characters to wear';[7] and the début of a new Clown, especially one with so famous a name, was an event of some consequence to the patrons of the pantomime.

To no one, of course, did the first performance of *Peter Wilkins* seem of such historic significance as it did to Joe and Maria Grimaldi. While the last rehearsals were bustled through that Easter Monday, Maria stayed in the theatre, bringing Joe lunch and moral support, for the young pantomimist was racked with first-night nerves and bouts of depression. For the first time, at any theatre, he was taking the lead in a pantomime, sharing the billing with London's leading clown; and the ghost of his grim old father, in his working clothes as clown, seemed to be challenging Joe's daring in stepping out of line. Right up to the time when he stood ready in the wings, with painted face and multi-coloured flaps and frills, Grimaldi was in a fever of nervous apprehension, intensified by the good wishes of his friends backstage and the avuncular advice — half kindly, half malicious — of old Dubois. Yet once he was out upon the stage, with the holiday crowd's shout of pleasure ringing in his ears, all constraint vanished and he plunged into the violent capers of the harlequinade with the assurance of a born clown. In her father's box, sitting anxiously behind the family, Maria unclasped her hands and relaxed a little in her chair, although not until the performance ended could she assume that all was well — so many things could, and did, go wrong on the opening night of a pantomime. Old Banks, one of the Harlequins, was somewhat stiff and slow for active service, but his younger rival, Simpson, made up for that by his grace and speed; Charles Dibdin's wife, billed as 'Female Volunteer with a Song', was barely tolerated by the crowd, but 'Jew' Davis restored the balance with some low comedy songs in his usual suggestive style; and although there were some snags in the machinery and stagecraft, these had become almost a first-night convention at every London theatre, and the 'tricks' and 'changes' were generally applauded. Both Clowns worked desperately hard for their laughs — too hard, perhaps, on that first night. Dubois guzzled pies and sausages, while Grimaldi downed quarts of stage beer, competing for applause; they chased Harlequin and Columbine through a score of comic misadventures, deceiving and being deceived, robbing and being robbed, thrashing and being thrashed; until at last they stood together, panting with exhaustion, in the final tableau of the pantomime, watching the audience cheering and applauding in the usual Easter Monday way. *Peter Wilkins* was a success and, although Joe Grimaldi was not immediately hailed by the press as a new star in the firmament of fun, he had made his impression upon the management and the audience.

There was, it seems, no reference in the press to the innovations at the Wells, and indeed it was not until nearly a month later that the name of Grimaldi was so much as mentioned. In its report on

FOUR FACES
Above. Left: Engraved by T. Blood, from a drawing by T. Wageman (1820).
Right: Engraved by H. Brown, a musician in the Sadler's Wells orchestra.
Below. Left: Engraved by W. Greatbach, from a drawing by R. Raven (1846):
the frontispiece to the *Memoirs*. Right: Artist unknown: this is, in the author's
opinion, a portrait of J. S. Grimaldi, Joe's son.

The central quartet of the Regency harlequinade, with Ellar, Blanchard and Grimaldi, as illustrated in a Toy Theatre sheet. *From the Beard Collection in the British Theatre Museum*

the first night *The Times* observed, with a perfunctory puff, that the entertainment was excellent (a standard verdict on 'minor' harlequinades at this period in the Thunderer's history), and devoted its attention to *Boadicea* as 'a chef d'oeuvre of serious Pantomime'; but a week later it returned to *Peter Wilkins*, singling out the comic singing of 'Jew' Davis and 'some very curious pieces of mechanism' for praise. The transformation of a box of pills into a basket of ducks seemed to *The Times* quite the most remarkable feature of the whole piece; and another critic solemnly observed that 'The transition from Ward's Medicine Shop to Jarvis's Coffin Shop is one of the prettiest scene changes we ever saw.' Yet the Grimaldis, reading the papers next morning in Penton Street, can scarcely have been surprised at the uncritical brevity of the reports or the absence of Joe's name. What counted was the appreciation of Charles Dibdin and Richard Hughes, and that had been given in full measure the previous night after the show was over. 'From that time — at the Wells at least — the Costume of the Clown was completely changed,' Dibdin says, 'and a whimsical mixture of colours and compositions invariably studied.'[8] From that time, too, Joe was recognized as the heir to Dubois's throne, and his name gained new lustre; news of his clowning spread by word of mouth, the best of all theatrical advertisements, and among the distinguished customers who came to Islington that summer were the Duke of Norfolk and the Lord Chancellor; not to mention the clowns of other London theatres who, when they could contrive an opportunity, studied the new-comer's costume and technique to see what they could borrow for their own routines. 'The new entertainments of Sadler's Wells,' runs a newspaper puff of the time, 'are now become a universal topic of conversation in all fashionable companies; and the first salutation after "How d'ye do?" is generally "Have you seen Boadicea and Peter Wilkins?" If the answer is No, the reply is sure to be, "Then, if you have any taste, never lose the opportunity." '

Under Dibdin's tuition, Grimaldi was given the opportunity to show the variety of his comic talent to a public which still regarded him as a young 'character' actor of serious pantomime; and in August he was billed for the first time as a comic singer, sharing the honours with 'Jew' Davis, who had ruled the roost in this department since he arrived from the Circus in 1797. The rapid growth in Joe's popularity is illustrated by the changes in his billing, for his name was now invoked more frequently as a bait in advance announcements not only at the Wells but also, very soon, at Drury Lane itself.

* * *

The young Grimaldis had another cause for celebration in that momentous spring of 1800: Maria was expecting a baby. The house in Penton Street was now the scene of eager family conferences, and Mrs Brooker, Mrs Lewis, and the Hughes girls all applied themselves to knitting clothes and choosing names, while Joe and Maria, whose cup of joy was now filled to the brim, discussed the future of the unborn child, due to make its entrance in October. Would he be an actor ... or a gentleman? Where would they send him to school? Could they afford to give him brothers and sisters? Or would it be a girl? At least, Joe thought, the child would be born in wedlock — for whatever good that might do it — and it would be assured of a happy home life, near the countryside, with young and devoted parents to look after it: young Joe (they had already decided on the name) would have a childhood very different from that which the Signor had allowed *his* son. The natural anxiety of a loving husband was, however, reinforced by Grimaldi's inherent melancholia as the months went by, for it proved to be a sickly pregnancy and Maria often had to take to her bed. There was, perhaps, some constitutional weakness in the Hughes family, for three of the girls died in the space of a few years, and though his mother and his friends assured him that Maria's illness was a common accompaniment of pregnancy — especially with the first child — Joe often found it hard to keep his fears to himself.

Yet, in spite of his anxieties and Maria's ill-health, those were exciting months for the Grimaldis. Joe's success as a Clown in *Peter Wilkins* had repercussions at Drury Lane, to whose management John Philip Kemble returned that autumn; and although the relative merits of buffoons were usually matters beneath Kemble's notice, he seems to have agreed that it was time for the Lane to stage another Christmas pantomime — after a three year gap — and that Joe Grimaldi, already under contract to the Lane, should be the new Clown. Preparations began that summer, while

Joe was still performing at the Wells, and whenever it was possible and permissible he would call in at Drury Lane (closed from July to September) to see what was happening in the paint-room and the workshops. Sometimes Maria was well enough, in spite of her husband's insistence, to watch him from her father's box at the Wells, as she had watched him so many times before; but more often she stayed at home, to wait eagerly until Joe came back — often not until one o'clock in the morning — primed with back-stage gossip, news of whom was 'out front', and rumours about the new pantomime.

When the Drury Lane season of 1800–1 opened in September, Grimaldi was cast, for the meantime, in a few small roles of the legitimate repertory, such as an officer in Cumberland's *The Wheel of Fortune* and a Jew Pedlar in a farce called *The Indian*; and he later rehearsed for the Sheridan pantomime of *Robinson Crusoe* (to be staged before Christmas), in which his father had appeared nearly twenty years before, while still performing many evenings at Islington. Overworked and over-anxious, his hopes and fears intensified as Maria's time drew near; and his double career at the Wells and the Lane kept him away from home.

Then, in October, the blow fell. Maria Grimaldi died in child-birth. It happened on St Luke's Day, Saturday, 18th October.

In his first agony of bereavement, Grimaldi's mind plunged into darkness. His friends feared for his sanity and even for his life. He talked wildly, with frequent fits of crying, and called out for Maria: 'nothing but the constant attention and vigilance of his friends, who never left him alone, would have prevented him laying violent hands upon his life.'[9] For seventeen months he had found happiness with the girl he loved, in an idyllic dream of contentment and success. Now the dream was over, the future was dissolved. There was no wife and no child. Success was hollow and meaningless, when there was nobody to share it, and all the plans they had made together were destroyed. The little house in Penton Street, stocked with memories, was unbearable, and Joe spent his time with the Hughes family, or the Lewises, or at the theatres and the nearby taverns. Maria's last words, addressed to her brother Richard, were: 'Poor Joe! Oh, Richard, be kind to poor Joe!' Better than anyone, she knew the anguish which this final parting would bring to her beloved husband; how much hope he had invested in their future and their child; and how precarious was his confidence and cheerfulness, in such a crisis as this. Maria knew that the inheritance of the old Signor was expressed not only upon the stage but also in Joe's private life.

Yet two days after his wife's death Joe Grimaldi was acting at Drury Lane. The play was *Hamlet*. The role was that of the Second Gravedigger.

That night, for one appearance only, Mrs Stephen Kemble was playing Ophelia to the Hamlet of her brother-in-law, John Philip; and perhaps it was, in some degree, to mark this event that Grimaldi was cast for the first time in *Hamlet*, and indeed in any Shakespearian play. Notoriously slow of study, he had been conning his part for weeks before the event, and Maria, as always, had held the book and prompted him at home.

Perhaps we may see him again, with the mind's eye, in the stage churchyard of Drury Lane, watching his comrade peel off and fold the traditional comic waistcoats (eight, at least), wielding his spade with a will as he proposes, with dutiful stupidity, a riddle to which he knows the answer only too well:

'Who builds stronger than a mason, a shipwright, or a carpenter?'

'Ay, tell me that and unyoke,' says the First Gravedigger.

'Marry, now I cannot tell.'

'To't.'

'Mass, I cannot tell.'

'Cudgel thy brains no more about it, for your dull ass will not mend his pace with beating; and, when you are asked this question next, say, "a grave-maker": the houses that he makes last till Doomsday. Go, get thee to Yaughan; fetch me a stoup of liquor . . .'

And Grimaldi staggers off into the wings, where the Court of Denmark waits to make its entrance. 'Say, a grave-maker,' the words echo in his head, 'the houses that he makes last till Doomsday.' The traditional horseplay of the grave-diggers must have been weak in comedy that night at Drury Lane, for as he stood in the make-believe grave near Elsinore the new Clown thought of the real graveyard of St James's, Clerkenwell, and of the lines which Maria had chosen as her epitaph:

Earth walks on gold like glittering gold;
Earth says to Earth, we are but mould:

84

Earth builds on Earth castles and towers;
Earth says to Earth, all shall be ours.

As Kemble stands above the grave, pronouncing measured, noble grief about the fate of Yorick, the Second Gravedigger is sobbing bitterly in his dressing-room. It is hard to bear, even for a veteran of 21.

* * *

As soon as it could be arranged, Grimaldi gave up the house in Penton Street with all the bitter-sweet memories it contained, and took another house on the other side of Sadler's Wells, 4 Baynes Row across Coppice Row (now part of Mount Pleasant).[10] There he sometimes entertained Bob Fairbrother, Richard Hughes, or the Dibdins, and his mother and sister, Mary Williamson, did what they could for his comfort; but Mrs Brooker, it seems, still lived apart, and in his leisure hours Joe did not seek out company. He went home to his pigeons, instead. At the top of the new house he contrived a pigeon-loft, where he would sit for hours at a time watching the comings and goings of his prize birds; he spent much time and trouble in coddling his collection, enlisting in that back-street fraternity of fanciers which still claims its lonely, dedicated, clannish connoisseurs; and into the welfare and training of these plump little birds — he had as many as sixty at one time — he poured all the energy that he could spare from acting. For, after Maria's death, Joe threw himself with new fervour into his work. Always conscientious, he became fanatical, and the daemonic energy which he released upon the stage served to build up the second personality of Joey the Clown.

But Maria was never forgotten. Thirty-six years later, alone and ill, after the death of his second wife and his son, Grimaldi made his will; and among other bequests he left to Dayus, the treasurer of Sadler's Wells, the prized possession of

two patchworked quilts . . . the largest made by my first wife, poor dear Maria, and the smaller one by her sister Julia now Mrs Bennett which I hope will be received out of respect to her dear memory.

Poor dear Maria, I think, always came first.

85

Eight

The more one suffers, the more, I believe, one has a sense for the comic. It is only by the deepest suffering that one acquires true authority in the use of the comic, an authority which by one word transforms as by magic the reasonable creature one calls man into a caricature.—KIERKEGAARD

DRURY LANE ENGAGED A NEW BALLET-MASTER for the season of 1800–1, a sturdy, agile man of 44, who had recently returned from America with a new wife and new ideas for the pantomime. Although this was James Byrne's first adult season at the Lane, he had danced here with his sister thirty years before as a pupil of Signor Giorgi, in the days of old Grimaldi; and after touring the provinces as a dancer, and scoring some success at Covent Garden, he had decided to try his luck abroad and had plunged into what was then the rare adventure of a transatlantic trip. To Drury Lane in 1800 he brought not only a number of talented children but a new kind of choreography, shaking up the somewhat venerable *corps de ballet* with his enthusiastic innovations; and when John Philip Kemble put him in charge of the next Christmas pantomime Byrne not only helped to make that season a landmark in the history of the harlequinade but he also helped to save Joe Grimaldi from what we should now identify as a nervous breakdown. The usual difficulties of pantomime rehearsals were complicated that autumn by Byrne's unfamiliarity with the company, the management's resistance to his new ideas, and the recurrent melancholia of Grimaldi, who, having reached his ambition of playing Clown at Drury Lane at the early age of 22, had lost interest in his great opportunity when Maria was no longer there to watch and pray for his success. Yet, for all his private misery, Grimaldi attended rehearsals as punctually as ever — he was a professional to the bone — and the personal importance of the approaching production was enhanced for him by the sympathy and enterprise of James Byrne, who planned to do for Harlequin what Joe had already begun to do for the Clown.

The new pantomime, *Harlequin Amulet: or, The Magick of Mona*, which was apparently written by William Powell (1754–1836) the prompter of the Theatre Royal, was staged for the first time on 22nd December, after Mrs Siddons had appeared in *The Stranger* (Boxing Day productions were still not *de rigueur*.) Like many pantos of that period, it made a feature of its topographical novelty: geography had a glamour for Georgian audiences, and Wales — the setting of Mr Powell's entertainment — was still an exotic country, whose customs and language were shrouded in romantic mist. *Harlequin Amulet* began in a subterranean temple, where 'several Welsh Bards had taken refuge from their persecutors, having been informed that Morcar, the evil genius of their race, had meditated their destruction'. After this precursor of the Demon King had appeared, with appropriately sinister effects, Iris, a counterpart of the Fairy Queen, made her entrance in company with a rainbow; and having promised protection to those who pursued her enemies she waved her scarf, a bright cloud descended from the flies, and Harlequin stepped out with his attendant, Punch — Mr Byrne and Mr Grimaldi, no less, ready to begin the harlequinade.

Harlequin? But how differently he was dressed from the orthodox 'parti-coloured gentry' of the pantomime! The pit buzzed with astonished talk at Byrne's entrance, for he was dressed not in the traditional loose jacket and trousers but in a skin-tight silk costume, covered with glittering spangles; and once the comic business began it was evident that he had abandoned much of the usual miming routine. Until that time Harlequin's movements had been, to a large extent, stylized in formal patterns and figures, and in certain pauses of the action he was expected to strike one of the 'attitudes' which Harry Woodward had established some forty years before; but Byrne introduced new attitudes and new dance-forms, and in spite of his age he dazzled the audience — in many ways so jealous of its Christmas traditions — with his athletic vigour, making an especial impression by apparently running up a perpendicular wall and over the side of a house 'with such amazing velocity that it was impossible to detect the means by which he was assisted'. Grimaldi recorded in his retirement his unchanging opinion that 'in my judgment Mr James Byrne was at that time the best Harlequin on the boards, and has never been excelled, even if equalled, since that period'; and Byrne was helped by his Columbine, Bella Menage, one of the few dancers to bring any distinction to this thankless role. 'Taking them together,' wrote Grimaldi in

1836, 'I never saw so good a Harlequin and Columbine; and I still entertain that same opinion.'[1]

Among other features of this historic pantomime were the 'characteristic Welsh airs', selected by Byrne, which were played on a harp by Mr Weippert; 'a dragon of surprising terror' made by the famous machinist, Alexander Johnstone; and the appearance of Pero, Scaramouch and Punch, who still lingered on the English stage. (Pantaloon, Pero and Scaramouch — as well as Harlequin and Clown — were played by actors new to the roles, and the production seems to have been an experiment for all concerned.)

Grimaldi himself scored so great a success as Punch — notably in his comic rivalry with Harlequin for Columbine's love — that Sheridan wanted him to continue in the role throughout the piece, instead of changing into Clown's dress; but Joe refused (so he would have us believe) because — even for him — the part was too arduous. As Punch he had to wear a big, heavy hump on both back and chest; a high, sugar-loaf hat; heavy wooden shoes; and a long-nosed mask, 'heavy from its machinery of springs to produce grimaces.'[2] But his india-rubber countenance needed no machinery to make the audience laugh, and the costume was so cumbersome that he changed into Clown's dress by the sixth scene: moreover, he was anxious to match Byrne's novelties with his own, and Punch restricted his opportunities and his range. Sheridan yielded, but not, one would imagine, before Joe's intransigence had provoked some bad temper among his more immediate superiors, Kemble in particular resenting breaches of stage discipline by mere pantomime buffoons. One of Grimaldi's stories, in which the proprietor of Drury Lane often featured as a friendly hero, concerned Sheridan's pun:

Grimaldi, your Punch was so good that I have lost all taste for the spirit of the pantomime.[3]

The new Harlequin at the Lane, like the new Clowns at the Wells, proved to be very successful, and the innovations of Byrne and Grimaldi were after some experiment accepted as the standard patterns. Yet little is known about the detail of either *Peter Wilkins* or *Harlequin Amulet*, and no indication of their significance may be found in the press. The following notice of *Harlequin Amulet* is characteristic:

The fact is, there is very little of novelty or experience to

CHARM the town. There is some good acting and dancing by Byrne, but that is wanting, without which Harlequin is merely 'Leather and Prunella'; the TRICK and cunning of the scene, to render the business comic as well as interesting.

Can this be the same pantomime — with a revolutionary Harlequin and England's greatest Clown? Again, *The Times* was at its frostiest:

> It is stated in the Play Bill to be a *Pantomime*, but it may as justly be called by any other title, as it has no claim either to humour or contrivance. The imperfection in the performance throughout added to the disgust of the entertainment itself, as there was scarcely one scene given in a neat and finished style. . . . This is the fifth new representation at this Theatre during the present season, every one of which has failed.

The critic of *The Times* went on to say that the music was 'not destitute of merit', and acknowledged that Weippert's harp was 'universally applauded', but of the new Clown and the new Harlequin he said not a word. He had noticed no difference.

Such hostility and misunderstanding in the newspapers were by no means unusual, while accompanied at the same time by an often meaningless eulogy of entertainments at the 'minor' theatres, and several years elapsed before Grimaldi's name was so much as recognized by the respectable press, because of this resistance to pantomime at Drury Lane and Covent Garden and the irrelevance of the old-fashioned demand for tricks and changes. Apart from its indication of the fallibility of dramatic critics, this inability to recognize comic genius lights up the gap between popular culture and educated taste, in an age when it was proper to discuss only 'legitimate' comedians in publications only a small minority could afford or were able to read.

In spite of such press reports, the influence of *Harlequin Amulet* was considerable in the theatre, and it enjoyed a tolerably successful run of thirty-three performances. When it was revived the following season, instead of a new pantomime, it was honoured by a royal visit, and it was on this occasion, perhaps, that George III, buttoned tightly into the general's uniform that was conventional wear for such appearances, 'laughed almost to suffocation' at Grimaldi's 'mimic exhibition of swallowing a quantity of long puddings':[4] this was the kind of acting which Farmer George understood and enjoyed. So did most of his subjects. From 1800 onwards — within a year of his first appearance in the role — Grimaldi was recognized as one of London's leading clowns. The town went to see the old Signor's son out of curiosity, but soon the news spread that he was a merryman in his own right and his own original kind. He had reached the top of the ladder — alone.

*   *   *

That first successful season of clowning at Drury Lane, however, was nearly Grimaldi's last, for the young man had the effrontery to disobey the great John Philip himself. In March 1801,[5] it would seem, Joe saw that the Drury Lane bills announced his forthcoming appearance at Easter in *Harlequin Amulet*, and as he regarded this as a breach of his articles, under which he was engaged to play in 'last pieces' at and after Easter, but not in pantomime, he sought an interview with Kemble and told him that he could not appear. According to the *Memoirs*, Kemble,

> who received him with all the grandeur and authority of demeanour which it was his habit to assume when he was about to insist upon something which he knew would be resisted . . . rose from his seat, and said in a solemn tone, 'Joe, one word here, Sir, is as good as a thousand — you *must* come!'
>
> Joe felt excessively indignant at this, not merely because *must* is a disagreeable word in itself, but because he conceived that the tone in which it was uttered rendered it additionally disagreeable; so, saying at once what the feeling of the moment prompted, he replied, 'Very good, sir, in reply to *must*, there is only one thing that can very well be said — I will *not* come, sir.'
>
> 'Will not, Joe, eh?' said Kemble.
>
> 'I will not, sir,' replied Grimaldi.
>
> 'Not!' said Kemble again, with great emphasis.
>
> Grimaldi repeated the monosyllable with equal vehemence.
>
> 'Then, Joe,' said Kemble, taking off his hat, and bowing in a ghost-like manner, 'I wish you a very good morning!'
>
> Grimaldi took off his hat, made another low bow, and wished Mr Kemble good morning: and so they parted.

The Second Gravedigger had no right to challenge the Prince of Denmark in this way, by the theatrical etiquette of the time, and to oppose Black Jack required considerable courage for a performer in Grimaldi's position; yet, according to the *Memoirs*, his defiance succeeded — for the moment — and his name was taken from the bills. The encounter, however, had a sequel. Three months later Joe received a letter, signed by the prompter, informing him that his services would not be required in the following season: he was, after twenty years' service, to be dismissed from Drury Lane.

In later life Grimaldi was a victim of what modern jargon labels a 'persecution complex', which was established by experiences such as these. At the Wells before his marriage he had met the open hostility of enemies in power who had tried to secure his dismissal, and at Drury Lane, it was clear, he had foes in high places, although if he had antagonized Kemble it was only because he had spoken the truth, in defending his rights as a man and an actor. This shock, coming so soon after his bereavement, weakened Joe's resistance to his family inheritance. As one biographer says:

> To apology and explanation he was always open and plausible, but an unmerited injury seemed ever present to his imagination; and this medium magnified the animosity which he supposed the party to bear towards him, until it positively absorbed every other idea, and every action of the party was attributed to this never-dying hate. Revenge, however, never entered Grimaldi's ideas — he was incapable of the feeling.[6]

Although he now did not seek revenge upon Drury Lane for this abrupt dismissal, he thought at first of bringing an action against Sheridan, until Maria's father talked him out of so wild a scheme. Richard Hughes offered Joe an engagement at his Exeter theatre as soon as the Wells closed down that autumn, at a weekly salary of £4 with a clear benefit, and the Clown, though nursing a deep sense of 'unmerited injury', turned his back on Drury Lane. How quickly his success and happiness had been destroyed: first, his wife and child had died, and now his career had been broken. What had he done, Joe asked, to deserve this punishment?

Joe knew that he could never find another Maria, yet he might salvage his career by going to Covent Garden the following year; there was a gentlemen's agreement between the two patent theatres that a year must elapse before an actor could transfer from one to the other. If Kemble was his enemy, however — and Joe's imagination 'magnified the animosity' of the great tragedian — that might be impossible, so he resigned himself to making a new start and to the prospect of playing in the provinces for the first time. From now on, he decided, his life would be divided between the Wells in the summer and Hughes's West-country theatres in the winter. At least, Joe thought, he would be working for Maria's family: but who would look after the pigeons at home?

Was his dismissal so tragic? To most of his contemporaries, Grimaldi's position would seem highly enviable — with powerful connections in management, guaranteed employment all the year round, stardom at Sadler's Wells, and all this at the age of 22. Yet Joe had set himself to expect the highest, and to his anxious, melancholy, lonely disposition such summary treatment at the Lane — his father's theatre — appeared too cruel a rebuff, a confirmation of his worst suspicions that he was in some way marked for suffering.

*　　*　　*

When the run of *Harlequin Amulet* ended at Drury Lane, Grimaldi returned to Sadler's Wells for the summer with increased prestige. He still shared the honours with Dubois, and their rivalry — 'Antics striving to outstrip each other'[7] — was symbolized by a comic scene in which they disputed as to who could make the ugliest face; after appeals to the audience — one enlisting the pit's support, and the other the cheers of the gallery — they exchanged cards and prepared for a burlesque duel. But when both men appeared in Charles Dibdin's *Harlequin Benedick: or, The Ghost of Mother Shipton*, Dubois took the role of Pero while his junior played Clown. This production continued the experiment of *Peter Wilkins*, for it included not only two fully-grown Harlequins but a junior edition as well (played by Master Charles Dubois), two Columbines (good and evil) and a female Pantaloon. Mrs Brooker was appropriately cast as a Butcher's Wife, with a duet on the cymbals, 'vulgarly called the marrowbone and cleavers'. As a result of this fateful season she was soon to become a grandmother once again, for during its course Joe Grimaldi found a new wife.

On 17th August the Wells staged a new serio-comic panto-mime, *The Great Devil*, based by Dibdin upon 'a character who is now committing great Depredations in and about the City of Genoa, at the head of Thirty Desperadoes, and for whose Apprehension the Doge and Council of Genoa have offered great

Rewards'; topicality, however tenuous, was always in favour at the Wells, whose customers liked to see 'recent things yet warm with life', as Wordsworth put it. The second-in-command of the Desperadoes was Grimaldi, armed to the teeth and heavily disguised, but one night on the stage, just as he was pulling a pistol from his boot to begin some mute villainy, the trigger caught and the weapon fired down at the unfortunate actor's foot. Joe was in agony, but he insisted in carrying on — limping the while — until the final curtain. When his boot was cut off, his foot was found to be severely burned; for although the pistol was, of course, unloaded, the explosion had set fire to his stocking, which had been smouldering all the time he was on the stage. Even Grimaldi had to acknowledge that he could not act again until his foot was better, and for a week or two he was obliged to stay at home in Baynes Row, fretting to be back in harness with the Desperadoes, brooding over his own misfortunes, hobbling up, as soon as he was able, to the pigeon-loft to watch his beloved birds. Mrs Brooker and Mary Williamson often came to visit him, with many friends from both theatres, and perhaps it was Joe's mother who brought along a young girl from the Drury Lane chorus, Mary Bristow, who had joined the theatre the previous autumn and appeared in *Harlequin Amulet* among the assorted peasants and gypsies. After her first visit to Baynes Row Miss Bristow frequently returned, chaperoned by Mrs Brooker or by one of her sisters, and in nursing Joe through this convalescence she cheered him by her company and conversation, rousing him from his fits of depression and despair.

In gratitude for her kindness, Grimaldi married her on the following Christmas Eve, and it may be as well to state in this place that with her he lived very happily for more than thirty years, when she died.

That is almost all we learn from the *Memoirs*, or from any other source, about the courtship, marriage and wedded life of the second Mrs Grimaldi, and with that brief introduction Mary Bristow sinks back into obscurity. 'In gratitude for her kindness, Grimaldi married her. . . .' Is that touch of condescension the inadvertency of patchwork editing, or does it reflect the truth — the truth of a lonely, vulnerable man, still mourning the loss of his adorable Maria but yearning for affection, comradeship and children? All we know is that Mary Bristow, during those summer days in Islington, won Joe's heart; that, by marrying the Clown of Drury Lane, she gave him the chance of a new security; and that, in marrying Mary, he also married her family — one of those feckless, friendly, hard-working, poverty-stricken tribes that peopled the English stage, and made frequent calls upon the purse and influence of their more prosperous relations.[9] Mary was the least talented of the Bristows, but one of the most persistent: after she married she continued to work at Drury Lane, and although in spite of her opportunities she never emerged from the anonymity of the chorus she was still in the company twenty years later, long after the names of the other Bristows had vanished from the London stage.

*　　*　　*

When Drury Lane opened for the season of 1801–2, Grimaldi had recovered his health, if not his heart, and was back in harness at the Wells; but his absence from the Lane was soon publicized, with fortunate results, when a melodrama was revived in which he had made a special, small success with one particular scene.[10] This was a 'combat' which gave Joe the chance to exhibit his swordsmanship, and gave the stage-hands the chance to set up the last, spectacular scene behind a front cloth; but as the stage management had neglected to find a substitute for Joe the scene was dropped at rehearsals. As a result, there was no distraction to hold the audience's attention while the last scene was being prepared and, as the temper of the house rose, some pittites remembered the stage fight which had been included in previous performances and loudly demanded its restoration. In a few moments the whole theatre was roaring with excited indignation, an endemic condition among playgoers of the time: some were shouting for an apology, some shouted for Kemble to fight in the combat himself, and others just shouted. The tardy unveiling of the last scene's splendours did not placate the angry house, and the curtain fell to the accompaniment of boos and hisses and cries of protest.

Before the humiliated players had left the stage, they were confronted by the rare spectacle of Richard Brinsley Sheridan, their employer . . . and Sheridan was in a towering rage. That evening he had been entertaining a party of friends in his private box, showing off the beauties of his beloved white elephant of a theatre, assuring them of the expertise and popularity of his company, in whose success he took some pride. The sudden storm in a teacup took him by surprise, and to his annoyance he was quite incapable of explaining it away to his friends, as he had no idea of what had gone wrong. As soon as the piece was over, 'he made one of his most imposing sweeps from the fourth wing, cutting the stage with a majestic curve ... and in a loud and alarming voice exclaimed "Let no one stir!" '[11] Standing with his back to the curtain, Sheridan demanded and received an explanation; at the news of Grimaldi's dismissal he became even more enraged and, after haranguing the hapless company upon the rights of the proprietor to know what was happening in his own theatre, he ordered the call boy to go to Grimaldi's house immediately and tell him to be on the stage next day at twelve o'clock.

What a night that was for Grimaldi! Knocked up at Baynes Row at midnight, he learned from the call boy, soon followed by friends in the company, of the hubbub at Drury Lane and of Sheridan's intervention. Right had triumphed over might, and the conspirators had been foiled: he would not have to go to Exeter after all. Next day Joe returned in triumph to the Lane and was reinstated with apologies by Sheridan, who increased his weekly salary by a pound; and at a rehearsal the following day Kemble went out of his way to meet Grimaldi and to say 'with great good humour, that he was very glad to see him there again, and that he hoped it would be very long before they parted company'.[12] Perhaps John Philip was not, after all, the villain of the piece? Or did such affability show all the more clearly his guilty conscience and his sinister intentions? It was hard for a Clown to tell.

*　　*　　*

Within three years Grimaldi had risen to stardom in pantomime, and his pay at Drury Lane had been trebled. For a full week of six days — although this was by no means the regular working week for a pantomimist — he earned £4, to which must be added the new Mrs Grimaldi's weekly £1. In the summer he earned a higher salary at the Wells — if not twice as much in 1802, as the

Memoirs say, it was probably in the region of £6, apart from the profits of benefits. To the farm labourer, whose average wage was eight shillings, or the miner, who earned sixteen shillings a week, a family wage of £5 was prosperity beyond his reach; and it is an illuminating sidelight on theatrical affairs that Grimaldi already earned more than the stage manager of the Wells, Charles Dibdin. In 1801 Dibdin was paid three guineas a week in summer (with two guineas for his wife) and two guineas a week in winter, a salary for which he not only wrote pieces to order — burlettas, songs, serious pantomimes and harlequinades — but also invented the necessary machinery, supervised the conduct of rehearsals, and performed other backstage duties of a more or less managerial nature. Yet although Joe was high up in the scale among the Drury Lane company of eighty-five, his weekly wage seemed less magnificent when Byrne earned twice and Suett three times as much money.

About this time, however, Grimaldi began to supplement his regular wages by brief visits to country theatres. It was a recognized practice for London stars to make provincial solo tours, appearing for a night or two in their favourite roles with a local stock company, and often earning considerable sums of money thereby. Mrs Jordan, for example, made 800 guineas in three weeks at Bath in 1809. Such excursions were to prove the most profitable evenings in Grimaldi's long career, although it was not until some ten years after his second marriage that he began to visit towns such as Birmingham or Liverpool, when in two nights he might take as much as he earned in a year at Drury Lane or Sadler's Wells; and his first performance outside London was, according to the *Memoirs*, at Rochester in November 1801, when for playing Clown and Scaramouch he earned £160, a windfall which may well have influenced his decision to marry Mary Bristow the following month. When he returned to the same Kent circuit in March 1802 he played two nights each in Canterbury and Maidstone and brought home over £300 to his new bride. Grimaldi had never seen so much money before in his life, except perhaps in the treasury of Drury Lane, and it was all his, to spend as he liked, in whatever way he chose. He spent it with the same prodigal intensity that he spent himself upon the stage; and Mary helped him with a will, making up for all her years of poverty and hardship, buying things for the house and herself and Joe and her family, buying until the bounty had disappeared and the bills ran high.

After being lionized in Kent, however, it was all the more difficult for Joe to endure the inefficient tyrannies of Drury Lane. Now that he had tasted the fullness of his own power, and had reaped a golden harvest by his own reputation he began to question the assumed superiority of some of his 'legitimate' colleagues with talents patently inferior to his own: he was inclined, in other words, to 'get above himself' — to use the management's diagnosis. In spite of the dramatic reinstatement by Sheridan, or because of it, life for Joe was rather uneasy at the Lane. Things were very different at Sadler's Wells. The old play-house had been redecorated and redesigned for the 1802 season by Cabanel, who altered its shape 'from square to semi-circular', and it came under new management; for with Hughes were now two City gentlemen, Barfoot and Yarnold; the composer, Reeve, and the scene-painter, Andrews; and the Dibdin brothers, Charles and Tom. Among the company was that boy prodigy, Master Carey; a new Harlequin arrived from Covent Garden in the person of Joe's old friend Jack Bologna, who returned to his theatrical *alma mater* as a star in his own right; and another landmark was the disappearance of Jack Richer, 'and with him Rope Dancing: which had been, time out of mind, an integral and indispensable part of the amusements of Sadler's Wells.' The Clown to the Rope had disappeared, too, for old Dubois left the company at the end of the 1801 season. From now on Grimaldi was in sole and undisputed possession of the Clownship of the Wells, and here he reigned for the next twenty years of his professional life. In this season of 1802, moreover, he carried his innovations a stage further and consolidated his experiments in make-up, costume and technique: according to Charles Dibdin,

> the present mode of dressing Clowns and painting their faces, was then invented by Mr Grimaldi, who, in every respect, founded a *New School* for Clowns.[13]

Ten days after the Wells opened its doors at Easter, the short-lived Peace of Amiens was declared. After nine years of war, nine years of heavy taxation and starvation prices, the people of London rejoiced ... and the new Clown of Sadler's Wells was there to help them to celebrate.

97

Nine

*No clown can be a real clown without the help of tradition
and method, and an exhaustive technical training for his
profession. Your clown, just as much as any other artist, is
the product of tradition.*—GROCK

THROUGHOUT THE PEACEFUL SUMMER OF 1802, while Napoleon
made his plans for world conquest and England relaxed in the lull
before the storm, a child ripened in the womb of the second Mrs
Grimaldi. These were anxious days for the Clown of Sadler's
Wells. Mary Bristow, however, was a hardier, healthier woman
than her predecessor. When the autumn season began at Drury
Lane she resumed her usual place in the chorus, and kept at work
until at least three weeks before her confinement. In this persistence
Mrs Grimaldi followed the example of such productive contemporaries as Dorothy Jordan, whose continual pregnancies seldom
prevented her from playing in breeches and were tolerated by
the audience, it seems, as an occupational disorder of English
actresses. Sometimes the ladies of the stage went too far in their
determination that the show must go on; thus at Astley's in 1807
Madame Mercerot was 'too big with child to take the sword and
mingle in the fight. Though she conquers her man, and the odds
are we know not how many in her favour her feats are more
alarming than agreeable;'[1] but for such feats Mary Grimaldi
had neither the talent nor the opportunity, and, undisturbed by
pre-natal combats on the stage, she presented her husband on 21st
November 1802 with a son.

Joseph Samuel William Grimaldi, the Clown's first and only
child, brought new happiness to the house in Baynes Row, and
Joe plunged with nervous enthusiasm into the mysteries of father-
craft. His talent for 'mug-cutting', or pulling funny faces, had at
first to be restrained, but soon he was able to display his son with
practised pride to all and sundry. Private bliss was accompanied
by public prosperity, and his own popularity was, in part,
reflected on the opening night of the Christmas pantomime,
when the crowds were so great outside the theatre that many
people were seriously injured. 'The scene was dreadful', as one
reporter noted. 'Many in the lowest class of life paid six shillings

to the boxes, rather than be disappointed.' Grimaldi was already a favourite of the holiday crowds.

At Sadler's Wells the following spring his contract was renewed for another three years at a high and rising salary, and this, together with his benefits, his country visits and his increased salary at the Lane, ensured that young Joe was brought up in a comfortable if unconventional home. Mary herself returned to work at Drury Lane a few weeks after Joe was born, and she remained there year after year, even in the heyday of her husband's glory, unremarkable, unsuccessful and underpaid. There seems to have been no urgent financial reason why she should have carried on in the chorus; and life in these lower depths cannot have been as grim as it appears, from this distance in time, if an apparently happily married, fairly prosperous woman could continue to work there by choice. Mary Grimaldi was, it seems, a slave of the theatre, and could not surrender herself to respectable domesticity at Clerkenwell.

A month after Sadler's Wells opened its doors for the season of 1803, the short-lived peace was ended. On 18th May war was declared, and Britain entered the second phase of the long struggle against Napoleon. The war-weariness of the previous year was forgotten, and with it the sudden gust of Francophilia that had blown through the interval of armistice. During the summer, the hatred of 'Boney' blazed up throughout the nation, and was fanned in the theatres and newspapers, while caricatures and pamphlets filled the booksellers' shops. The invasion of England was, with some reason, expected at any moment, and men crowded to join the Volunteers: at Drury Lane one night the performance was cancelled because so many of the company were under arms. Grimaldi does not appear to have served as a Home Guard,[2] but on the stage he did his patriotic duty in his own particular way; at Sadler's Wells, for example, he took the role of Rufo the Robber in *Red Riding Hood* and distinguished himself as a British tar with a wooden leg and a repertoire of belligerent ballads; and it seems to have been accepted as an admirable piece of casting that in Dibdin's prelude *New Brooms* this half-Italian clown should have appeared as Sir John Bull, singing:

John Bull is my name,
None my spirit can tame,
I'm upright and downright with all.
I laugh and grow fat,
Crack my joke and all that,
And live at old Liberty Hall.[3]

Joe Grimaldi was expected to provide pleasure, not propaganda, and with a few perfunctory acknowledgments of the war he continued his career in serious and comic pantomime uninterrupted; yet his creature Joey was animated by the wartime pride in being English, reflecting in caricature the new sense of national distinction and John Bull-ishness which Napoleon had helped to foster. Whatever his cosmopolitan parentage and his criminal habits, Joey the Clown was regarded as a true-born Englishman in the looking-glass world of pantomime.

During the war years, Sadler's Wells provided patriotic propaganda even more assiduously, perhaps, than did Covent Garden or Drury Lane: thus the Islington season of 1811 opened with *Dulce Domum: or England the Land of Freedom!* designed 'to prove the Superiority of our Native Country over all others, by a Comparison of Existing Circumstances (in general too palpably true to be contradicted). Harlequin and Columbine (a married Pair) are represented as being excited by the Sprite Curiosity, to relieve the ennui that might naturally be supposed to take place after the Honeymoon with such a fantastical Pair, and which makes them tired of their Home, to visit Foreign Climes; and, from ocular demonstration of the imperfect state of Foreign Liberty, to learn how to prize British Freedom and Domestic Happiness.' Both Joe Grimaldi and his brother-in-law George Bristow appeared as the main enemy to that Freedom and Happiness — Napoleon Bonaparte — and were soundly hissed by the loyal audience of the Wells. During a song in the same bill, Grimaldi broke off into patter with: 'O give me little England, where a man's head is his own freehold property, and his house is his castle; and whoever touches a hair of the one, or the latch of the other without leave, is sure to get the door in his face and his head in his hand.' These were sentiments to be loudly cheered at the Wells, and there was no sense of incongruity that they should be voiced by the Clown.

It seems appropriate that, as Joe was accepted as an embodiment of English character, the only 'straight' part in his repertoire should be that of Bob Acres in *The Rivals*. He played this role for the first time in the summer of 1811, at his Covent Garden benefit, with a distinguished cast which included Charles Kemble as Captain Absolute, Munden as Sir Anthony, Charles Mayne Young, the new star of the season, as Falkland, and Farley and Emery as Fag and David; and from that time onwards it was one of his most popular roles in his provincial tours. Did Grimaldi, one wonders, often repeat the buffoonery of an early performance at Covent Garden? In the famous duel scene, when Sir Lucius O'Trigger instructs Acres how to 'receive the gentleman's shot', one playgoer says, 'the whole soul of the clown came over Grimaldi.' Sir Lucius placed Acres in position and measured out the distance a few paces away, but on turning round and levelling his pistol he found that Acres was nowhere to be seen. Grimaldi, unable to resist a gag, had walked along behind his back, and turned around with him, to the delight of the audience. He was at home in comic duels: in one of these at the Wells, he and his opponent shot their seconds and shook hands over the bodies. Whatever he did, seemed in character.

* * *

There was no harlequinade at Drury Lane at the Christmas of 1803, but in its place 'A New Grand Allegorical Pantomimic Spectacle' — *Cinderella, or the Little Glass Slipper* — was presented on 3rd January 1804. As the first British *Cinderella*, this was a production of some historic importance (in which Grimaldi took a leading role); but it differed in many ways from the fairy-tale pantomime which for nearly a hundred years has been the most popular of all the Christmas mixtures of transvestite romance and music hall fun. The Prince was played by a man (James Byrne) and Cinderella's sisters by women (Mrs Byrne and Mrs Vining); there was no Baron, Baroness or Broker's Men; Stony-broke Hall had not yet been built, nor Dandini created; and the Fairy Godmother was usurped by Venus, chiefly in order to provide a cue for Byrne's ballet of Loves and Graces in the Island of Cytherea. (The ballet-master's two sons were Hymen and Cupid, and Grimaldi's sister-in-law Louisa appeared as one of the

Graces.) The management explained that 'the Heathen Mythology laid open a wider field for striking scenery and attractive agency — and therefore, though its admission be critically incorrect, it is hoped the public will excuse it in consideration of the effect'; and although this deviation was sharply censured by some critics, the public excused the Heathen Mythology so far that the piece ran for fifty-one nights and brought a big profit to the Drury Lane treasury. Joe Grimaldi played the part of Pedro, servant to Cinderella's sisters and ancestor of Buttons; it is tantalizing to think what his genius might have made out of the stock pathos of the page's unrequited love, which now colours the entire panto-mime, but this was a Victorian embroidery on the old, plain tale and Grimaldi played Pedro as a straight, comic servant, a role which gave him scant opportunity to shine. Drury Lane, it is clear, was wasting one of its prime assets.

The success of *Cinderella* — for which Michael Kelly wrote the music — foreshadowed its institutional popularity in a later generation, and this version has one attraction in common with its modern descendants. When *The Times* said of the 1804 production that it possessed 'almost as much merit as a Panto-mime', it was referring specifically to the mechanical 'changes', and it gave high praise to the transformation of Cinderella's kitchen table into a 'toilette', a pumpkin into a pavilioned chariot, mice into horses, and lizards into footmen. Today the *pièce de résistance* of any Christmas *Cinderella* is the same magic metamor-phosis. Whatever economies a provincial manager may make in the supply of fairies or footmen, he is sure to succeed with the essential minimum of two ponies and a carriage; and every year, with unfailing admiration, critics single out for commendation the moment when the hired Shetlands draw on the Magic Coach, glittering with spangles and perspex, in which the universal heroine will travel to the fateful ball. In such a setting, Buttons is expected to conceal his broken heart with some mild slapstick and comic singing, until the time for his 'speciality' arrives and he steps out of whatever shreds of character he has pinned to his sleeve. Grimaldi's genius today might find better scope as the Baroness or a Broker's Man, outside the 'tradition' of Buttons's tearful puppy love.

Meanwhile, there was a transformation scene at Sadler's Wells itself in the winter of 1803–4. As soon as the theatre closed in

October, Hughes and his associates put into operation a secret plan for an amphibious playhouse, inspired by the success of aqua shows — as we should call them today — in the circuses of Paris; and, as the work proceeded behind locked doors at Islington, elaborate precautions were taken to prevent the news from reaching rival managements. Workmen ripped up the old stage, with all the traps and cellar work from which a thousand ghosts and demons had sprung into view, and built a long, shallow reservoir, three feet in depth. In the roof a square tank was installed, and both containers were filled with water from the New River, which once again proved a valuable ally to the Wells. While the mimic sea was being commissioned, shipwrights and riggers from the Woolwich dockyard were building a fleet of model ships; Dibdin was planning the scenarios of the new aquatic dramas; and a new drop scene was prepared in the painting-room, which showed the English Grand Fleet drawn up in battle line against the combined fleets of France and Spain. On 2nd April, the new wonders of the Wells were exhibited for the first time with *The Siege of Gibraltar*, and the stage navy of Islington — pushed across an ocean on which it fought again the great battles of the day — became the talk of London. The Clown had to face the competition of the Water; and, indeed, Grimaldi often took part in these waterborne melodramas, as a villain doomed to drowning, though it was only by accident that he ever suffered the penalties of immersion.

To some extent the naval manoeuvres of the Royal Aquatic Theatre, as the Wells was now called, were the consummation of a popular island cult, the cult of the British Tar, commemorated in so many hymns of praise by the elder Dibdin. For years this golden-hearted hero had rushed in at the last minute to rescue the poor and oppressed; a symbol of English liberty, he stood for democracy against the upper classes (and their predilection for seducing working girls); but he had never been seen in his element — the water that defended the fortress of freedom. As the danger of invasion grew, the popularity of the stage sailor boy was obscured by the popularity of the Royal Navy itself; and at Sadler's Wells, where fourteen years before the customers had applauded the fall of the Bastille, audiences could enjoy the vicarious excitements of Trafalgar or Cape St Vincent — without real blood but on real water. By the end of the 1804 season, the theatre had made about six times as much profit as in the previous year, and from now on, as Charles Dibdin said, 'Grimaldi and the Water were the Alpha and Omega.' When both were exhausted, Sadler's Wells failed.

The year of the water at the Wells was also the year of the Young Roscius at the Lane. Master William Betty had begun his remarkable career in 1803 at the age of eleven, after watching Mrs Siddons on the Belfast stage, and, having toured the provinces in triumph, he reached London in December 1804 with a fanfare of publicity. At once the little boy became the new idol of society; the Kembles were put in the shade; and although Spain declared war on Britain a few days after his sensational début at Covent Garden, there was little reflection of such events in the busy, elegant world of the capital, where the Young Roscius was the main topic of well-bred conversation. 'You would not suspect,' wrote Lady Bessborough, 'that Europe was in a state of warfare and bondage.' Grimaldi himself appeared twice in 1805 with Master Betty, as the Second Gravedigger in *Hamlet* — a role which he had only played once (in the previous December) since the death of his first wife. By the end of the 1804–5 season Betty had earned nearly £35,000 for Drury Lane and Covent Garden, and he himself had drawn £50 a night, with a clear benefit every week (worth, perhaps, another £250). Many managers and fathers tried hopefully to launch children of various ages and abilities in his wake, but the Infant Billingtons and Infant D'Egvilles never succeeded in winning a hundredth part of the fame which the little boy from Ireland enjoyed for one glorious and ridiculous season.

It may have been the Roscius craze which helped to kill Drury Lane's pantomime in the Christmas of 1804–5, but, whatever the reason, *Old Harlequin's Fireside* did not reach thirty performances. Among the cast were two Young Harlequins and Young Columbines, for which Master Betty may have been responsible; Byrne and Bella Menage (now Mrs Sharp) appeared as senior Harlequin and Columbine; and there were two Bristow sisters in the rank and file, one of whom, Charlotte, took several small parts in the legitimate repertory that season. Grimaldi appeared again as Punch, a piece of casting which indicates the inability of the Lane's management to capitalize the popularity of the new Clown or to understand the difficulties which he had found in the Punch of *Harlequin Amulet*, and their blunder may well have contributed to the pantomime's failure. This was, however, the last harlequinade in which Grimaldi was to appear at Drury Lane. Before the year of 1805 was out, he left the theatre for good.

*   *   *

When the 1805 season began in September, on the day that Nelson boarded the *Victory*, James Byrne was no longer on the Drury Lane payroll; he had followed the Kembles to Covent Garden, and James D'Egville was to take his place as ballet-master. In the meantime, however, Wroughton found that there were some incidental dances to be arranged, and as D'Egville had not yet taken up his duties he asked Grimaldi to help him in this emergency. When the bait of an additional two pounds a week was offered, Grimaldi agreed — according to the *Memoirs* — on condition that this was confirmed as a permanent increase in his salary, and this was agreed by Aaron Graham, the Bow Street magistrate, who was then in active control of Drury Lane's affairs. Some weeks later, Grimaldi began rehearsals for D'Egville's new ballet *Terpsichore's Return*, designed as a vehicle for the celebrated dancer Parisot, whom the new ballet-master had brought from the King's Theatre at a fee of a thousand guineas. The Clown of Sadler's Wells was, appropriately enough, playing the role of Pan (who has been described as the divine ancestor of all clowns)[4] but although he considered this to be one of his best parts in any theatre, he was not destined to appear in it for long. The ballet was first staged, after a week's postponement, on 4th November — outside, the heaviest fog for twenty years filled the London streets — and made a considerable success, in spite of the weather. That was a week of mingled grief and rejoicing in England, for it was the week that the news of Nelson's victory and death at Trafalgar was received; the fog dispersed in time for the illuminations on Thursday (the 7th), when Drury Lane displayed Nelson's initials, surmounted by an anchor and enveloped in a wreath of palm and laurel; and on Saturday night the whole company and the audience joined to sing *Rule Britannia*, with special new verses to commemorate the great victory over the French. As the local Pan stood on the stage among his band of shepherds, singing lustily that Britons never, never, never should be slaves, he may well have felt that he was celebrating his own liberty — for that was Grimaldi's last night at Drury Lane.

The break with the Lane was due, so he said many years later, to a 'very trifling misunderstanding', but it was big enough to make Grimaldi look for work at Covent Garden, and to sever his connections with the theatre where he had worked for twenty-four years. The immediate cause was Aaron Graham's refusal to continue the £2 weekly bonus, but behind this incident, it would seem, lay several years of frustration and resentment; Joe always felt that he was undervalued at the Lane, and that, in comparison with his opportunities at the Wells, he was wasted in the pantomimes. At Covent Garden, on the other hand, there were the Byrnes, the Dibdins, and — for the following season — the Bolognas, and it took little urging from Tom Dibdin to make Grimaldi accept an offer from Thomas Harris, principal proprietor of the rival theatre. John Philip Kemble was present at the interview, and may well have cleared Joe's suspicions of his malignity by his praise of Grimaldi as 'a true chip of the old block and the first low comedian in the country'.[5] Moreover, Joe stood to gain financially by transferring to Covent Garden, which not only paid more punctually but more generously. He was engaged to play at £6 a week for the first season, £7 for the second and third, and £8 for the fourth and fifth — a substantial inducement to leave a theatre where he was no longer eager to stay.[6] After a fierce quarrel with Mr Graham in the green room, Grimaldi gave in his notice, and left Drury Lane in a blaze of glory. A few days later he set off with his wife and son to Dublin, where the Dibdin brothers had taken Astley's for a short season; and by far the highest paid artists in the company were the Grimaldis, with fourteen guineas a week, half a clear benefit, and all travelling expenses paid — more than double the salary of Jack Bologna. The monetary difference indicates Joe's new status in the theatre, achieved since his first season of clowning in 1800, a status which the management of Drury Lane had failed to recognize.

There is some contradictory evidence about the sequence of these events. According to Tom Dibdin, it was *after* Grimaldi's visit to Ireland, which proved a disastrous one for his pocket, that he was engaged to play at Covent Garden; and it is likely that the Irish expedition may have helped to provoke the quarrel with Aaron Graham. Yet a job at Covent Garden was almost inevitable for Joe, and he need have been in no danger of unemployment. Good clowns, then as now, were in short supply, and at Covent Garden the last three pantomimes had suffered for want of one. Delpini, Dubois and old Bologna were all in decline, belonging as they did to the old-fashioned tradition of 'foreign fooling', and Farley himself, the producer, had been obliged to try his hand at clowning; so he and Dibdin were only too eager to seize the opportunity of recruiting the Clown of Sadler's Wells.

For twenty years, Drury Lane never really succeeded in matching the pantomimes at Covent Garden. In part, it was because Sheridan's Grand National and its successor were too large, for, as the *Monthly Mirror* said in 1806:

> This stage is not the land of pantomime; its vast dimensions preclude the possibility of giving that apparently magical quickness and variety peculiar to the excellence of these performances.

Yet that criticism was also partially true of the 'vast dimensions' of Covent Garden, whose stage was better adapted to spectacle than to comedy. The difference between Covent Garden and Drury Lane, from now on, was not in size or policy or management; the difference was Joe Grimaldi.

Ten

Poor Joe! It was like the boys and the frogs; it was sport to us, but it was death to you.—WILLIAM ROBSON (The Old Play-Goer, 1854)

WHEN JOE GRIMALDI CAME TO COVENT GARDEN in the autumn of 1806, he found a theatre whose prosperity and efficiency contrasted sharply with the state of Drury Lane. Much of the credit was due to the continuity in its administration and the personality of the chief proprietor, Thomas 'Jupiter' Harris. For forty years Harris had known the world of London theatre inside out, through all its vagaries and vicissitudes; and although he had entered the trade without experience — he was, it is said, a soap-boiler — he soon acquired a sufficiency of it in the hurly-burly of theatrical partnership. Unlike Kemble, who had bought a sixth interest in the theatre for £23,000, Harris was not known to stand on his dignity. After attending rehearsals for an hour or two he would walk into the centre of the stage, put his hands in his pockets, and announce: 'I am now going away. Has anybody anything to say to me?'; and if there were any complaints from any member of the establishment, no matter how lowly, Harris answered them promptly and justly. Among his eccentric habits was his well-known addiction to shaking hands in stages: on first meeting, he would probably offer you one finger, but as acquaintance ripened in your favour more fingers were proposed, until the presentation of the whole hand 'denoted a perfect climax of applause, sometimes accompanied with "Good boy! good boy!" '[1] Harris was a hard man, but a man who was honest, shrewd and kind, and Grimaldi, who met him in his mellower years, was not the only performer who held the 'dear old master', as Joe called him, in affection and respect.

During the 1805–6 season, Tom Dibdin, who had been writing pantomimes for eight years at Covent Garden, besought Harris to release him from this 'drudgery'; and when his request was granted, Dibdin spent his summer 'free from the everlasting dream of traps, flaps, daggers of lath, and parti-coloured jackets', although he took some credit for persuading his old employer to engage Grimaldi.[2] He was eager to be absolved of the duty, it seems, not only from occupational fatigue but from political caution, for pantomimes were becomingly increasingly unpopular with 'the head of the stage management' — by whom he appears to mean John Philip Kemble. Dibdin assumed, however, that Harris would engage a successor, and was surprised during his summer visits to Covent Garden to see no sign of the pantomime. He himself usually submitted an 'outline' in June, discussions with the machinists, scene-painters and others followed, and five or six months in all were frequently spent on preliminary planning; but he held his peace, and helped to make Grimaldi feel at home in his new theatre. Joe had left his mother behind, with Charlotte Bristow, at the Lane, while Mary brought several other sisters to Covent Garden; and it may have been difficult for the Clown, after so many years at the Lane, to settle down in the rival camp, though he found there several old friends in harness.

The Covent Garden season opened on 15th September, and most of the Grimaldis and Bristows took up their stations right away in the theatrical hierarchy. Mrs Grimaldi, who resumed her anonymous career among the ladies of the chorus in *Pizarro*, *Coriolanus* and *The Tempest*, stepped for a few nights into the individual glory of a part — Dolly Trull in *The Beggar's Opera* (with Incledon as Macheath, Munden as Peachum, Emery as Lockit, and Simmons as Filch — what a starry cast!); but she was never given another opportunity in the next twenty years, and this proved to be the only part which she was ever allowed to play. Other newcomers that season were Mary Bolton, later the Countess of Thurlow, who made her début in another of Gay's pieces, *Polly*; and Miss De Camp, who three months before had won new honours by becoming the wife of Charles Kemble, the manager's brother. Grimaldi himself made his début on 9th October, in the role of Orson, and he was received with enthusiasm by the audience, although some critics inevitably expressed their preference for Dubois, from whom Joe had inherited the part. It was at the suggestion of Charles Farley, the producer, that Grimaldi chose the role as his first on the Covent Garden stage, and Farley coached him carefully in the antics of the wild man. Farley, a big-nosed, rough-voiced, warm-hearted little man, was then 35, and had worked at Covent Garden since his childhood — he was born in one of the slum streets nearby. From appearing as an 'extra child' in processions and tableaux, he graduated to the post of call-boy and prompter's assistant, and he made a name for his skill in producing pantomime, both in melodramas and harlequinades ('A great author of helmets and battle-axes ; — a huxter of black dwarfs and giants,' said *The Champion*, in 1817). He and Grimaldi established a close professional *rapport*, and according to the *Memoirs*,

> if he can be said to have been the pupil of anybody, Mr Farley was certainly his master, as he not only took infinite pains to instruct him in the character of Orson, but afterwards gave him very valuable advice and great assistance in getting up many other parts . . .

About six weeks before Christmas, Thomas Harris called on Tom Dibdin, and the following conversation took place:

HARRIS: Well, my dear Dibdin! We cannot do without a pantomime from you, after all.

DIBDIN ('thunderstruck'): From me, sir? A pantomime, and to be acted in six weeks? It is impossible. I grant I might write one: but how is its scenery to be painted? what time for machinery, practice, composing the music, etc., etc.?

HARRIS: Well, but have you not some sketches by you?

DIBDIN: Yes, sir, I have shown them to you often; and often strongly recommended one in particular, which you have for five years refused.

HARRIS: O, what? that damned Mother Goose, whom you are so wedded to! Let's look at her again: she has one recommendation; there is no finery about her; and the scenery, in general, is too common-place to take up much time: so, e'en set everybody to work: I need not again see the manuscript. I will speak to Farley, and you must lose no time.

DIBDIN: But sir, our late agreement, and the difficulties thrown in my way . . .

HARRIS: You are too good a fellow to talk about agreements when I want you to do me a service; and as for difficulties, you shan't meet with any: I won't suffer it. Here (and Harris gave Dibdin his *whole* hand to shake) call everybody about you, and order every thing you like: I cannot expect you to effect much, especially with such a subject, but do the best you can.[3]

Covent Garden (*above*) and Sadler's Wells theatres in Grimaldi's time

A print of Grimaldi in one of his most famous scenes from *Mother Goose* ('Sir, I'll just trouble you with a line') is here imposed upon a contemporary writing-sheet, whose decorative border consists of scenes from the Covent Garden pantomime instead of the more customary Biblical texts. *From the Raymond Mander and Joe Mitchenson Collection*

It was in this way that the most famous pantomime in our history was produced: *that damned Mother Goose*, as Harris called it — *Harlequin and Mother Goose: or The Golden Egg* — proved to be the most successful harlequinade which Covent Garden ever staged, and its popularity spread from America to the Antipodes.[4] Yet it was apparently staged as a stopgap piece, against Harris's better judgment, and the proprietor never really forgave the pantomime for proving that his judgment was wrong. Would it have been a success five years before, when Tom Dibdin first put it forward, or did it require the genius of Grimaldi to carry off its simplicity and charm? One can only say that the timing of its production was a happy coincidence, both for Joe and the theatre. But it seems strange that Harris should have taken no better precautions for the exhibition of Drury Lane's Clown, and that, once in rehearsal, he took so little interest in the piece. Every year, until *Mother Goose*, Harris had paid close attention to the progress of the pantomime, from the first plans to the last rehearsal, but now he ignored the frenzied activity at the theatre. In the wardrobe and the paint-room, costumes and scenery were being prepared; the orchestra was rehearsing the music which its leader, Mr Ware, had written for the piece; in one room the chorus was going through its paces, and in another morris-dancers were practising their steps; Joe Grimaldi was directing the business of the harlequinade, while Farley and Tom Dibdin rushed from one piece of the jigsaw to the other. It was not until the Sunday night before its première that *Mother Goose* could be pieced together on the stage, and only then did Harris put in an appearance, when he arrived with Kemble after dinner and watched the proceedings for nearly an hour. Even after the pantomime he despised made so great a success, and so large a profit, he was reluctant to change his former opinion of its merits, and Dibdin records that Harris never gave him 'the usual cheering clap on the back . . . though his kindness and liberality, in all other respects, rather increased than abated.'

Many of the cast appeared to have as little confidence in Dibdin's ugly duckling as their employer, whose defection from rehearsals increased their anxieties. These were sharpened by stage superstitions. Thus, at the first rehearsal Farley appeared without the red cap which he always wore during the preparations for a new piece. There were murmurings among the cast, but when

Grimaldi pointed out his omission, with a protesting 'Farley, you have not got your red cap on!' the amiable producer sent out the call-boy to buy a new one immediately, saying: 'I will not go on without one, we shall have no luck with the pantomime if I do.'[5]

At Drury Lane the panic was even worse for, by some mismanagement, the new pantomime was 'thought of, planned rehearsed and produced in less than a month'. According to "Captain" Everard, who played Pantaloon,

> there was no time to paint a scene, invent or bring forward any thing new; even the music was taken from the old pantomimes of the 'Genii', 'Fortunatus', 'Queen Mab', the 'Elopement', etc., and adapted to the business and cunning of the scenes, as well as they could: the principal character in this, the Clown, was not provided till within a week of its being brought out, and, then, what we had done, was all to do over again.[6]

It seems likely that the decision to stage a pantomime at Drury Lane this Christmas was made only after the news that *Mother Goose* was already in rehearsal, and the management obviously found it difficult to fill Grimaldi's shoes: it was a difficulty which they never overcame while Joe was still in power. The Drury Lane pantomime — *The Enchanters: or Harlequin Sultan* — was brought out on Boxing Day, three days before *Mother Goose*, with Montgomery (from the Circus) as Clown, Bella Menage as Columbine, and Fred Hartland (for many years Grimaldi's stand-in at the Wells) as Harlequin. Montgomery was a crude buffoon, unaccustomed to the techniques or traditions of the Lane, and if it is true that he had only a week's rehearsal, it is scarcely surprising that he was booed by the audience. The comic business in general, however, was so poor that the hissing began to increase in volume half way through the piece, until there was so much hubbub that the curtain was dropped before the last scene. Grimaldi sat in the pit that night with Jack Bologna, among the booing, noisy customers, and although he had the sympathy of an actor and a friend for the feelings of the company, it would be surprising if he did not also derive some satisfaction from the fiasco. (*The Enchanters* ran for only fifteen performances.)

The failure of their rival, however, increased the fears of many of his colleagues at Covent Garden. If *The Enchanters*, which, for all its weaknesses, boasted some spectacular scenery and display, did not please the customers, what would they say to *Mother*

Goose, a piece produced on the cheap, so it seemed, deliberately and resolutely austere by pantomimic standards? The people who booed at Drury Lane might show even more violence at Covent Garden. In the green-rooms there were angry complaints about the apathy and niggardliness of the management; if only Harris would spend some of his fortune on the piece, everything might be all right, they said, but if *Mother Goose* were goosed then *they* had to take the blame.

The evening of 29th December 1806 began with the production of *George Barnwell,* which had been a conventional item of Christmas diet since 1759: for many years a new pantomime was preceded by this domestic drama, or, less frequently, by *Jane Shore* and other solemnities. Charles Kemble, who was then 31, played the apprentice hero, and went through the usual ordeal of such performances, for the old play was treated that evening with a traditionally rowdy contempt, and there was so much noise in the pit and galleries that most of the lines were inaudible. At last, among a torrent of booing and applause, *George Barnwell* ended and Charles Kemble escaped. The green carpet — still laid down for the performance of tragedies — was rolled up and taken away by the liveried stage servants. Now the serious business of the day was about to start, and the audience in readiness laid in new stocks of food and drink, waiting for the revels to begin and encouraging all concerned with loud and impatient whoops and applause. Soon the orchestra struck up Mr Ware's overture, the hubbub was hushed, and *Mother Goose* began. Let us revisit the theatre, on that historic evening, to see what happens in that vanished world of laughter . . .

When the curtain parts, the Covent Garden audience see, instead of the usual supernatural haunt or romantic landscape, an English village on a summer's morning. There are a church, a thatched cottage, and a distant view of the river, with a bridge across it; the church bells are ringing, the sun has just risen, and the villagers, dressed with favours, are singing and dancing in the market-place:

> *Neighbours, we're met on a very merry morning,*
> *Lads and lasses dressed in all their pride so gay,*
> *To celebrate the happy hour when, maiden shyness scorning,*
> *Sweet Colinette is married to the Squire today.*

Suddenly the sky is overclouded, a hailstorm begins, and as it ends
the figure of an old woman riding on an airborne goose is seen
in the distance — Mother Goose herself (Samuel Simmons). Sweet
Colinette, who soon appears in the person of Miss Searle, is the
pretty young ward of old Avaro (Louis Bologna), and is being
compelled against her will to marry Squire Bugle, the rich and
ugly villain whose wife had died only seven weeks previously.
On the right are the entrance gates to the Squire's mansion, and
soon he enters 'equipped for hunting', preceded by huntsmen,
jockeys, grooms and servants. As the Squire at last comes on to
the stage, he is greeted by the audience with a resounding cheer
of welcome, for under the huntsman's hat and mask is the
grinning face of Joe Grimaldi. It is like the Squire's entrance
described by Pope in *The Dunciad*:

> *Six huntsmen with a shout precede his chair,*
> *He grins, and looks broad nonsense with a stare.*

Avaro presents his reluctant ward to the Squire, but she turns
away in disgust and waves to her lover Colin (Jack Bologna) a
village boy who appears at the window of the thatched cottage.
When the Squire persists in his advances, she points dramatically
to a tomb conspicuously displayed on the stage, with its inscription: 'In memory of Xantippe, wife of Bullface Bugle, Esq.'; but
to this reminder of mortality (shades of Maria Hughes!) he replies
with a jocular song:

> *First wife's dead,*
> *There let her lie.*
> *She's at rest*
> *And so am I . . .*

Colin soon appears on the scene to interrupt the festivities, but at
that moment Mother Goose arrives, dragged on by the beadle
and the parish constable; she is condemned as a witch, for interfering with the weather, and the Squire sentences her to be ducked
in the village pond. Colin, however, proves 'that there is no Act
of Parliament to prevent people flying if they can bring it about',
and when the beadle and his men try to drag Mother Goose away
he thrashes them single-handed and allows the old woman to

escape. In gratitude for his chivalry, Mother Goose breaks up the wedding party by raising the ghost of Xantippe, who appears clad in white satin and poppy ribbons, shakes her fists at the Squire, and descends through the trap — an apparition which drives Bullface Bugle off the stage in terror. Moreover, Mother Goose presents Colin with a considerable social asset in the shape of a magic goose, which lays a golden egg at 7.30 every morning, holidays and Saturdays excepted. The scene in which this happens has many echoes in our own experience of pantomimes. Colin appears, despondently, in front of Mother Goose's 'Habitation', and the enchantress says, 'with action appropriate' — and music:

> *Youth, why despair? the girl thou shalt obtain;*
> *This present shall her guardian's sanction gain.* (Goose appears)
> *Nay, doubt not, while she's kindly used, she'll lay,*
> *A golden egg on each succeeding day:*
> *You served me — no reply — there lies your way.*

In modern versions of *Mother Goose*, the goose is presented by a high-ranking fairy and is usually called Priscilla; the man (or woman) inside her skin sometimes earns more than the principals of the pantomime; and Mother Goose herself is usually Colin's mother, an everyday mortal Dame in middle age. Yet the lines above might be heard in any provincial production of today, and the red-coated Squire, the opening chorus, and the village market place are all standard ingredients of the traditional panto.

The gift of the goose provides Colin with bargaining power in the matrimonial market, and, as Mother Goose predicted, Avaro relents. His condition for surrendering Colinette, however, is that Colin should give him the miraculous bird, and that he should be allowed to cut the bird open immediately: he cannot, it seems, wait until 7.30 the next morning. When Colin agrees to this infamy, 'the goose makes her exit through a panel in the back scene, which turns round and presents Mother Goose': the enchantress punishes them for their greed and cruelty by turning Colin and Colinette into Harlequin and Columbine, and the Squire and Avaro into Clown and Pantaloon. Under their costumes, loosely tied at the back, the characters wear their harlequinade dress, and in a few seconds — as Mother Goose chants her rhyming magic on a darkened stage — the strings are untied, the boots are kicked off, and the Squire's coat and hat are whisked into the wings. Grimaldi now steps forward in his red-white-and-blue motley. He wears a red shirt, frilled and decorated with blue and white facings, which is cut away at the chest and waist to reveal an ornamented shirt beneath; his blue-and-white-striped breeches end above the knee with a red-white-and-blue ribbon, which is repeated at his wrists; and beneath his blue-crested wig, his whitened face is daubed with red triangles on either cheek. He is a very English Clown, and he is ready for the English harlequinade . . .

*   *   *

The nominal pretext for the harlequinade on this December evening is, as usual, the pursuit of the lovers by Pantaloon and Clown, and the excitement of the chase lends zest to the buffoon-ery. But although the sympathy of the audience is officially with the runaways, and although a happy ending for Harlequin and Columbine is inevitable, the hero of the game is really the rascally Clown. Every one is on the anarchist's side. There is no end to his antics, and no particular continuity but the succession of familiar English scenes, as he races through Georgian London leaving havoc and destruction in his wake. He dodges a recruiting party, looking for men to fight Napoleon; he picks a fight with an innkeeper; he tries to steal some fruit from the basket of a St Giles street-girl, and performs a comic *pas de deux* with her in the street, until he discovers that the girl is Harlequin in disguise. In another scene, Clown enters an inn, and sits down at a table, which immediately rises into the air high above his head. Mystified, he looks at the floor in amazement: has it been swallowed up? He gets up and searches every corner of the room: perhaps somebody has moved it? With enormous labour, he stands in the middle of the stage and *thinks* about this extraordinary disappearance. Suddenly he looks up, sees the table, gives a shout of surprise, and quietly sits down again; down comes the table in front of him . . . and up goes Clown in his chair, to his own horror and astonishment. While he sits there in mid-air, squeaking for help, Pantaloon and the landlord come into the room; the landlord goes off to fetch some tools to cut him down, but meanwhile the chair descends of its own accord. Now Clown and the landlord sit down at the table together, but it begins to edge up into the air, very gradually, while they try to hold it down; underneath are three little tables, replicas of their parent table with two candles on each. There is one table apiece for each of the trio, but when they take their seats once more they are all carried six feet into the air. How Clown roars at the misery of his airborne neighbours, quite oblivious of the fact that he is in exactly the same position! (This table-lifting routine, and comedy on wires, was a feature of the entertainments in the Paris fairs of the late seventeenth century.)

In this scene Grimaldi shows the Clodpoll side of the Clown, as the butt and victim of circumstances. In others, however, he is very much the master of his fate and displays the eager mischief of the *zanni*. (For an explanation of Clodpolls and *zanni*, turn to Chapter 14.) One episode shows Vauxhall Gardens blazing with lights, as if on a gala night, and the Pandean Minstrels, a popular musical turn of the day, playing 'the favourite air'. The Clown joins in the music himself, by playing on a large tin fish-kettle hung around his neck, with the aid of a ladle and whisk, while he rests his chin on an inverted hair-broom, all in parody of the Pandeans. Then a country dance strikes up, in which the villagers of the opening scene, including Mrs Grimaldi and her sister, get another opportunity, and Clown rounds it off by stealing the table-cloths, pelting the waiters with plates, and knocking down the more elderly guests — this is always good for a laugh in Georgian times — while fowls fly off the dishes and other unusual phenomena are seen. In the next scene, a Grocer's Shop and Post Office, Clown continues his career of larceny by stealing some letters from the post box; he opens one of them and secretes some banknotes, opens another and reads out, 'Sir, I'll just trouble you with a line,' exhibiting a small hanging noose which is enclosed. Harlequin, however, changes the post box into a lion's head, and Clown's hand is caught in its jaws: as he struggles to release it, he pulls out a little postman who annoys him by ringing his bell all the time. Clown then steals a loaf from a baker's basket, throws the loaf to Pantaloon, and puts the basket over the little postman.

The harlequinade is not entirely given up to comedy. It is interspersed by country dancing and by at least one sentimental ballad which becomes the talk of the town. In the eighth scene, when the Clown tries to steal from a poor woodcutter's wife, her small son steps forward and sings 'The Cabin Boy', a pathetic ditty which wrings the customers' heart-strings. The boy is Master Smalley, who had made his stage début with Grimaldi that season on 9th October, and who enjoyed for a time a considerable vogue as the singer of 'The Cabin Boy'. Sympathy for the woodcutter's family, however, makes no difference to the audience's affection for their persecutor, the Clown.

Clown does not always go scot-free. In one scene he and Pantaloon are chased off the stage by bees, and in another he is caught in a steel trap and spring gun, set by Harlequin. The gun goes off and shoots Clown in the stomach, while Harlequin drags him off by the leg that is fastened in the trap. If any Clodpoll in real life had been caught in one of these man-traps, set for those criminals who trespassed on private property, he might have been transported for life to Australia: but this is the realm of pantomime. When Harlequin cuts off Clown's ear, a carpenter sticks it back with glue, and when Clown kills Harlequin with a red-hot poker he is speedily resurrected. No injuries are mortal here: there is no crime, and no punishment.

At last the chase is over, the lovers are united, and in the finale the company steps forward to sing the chorus:

> Ye patrons kind, who deign to view
> The sports our scenes produce,
> Accept our wish to pleasure you,
> And laugh with Mother Goose.

And Grimaldi, dripping with sweat, triumphant in his motley, concludes with:

> And let no critic stern regret
> What our petitions beg,
> That we may from your smiles collect.
> Each night some Golden Egg.

* * *

What applause there was that night! They stamped and cheered and shouted, in a way that had not been heard at Covent Garden for many years at Christmas time. When the curtain fell, what jubilant rejoicings there were in the green-rooms, with the Bolognas and the Grimaldis giving and receiving congratulations, and little Simmons taking his honours as pleased as Punch, and Farley shaking everybody's hand. Joe and Mary Grimaldi went home in triumph: the change to Covent Garden had done the trick, and their future seemed secure. The press was generally favourable. According to the *Morning Post*, 'everything combined to make this spectacle the most perfect, in all its accompaniments, of any thing of the kind we have witnessed for some time... Bologna and Grimaldi were excellent in Harlequin and the Clown'. The *Oracle* said: 'few productions of this description have ever been deservedly applauded, or promised to prove more generally successful, than the Pantomime of yesterday evening. It must every night produce a Golden Egg to the Treasury.' (The critic — writing before the era of entertainments tax — was referring to the treasury of Covent Garden.) Said the *Monthly Mirror*:

> With respect to pantomime this theatre is 'native, and to the manner born'. *Mother Goose*, however, outdoes almost all its former outdoings. This little fable of the nursery forms the leading interest of the exhibition which, considered in all its qualities, its innumerable tricks and metamorphoses, its excellent scenery, and appropriate music, humour and drollery, is admirable, and reflects infinite credit on the ingenuity and invention of Dibdin and Farley...but of all the whimsical beings that, by their contortions and vulgarities in pantomime, set the young, ay, and old folks too, in a roar, the clown of Grimaldi is the most surprising, diverting and effective. We can in no way describe what he does, nor give any idea of the inimitable style in which he keeps up the ball from the beginning to the end. He must be seen.

Here, indeed, was a 'rave notice'; yet it was some weeks before it came Grimaldi's way (if, indeed, he ever read it), and the daily press was less specific. The *Morning Herald*, for example, mentioned none of the artists by name, but singled out for facetious praise the small boy in the goose's skin: 'The introduction of the goose was extremely well managed, and the *feathered* performer was received with unbounded applause.' *The Times*, while praising the 'beautiful exhibition of scenery, which has seldom been equalled on any former occasion' (the one ingredient of the production which was *not* remarkable), omitted to notice the Clown or his colleagues.

Yet although the press might not publicize his triumph, a triumph it was for the Clown of Covent Garden. For in *Mother Goose*, as J.P.Boaden says, 'Grimaldi, who had been slighted at Drury Lane, at once proved himself the great master of his art.'[7] Fashionable London flocked to see the pantomime. Every print-shop in the city displayed prints of *Mother Goose*, and the most popular showed him holding the noose and the letter, 'Sir, I'll just trouble you with a line.' Lord Eldon, it is said, had never seen a pantomime before he became Lord Chancellor, but after he was persuaded to visit *Mother Goose* he returned for another eleven nights in order to watch Grimaldi. 'Never,' Lord Eldon said, 'never did I see a leg of mutton stolen with such superhumanly sublime impudence as by that man.'[8] Commoner people, too, took the Clown to their hearts, and *Mother Goose* was the subject of broadsides and ballads. One of these includes the magnanimous couplet:

> *Their fame it is great, and their pay is the same,*
> *And as they deserve it, there's none who can blame,*

but this estimation of the players' income was, by our standards, wide of the mark. Grimaldi was now earning £5 a week, a pound more than at Drury Lane, but still less than little Simmons, who drew £7; and on his benefit night, which he shared with Jack Bologna, he drew another £54 4s 6d. Bologna, whose wage was also £5, was paid £73 10s. for tricks in this and the previous year's pantomime.

Night after night through the season *Mother Goose* was staged to packed and approving houses. When the theatre closed on 23rd June, with *Hamlet* and *Mother Goose*, Dibdin's unwanted harlequinade had run for ninety-two performances, and during the years to come the memory of this season was to be preserved as 'the golden age of pantomime'. Already it was being copied throughout the provinces, and that autumn Edmund Kean, an unknown stroller, was making trick models for its production at Sheerness, among the other duties for which he was paid a full guinea a week.

What was the secret of its success? One reason seems to be that it broke away from the current vogue of exotic spectacle, and although it had scenes in plenty they were subordinated to the story, which was emphatically English. The austerity of the production has been exaggerated by stage historians, if we are to believe contemporary reports, yet its cost was relatively small, and by reducing display it could afford the time to concentrate on comedy. Moreover, its humours were plainly national, after so many overdressed excursions into foreign and fanciful parts.

Grimaldi himself, it seems, did not think highly of the piece which established him as the King of Clowns. 'He considered the pantomime, as a whole, a very indifferent one, and always declared his part to be one of the worst he ever played; nor was there a trick or situation to which he had not been well accustomed for many years before.'[9] It is strange that neither he nor Thomas Harris had a good word for Dibdin's pantomime in later life. It is said to have made a profit of over £20,000 for Covent Garden, and although Joe's immediate bonus was somewhat smaller — notably, a gold watch presented by his employer — it made his fortune as a Clown. It seems even stranger that the managers of the day never learned the lessons of *Mother Goose* — the lessons of simplicity, economy and the priority of humour — but continued to smother Grimaldi's comedy with exotic and expensive spectacle, as if *Mother Goose* had never laid such unexpectedly golden eggs.

As Munden's son said, in his biography of his father, 'All former pantomimes were eclipsed by this master-piece of fun, as all former clowns were by Joe. It is impossible to describe what he did. A thousand masks would not portray the grotesque contortions of his countenance; and his humorous and lively action drew shouts of merriment both from children who are young, and children who are old. It was the joint composition of Dibdin and Farley, and their memory deserves to be immortalised for hatching such a production.'[10]

*   *   *

Although Joe Grimaldi seemed now to be established as the new comic star of Covent Garden, he could not — it should be noted — ensure the good behaviour of the audience or the success of a show merely by his presence on the stage. Both the Easter pieces at Covent Garden in 1807 and 1808 were hissed off the stage, although he appeared in them. The 1807 piece was *The Ogre and Little Thumb: or, The Seven League Boots*, in which his sister-in-law Maria made her début as the hero, Little Thumb, one of the earliest Principal Boys. (She destroyed a three-eyed ogre, Anthropophagus, played by Farley.) This was a forerunner of the modern *Jack and the Beanstalk*; but although it included a Sylvan Bower and a Real Cataract (recipes for success 150 years later), it was frequently hissed, altered overnight and soon withdrawn. If Grimaldi had needed a reminder of the uncertainty of theatrical success, here was a sharp nudge in the ribs. The Easter piece of 1808 provided another. It was a burlesque by Tom Dibdin of the current vogue for melodrama, with the laboriously comic title of *Bonifacio and Bridgetina: or, The Knight of the Hermitage: or, The Windmill Turret: or, The Spectre of the North East Gallery*. Although the author had high hopes, it was 'completely damned' by the audience and by such critics as Leigh Hunt, who called it 'the most stupid piece of impertinence that has disgraced the English stage for some years past'. On the day after its disastrous début the playbill announced that it had set the audience in 'universal and continued peals of laughter'; but this 'miserable artifice', as Leigh Hunt called it, had little effect, and Grimaldi was quickly released from his role as the Second Champion.

Eleven

I never saw anything funny that wasn't terrible. If it causes pain, it's funny: if it doesn't, it isn't. I try to hide the pain with embarrassment, and the more I do that, the better they like it. But that doesn't mean they are unsympathetic. Oh no, they laugh often with tears in their eyes. Only of course it mustn't be too painful.—W.C.FIELDS

> *Come all ye who love mirth and fun,*
> *No matter who ye may be,*
> *To Covent Garden all must run,*
> *Who merry would, and wise be:*
> *You'll of your time find no abuse,*
> *Since for your cash, i' fegs, sirs,*
> *Your old acquaintance, Mother Goose,*
> *Will give you Golden Eggs, sirs.*

That was one of the street ballads which the London hawkers were selling in Grimaldi's wonder year of 1807; and the triumph of Covent Garden's pantomime brought new business to Sadler's Wells, where:

> The Clown of Grimaldi . . . is the principal cause of crowded lobbies and scarcely standing room. . . . Many of our second and third rate tragedians would give their ears to meet with half the plaudits, which are every night conferred on Grimaldi for his inimitable exertions. His Clown has not been equalled — we never expect to see it surpassed. He has arrived at an *acme* of all clownery.[1]

It is not surprising that Thomas Harris, whatever his opinion of the pantomime, revived *Mother Goose* in the new season at Covent Garden. But before its second run began, the comic hero was plunged into another of those macabre incidents with which his private life seems to have been so insistently punctuated.

On the night of 15th October, Grimaldi went home early from the Wells, where the pantomime had been played in the first part of the programme, as sometimes happened on benefit nights; and as he was not yet working at Covent Garden he intended to enjoy the luxury of an early night. His sleep, however, was soon interrupted, for at midnight he was woken up by a hubbub in the street outside, and loud knocking at the door: there was trouble at the Wells, he was told, and many lives had been lost. In a few minutes Grimaldi had dressed, and he ran towards the theatre, from which he could already hear the noise of angry shouts and screams; but the crowd was so dense that it was impossible for him to enter the building in the usual way, and as he was feverishly anxious to find out what had happened and if any of his friends or relations were hurt, he ran to the other side of the New River, jumped in, and swam across to the back of the theatre, where Richard Hughes had his house. There was a light in the music parlour, and the window was unlocked, so the dripping, shivering Grimaldi flung up the sash and jumped in, 'à la Harlequin.' There, around him, were the corpses of men, women and children, stretched out on the floor and the furniture. Some of them had trampled faces and crushed limbs, and there was scarcely room for Grimaldi to move among them. This was a room of the dead, with the candles flickering in the breeze from the window, and not a living soul but the Clown, whose shadow loomed and lurched about the wall. Worse still, the door was locked on the other side: he was shut up in a tomb, the quick and the dead together. It was a nightmare terror which brought back to Grimaldi's mind all the obsessions of his superstitious father, and he began to shout and bang on the door, in rising hysteria, crying for them to let him out. But the Hughes family, in the neighbouring room, were so terrified to hear this screaming from a room which they had locked upon the dead, that they clung together in fear — there had been horrors enough that night — until someone recognized the raging, beseeching voice as that of Joe Grimaldi. Quickly and apprehensively — had Joe gone off his head again? — they opened the door of the music parlour, and Grimaldi staggered out into the world of the living.

The tragic accident, it seemed, was due to hooliganism and hysteria: no blame, said the Coroner, could be attached to the managers of the Wells. It all began when two drunken brewer's men, with their women, came in at half-price and created a disturbance: some of their neighbours took exception to their shouting and indecency, and with the help of the theatre police tried to throw them out. Cries of 'A fight! A fight!' were raised in the pit, and this was taken up in the gallery and boxes as a cry of 'Fire!' It was not long since Astley's had been burned down, and panic set in immediately: the customers rushed for the exits, and in the gallery this had fatal results, for people were thrown down the stairs in the rush and trampled to death. One girl threw herself out of the gallery into the pit, but miraculously escaped with a few bruises. Whatever the cause of 'The Accident', as it was always known thereafter at the Wells, it took Grimaldi some time to obliterate that room of death from his memory. Twelve days later *Mother Goose* reopened at Covent Garden, and he was back in his warpaint, in a world where death was just another practical joke.

* * *

The new pantomime that season, which opened three days after Christmas, was *Harlequin in his Element: or Fire, Water, Earth and Air*; and although it enjoyed a relatively successful run, it seems to have disappointed the critics. Louis Bologna's Pantaloon displeased the traditionalists: 'the hue and cry are not so well filled up by Sir Feeble Sordid, a foppish guardian, as by the usual accompaniment of the old father with his long chin and dagger, attended by the son-in-law of his choice.' Grimaldi himself was 'more confined in his drolleries, consequently less successful', according to one critic; while another complained that 'all the old contortions were practised, but every twist, turn and tumble seems to be exhausted, for nothing new appeared'. Disappointment, perhaps, was inevitable while *Mother Goose* was still running in the repertory: and from this time onward until Grimaldi's death, indeed until the turn of the century, all pantomimes were compared with that Platonic model. Yet it should be noted that Grimaldi himself, in retrospect, chose *Harlequin in his Element* as one of his favourites, and preferred it to the pantomime which made his name.

At the end of the 1807–8 season, Grimaldi added two more successful roles to his repertory: he played Baptist in *Raymond and Agnes: or The Bleeding Nun* — one of the popular penny-dreadful melodramas of the day — for Charles Kemble's benefit, and Skirmish in *The Deserter of Naples*, a comic role, for Taylor's benefit; but his refusal to essay a new role on another benefit night made him, according to the *Memoirs*, a powerful enemy at Covent Garden. One afternoon in March,[2] it seems, Grimaldi was visited at home by John Fawcett, the comedian, who asked him to appear at his benefit; Joe agreed at once, but then Fawcett revealed that he wanted him to appear not as Clown or Orson, but as Bowkitt in *The Son-in-law*, a two-act farce by O'Keeffe first produced in 1779. When revived in October 1807 at Covent Garden, Blanchard, Emery, Farley, Simmons, and Incledon appeared in the piece, and Bowkitt was played by Richard Jones: but for Grimaldi to take up the role would be an invasion of the 'legitimate' terrain, and though Fawcett may well have thought this a tempting bait both for the audience and the Clown, it was refused in a letter couched 'in respectful terms'. Grimaldi decided, after consulting his friends, that he should make no such experiments, for the moment at least, and he did not appear at Fawcett's benefit in May, although Emery and Liston did. This refusal so offended Fawcett that for three years he cut him dead whenever they happened to meet in the theatre, and — so Grimaldi believed — set out to injure his reputation when opportunity arose. He had joined the ranks of the enemy, and as he later became stage manager, he was a man to be feared.

This incident and its apparent sequels (see Chapter 18 of the *Memoirs*) served to strengthen Grimaldi's tendency to 'persecution mania', described in an earlier chapter. At Sadler's Wells and Covent Garden, he believed, there were dangerous men at work — insidious, malicious, jealous members of an anti-Grimaldi conspiracy, to whose machinations he ascribed many of his later misfortunes. There were, of course, grounds for his suspicions, for at all three theatres he was often treated shabbily and his success inevitably created enemies, but the root of the trouble was not in the man but in his occupation. He was a professional buffoon, and some leading figures in the theatre world despised pantomime and regarded its most successful artist as a thief who had stolen their thunder. In 1806 Tom Dibdin had wished to give up writing pantomimes at Covent Garden because of opposition in high places, and, in spite of *Mother Goose*, that opposition lingered.

About this time Grimaldi was allowed to play for Miss Bristow's benefit at Birmingham, where the theatre was under the management of Macready, the tragedian's father.[3] On his arrival, Macready asked him to play for a further three nights and, as the financial bait was large and he was not wanted at Covent

Garden for a week at least, Grimaldi accepted with pleasure. But on the fourth night of his appearance, just as he was going on the stage in the pantomime, a letter arrived post-haste from London. It was written by 'an old friend', who warned Joe to return to Covent Garden at once: he had been announced to play the following night, although the stage manager knew that he was still in Birmingham, and 'I fear it is done to injure you'. The conspiracy was at work again, and Grimaldi saw Fawcett's hand in it! He wanted to leave immediately, without giving his performance, so afraid was he of the shadowy cabal, but Macready persuaded him to remain, promising that a chaise and four would be waiting outside the stage door as soon as the pantomime was over. Within a few minutes of the final tableau, the Clown was wiping off his red paint, bundling his motley into a bag, pulling on his trousers and boots, and with a quick farewell to Macready — who pressed a package of banknotes into his hand — he jumped into the chaise and set off for London. He would foil the conspirators by reaching Covent Garden in time for the evening performance.

It was a rough journey. The night was stormy, and the wheels bumped and lurched along the potholed, rutted roads, squelching into the mud and out again, while the horses slipped and floundered in the slime. To make matters worse, Grimaldi in his anxiety to make good time treated the postboys so liberally — he had £294 for his four nights in Birmingham — that they got increasingly drunk at every stage. There the Clown sat, huddled in his greatcoat, jolted up and down like a sack of potatoes, while the chaise rattled on through the night, with the whips cracking and the rain beating down and the drunken drivers roaring songs above. The journey went on all through the next day, including a fourteen-mile diversion along the wrong road, until Grimaldi reached Salt Hill at seven o'clock the following evening. He had been nineteen hours on the road. At Salt Hill he jumped into another chaise, drove straight to Covent Garden, and ran up the steps to his dressing-room where Farley was already preparing to go on in his place. The overture was already playing but, with the practised rapidity of a quick-change pantomime artist, he was on the stage in his usual role, out of breath but in time. This was a victory over his enemies, and also over his constitution; for such feats of endurance served to shorten Grimaldi's life. It is typical of Joe — whether these be the facts of his life or the fantasy he spun around them — that the story of the Birmingham adventure is darkened by yet another betrayal. Shortly before his invitation by Macready, he asked a close friend

> to get his bill at one month for £150 discounted. The friend put the bill into his pocket-book, and promised to bring the money at night. Night came, but the money did not; it had not arrived when he returned from Birmingham; the friend was nowhere to be found, and he had soon afterwards the satisfaction of paying the whole sum, without having received a sixpence of the money.

Joe seemed to be doomed to misfortune: however much money he made, it was always disappearing by some mysterious agency or treacherous plot. That, at least, is the picture which the *Memoirs* present.

*   *   *

That autumn brought disaster to Covent Garden. On 12th September the great theatre opened its doors for the winter season: a week later, in the early morning of the 20th, the Grimaldis were awakened by the news that it was on fire. Like other members of the company, they quickly dressed and made their way towards Hart Street through a pall of smoke. All round the burning building thronged the crowds, with looters and pickpockets hard at work: it was a spectacle too good to miss, better than *Lodoiska* or any of those other Conflagrations of the stage; but for the Grimaldis and their comrades this burning splendour was a bitter sight. Joe was lucky, for most of his properties were at the Wells — he had played there in a pantomime and an aquatic drama that night — but his wife and her sisters had all lost clothes and personal possessions; and most of the theatre's scenery, properties, manuscripts and records went up in smoke, together with such treasures as original scores of Arne and Handel, at an estimated cost of £150,000. That was not all: twenty-two lives were lost.

The following morning, Boaden called on Kemble at his house in Great Russell Street, and was admitted to a room where the great actor was trying to shave. At length he turned round and, so Boaden would have us believe, delivered the following harangue:

Yes, it has perished, that magnificent theatre, which for all the purposes of exhibition or comfort was the first in Europe. It is gone, with all its treasures of every description, and some which can never be replaced. That LIBRARY, which contained all those immortal productions of our countrymen, prepared for the purposes of representation! That vast collection of Music, composed by the greatest geniuses in that science — by Handel, Arne, and others; most of it manuscript, in the original score! That Wardrobe, stored with all the costumes of all ages and nations, accumulated by unwearied research, and at incredible expense! Scenery, the triumph of the art, unrivalled for its accuracy, and so exquisitely finished, that it might be the ornament of your drawing-rooms, were they only large enough to contain it. Of all this vast treasure nothing now remains, but the Arms of England over the entrance of the theatre — and the Roman Eagle standing solitary in the market place![4]

Besides the Roman Eagle, however, there was the English Goose: Dibdin's pantomime and its properties had — out of 'all this vast treasure' — survived. It was, somehow, adding insult to injury.

*   *   *

Within a week of the fire the company was back in harness. The following Monday Kemble opened a season at the King's, where the Covent Garden players remained until the beginning of December. Grimaldi, however, was not in the repertory until Christmas, so he accepted more invitations from provincial managers. In October he appeared in Brighton for the first time, with Bologna as Harlequin in a pantomime, and it was also at this period, according to the *Memoirs*, that he made his first expedition to Manchester and Liverpool, an expedition that was nearly his last.[6] It began with an accident on the road, when Grimaldi's coach overturned and 'five stout men' fell on top of him — a Dickensian touch, this! That was not serious, but at Manchester he suffered a severe shock, of a kind which was not uncommon in his profession. The casualty rate among panto-mimists was high: when Harlequins jumped through windows, sometimes there were no stage-hands ready to receive them (like Tom Ellar): when Pantaloons performed in comic duels, their eyes were thrust out by swords (like James Parsloe); when Clowns shot up through stage-traps, the ropes were likely to break. This is what happened to Grimaldi at Manchester. Just as he reached the level of the stage, he fell back into the cellar below, stunned and shaken; although he was in acute pain he continued to play the scene as if nothing was amiss, and by the end of the evening — with the help, no doubt, of the Signor's embrocation — he had quite recovered. He had been his own doctor, but he was not anxious to test the cure again, and when he travelled with the company to Liverpool for a one-night stand he implored the master-carpenter to ensure that there was no recurrence of such an accident at that theatre. Nevertheless, it happened all over again. Just as Grimaldi's head showed above the stage, to be greeted with applause by the people of Liverpool, the ropes snapped, and after holding on for a few seconds to the edge of the trap he fell right down into the machinery below. Again, he was in agony; again, he insisted on continuing his performance, but with considerable difficulty. After the pantomime was over, he could scarcely walk to the stage door, and it took him some time to recover from the effects of his injuries.

He was back at work, however, by Boxing Day, when *Mother Goose* began its third lease of life — at the Haymarket. Three new scenes were added to the old favourite during the season, one of them representing the ruins of the old theatre transformed by a touch of Harlequin's wand into a new and splendid building; and four days later the foundation stone of that building was laid by the Prince of Wales himself, in a ceremony of great Masonic splendour. Neither to Kemble nor to his theatre did the Prince's blessing bring good fortune, and the new Covent Garden was no sooner opened than new troubles began for the management. To Grimaldi, the overstrain and injuries of these years brought premature old age. He frequently played Clown at both Sadler's Wells and Covent Garden on the same night, wrapping his sweating body in blankets, dashing into the waiting hackney, and driving through the bitter winter night to his next appointment with folly; on one occasion, at least, he even appeared at three theatres in one night; and another time — the subject of a celebrated anecdote — he *ran* in his Clown's motley from Sadler's Wells to Covent Garden, followed by a cheering gang of ragamuffins. In the long run, his body took its revenge.

Twelve

*We are not a nation of pantomimists, and but for Grimaldi
British pantomime would long ago have given up the ghost.*
—D.J.ANDERSON (1879)

IN SPITE OF HIS ENORMOUS SUCCESS AT COVENT GARDEN, it was as
'the Clown of Sadler's Wells' that Joe Grimaldi was still known
to most Londoners, and he retained that honourable title until his
retirement from the stage. Every Easter Monday he appeared in
his motley to launch a new pantomime on the Islington boards,
and from that time onward until the theatre closed in October he
appeared several nights a week in the summer repertory of
aquadrama and harlequinade. At nights he often travelled out to
Finchley, where in 1806 he leased a cottage at Fallow Corner,
which then enjoyed a semi-rural peace and prettiness as part of
the green belt of Georgian London. Here his son Joe, a rather
sickly child, spent most of his early boyhood. Grimaldi 'could
not bear to part with him, and was wholly unable to make up his
mind to send him to any great boarding school',[1] so the boy was
educated partly at home and partly at the Putney school which
his father had attended occasionally before the war — but not
upon the stage. Both Covent Garden and Sadler's Wells were
filled with the little sons and daughters of his relations and
colleagues, and Grimaldi must often have been rallied about the
way in which he mollycoddled young Joe and spoiled his chances
in the profession; but he kept him out of the theatre or, at least,
off the stage. Was it not the best way of training a child, to set
him in the business of the stage while his body was most flexible
and his mind most impressionable? Wasn't Grimaldi's own success
partly due, said Byrne, Fairbrother and other family men, to his
early start in infancy? Look, they said, at the success which
Laurent was achieving with his seven-year-old son at the Lane;
look how well the Dubois boys were doing, or Joe's own brother-
in-law, George Bristow. Grimaldi, however, kept his own counsel.
He wanted his son to be educated not only in stage-lore but also
in book-learning, and though he may have dreamed that one day
Joe might succeed him as leader of the Clowns he made no attempt
to force him into the hard world of the theatre until he was on

the edge of manhood. Joe was, in any event, too delicate for the rough-and-tumble of the 'variety' stage, or so his father considered; and he already showed a precociously alert mind which delighted Grimaldi, who did his best to share this childhood in the fields of Finchley. (According to the *Memoirs* he gave up the cottage in 1812, but in fact he did not surrender the lease until 1827.) Later, as the boy's skill developed and his health improved, Grimaldi taught him some of the secrets of Clownship, passing on the heritage of the old Signor and enriching it with his own experience and genius; he trained young Joe in acrobatic routine, trickwork, combats, and the elements of pantomime business, so that if the call came Grimaldi's heir would be prepared. Sometimes the boy was permitted to mix with the audience at the Garden, under proper supervision, and in the summer his mother sometimes took him to the Wells; but the stage was never allowed to interfere (in theory) with his schooling, and he was not allowed too often in the green-rooms and dressing-rooms, where manners and language were not always of the nicest. (Even on the public stage actresses were known to give voice, in the heat of emotion, to such unscripted expressions as: 'I'll give you a podger in the guts.') Grimaldi was determined that his son should have, as far and as long as possible, a gentleman's education; if he did decide to enter the theatre he need feel no inferiority to his so-called superiors in the 'legitimate' drama.

Superior? What legitimate actor could boast, with Grimaldi, that he could work a miracle: not even Mrs Siddons had healed the sick. (She might kill, but never cure.) It happened in this way. One summer night at Islington the gallery was filled with sailors, who were regular patrons of the Aquatic Theatre, and among them was a large party of men who had recently been paid off from a ship commanded by Captain George Harris, a son of Covent Garden's proprietor. Among these bluejackets, celebrating their leave in the usual naval way, was a man who had been deaf and dumb ever since an attack of sunstroke some years before. He sat in the front row of the gallery, and seemed to enjoy all the antics of Grimaldi's Clown, whose humour was indeed admirably suited to a theatre of the deaf, so little did it depend upon the spoken word: a blind man at the pantomime would hear nothing but stuff and nonsense. That night the deaf sailor, so long shut up in solitude, watched with delight the squat, grimacing figure on the stage below, convulsing the house with noiseless laughter; and so deep was his enjoyment that, after one violent burst of applause, he turned to the man beside him and said: 'What a damned funny fellow!'

'What, Jack, can you speak?' cried his neighbour, who could hardly believe his ears, with all the hubbub going on around them.

'Ay, and hear too!' said the sailor, to his own enormous surprise, and he proceeded to tell his shipmates and everyone else in the gallery.

Grimaldi and his colleagues on the stage must have imagined that some news of a naval victory had reached the 'gods' above, for the sailors gave three rousing cheers and the noise swelled to a tumult; but they continued to watch the pantomime, perhaps in order to see what other miracles the Clown could perform when he was in the vein, and as soon as it was over they marched over to the Myddelton's Head with the deaf and dumb man borne in triumph on their shoulders. There the sailors celebrated his recovery, and the news rapidly spread through the neighbourhood that Joe Grimaldi had restored speech and hearing to a deaf and dumb sailor, had given back sight to a blinded soldier, had raised a man from the dead. (Why not? A Clown could do anything: he broke the laws of life and death on the stage.)

Next morning, Grimaldi came to the tavern to meet his patient, and the celebration continued while the sailor answered the questions of his incredulous benefactor; but Grimaldi and Dibdin decided that he could not have counterfeited the unmistakable delight he took in the sound of his own forgotten voice, as he told his story in the crowded bar-room, and it was afterwards corroborated by his commander. What, one wonders, was the particular piece of buffoonery which broke down the barrier of years? And how was the news received in the green rooms of Covent Garden? Grimaldi must have felt some pride in his cure by clowning: had Emery or Munden done as much, let alone John Philip Kemble?

* * *

Even Joe Grimaldi, however, could make no impression upon the campaigners in that theatrical civil war known to posterity as the OP (Old Price) Riots, which broke out in the autumn of 1809.

It was not until 20th November, the forty-fifth night, that Grimaldi appeared before this rioting audience in the pantomime of *Don Juan*, with Louisa Bristow as Donna Anna. Covent Garden was as noisy as ever, but Joe was given a great reception by the rioters; the next night, it seems, 'the empire of tumult seemed to be on the decline. The play was heard through the fourth act, and even the fifth was pretty audible. There was considerable noise during the pantomime, but it was merely vocal.'[2] This was, however, a temporary recession, and was not, as Grimaldi himself believed, due to the influence of the Clown. The following week *Don Juan* supplied the OP-ites with a popular banner. During the play, Don Guzman's statue was seen with an inscription in letters of blood:

> *Don Juan, by thee*
> *Don Guzman bleeds,*
> *Heaven will avenge*
> *Thy bloody deeds!*

At this moment a whole posse of men with OP symbols in their hats raised a placard on which was written in huge letters

> *What are Don Juan's bloody deeds*
> *Compared with Don John's bloody deeds?*

Greeted with loud applause, this was maintained during the rest of the performance, until the curtain fell and the audience gave three hearty groans.

By Christmas, however, the row was settled for the time being, and the OP wars were over. Many later historians have dismissed the whole affair as a demonstration of vicious hooliganism and mob rule, and at the time even William Cobbett opposed the rioters because they were breaking the rules of commerce by dictating the price at which products should be sold. Yet one of the most interesting facts about the OP riots is that they were led by middle class and professional men, for no more sinister motives, it would seem, than a belief in the bad faith and bad manners of the theatre management. As the *Covent Garden Journal* said,

> The poor can have no concern in the business. It is for them, in the present unfortunate times, to consider rather the advanced

prices of provisions and necessaries than of admission to a theatre. . . . For the most part, it is the rich and better sort of people who are engaged in resisting the exaction complained of. Public rowdiness and militant demonstrations were by no means limited to the lower classes, for this was a time when public schoolboys revolted against their masters, when aristocrats at royal levees fought so hard for elbow-room that the casualty rate was often alarmingly high. The OP riots, indeed, illustrate the vigour, energy and tyranny of the Georgian audience, which suggests one reason for the enormous popularity of the harlequinade in which Grimaldi was the rebel incarnate; and they indirectly underline the incompatibility of theatre aesthetics and popular taste and the gulf between the management and the audience. Both Covent Garden and Drury Lane had been rebuilt after their most recent fires — by Robert Smirke and Benjamin Wyatt respectively — in the ponderous neo-classical style of the day, and decorated with statues of muses and poets ancient and modern, as symbols of their place in the nation's culture. Yet the true deities of both theatres were Harlequin and Columbine, the Bleeding Nun and the Spectre Knight, the Wild Man and the Clown; and of these there was no sign in stone. These temples of the drama were kept alive by the popular theatre of pantomime and melodrama, and their pseudo-Greek façades were as much of a sham as the Gothic shells of some of these new mills and factories which were now beginning to spread through the Midlands and the North.

*   *   *

During this eventful season of 1809–10 Louisa Bristow, one of Grimaldi's sisters-in-law, found sudden favour in the eyes of the management, and was promoted to nearly twenty roles, including Bridget in *Every Man in his Humour*, Helen in *The Iron Chest*, Anne Bullen in *Henry VIII*, Lady Percy in *Henry IV Part I* and Cordelia in *King Lear*. The OP rioters gave her little opportunity to show her mettle in the autumn, but by the time she made her appearance as Lear's youngest daughter the crowds were quiet at Covent Garden, and her performance could be heard and not only seen. The verdicts were not enthusiastic. As the *Monthly Mirror* said:

A prettier Cordelia was never seen than Miss Bristowe (*sic*), but to do her justice, a worse was never heard. Time and study may improve Miss Bristowe's qualities, but at present she bears a weight so *kindly* heaped upon her, with very feeble shoulders ... Much as we have always detested the tragic taste of Tate, for sparing the life of Cordelia, we never felt it more insupportable than on this occasion.

It was widely hinted that the pretty Louisa owed her rapid promotion to the intimate interest of John Philip Kemble, but whether the manager's admiration of her beauty — would he have made an alliance with the family of a Clown? — or merely his misjudgment of her talent was responsible for her sudden appearance in the limelight, it was all too brief. When the 1810–11 season opened her parts had been distributed among the other actresses and she, with her younger sister, had been dismissed. With relish, the *Monthly Mirror* noted that 'Mr Kemble's favourite, Miss Bristowe, has only been raised, it seems, to make her fall the greater'. Louisa's brief celebrity, however, was not entirely fruitless; she succeeded, for a time, to the role of Columbine in her brother-in-law's harlequinades, and when she married some years later it was to her former Harlequin, Jack Bologna. Grimaldi must have been in some delicate family embarrassments during this season; and towards the end of it his mother, Rebecca Brooker, disappeared from the bills of Drury Lane after some forty dancing years. It is a pity that we know so little of Mrs Brooker, for she must have played a big part in shaping her great son's character in childhood. But we know enough to hazard a guess that only serious illness could have kept her off the stage. With help from the Drury Lane fund she lived on in retirement for another nine years. She died on 23rd October 1819.

Thirteen

All things are big with jest; nothing that's plain
But may be witty, if thou hast the vein.
                              —GEORGE HERBERT

DURING THE EARLY DAYS OF THE 1810–11 SEASON at Covent Garden, the theatre, on which the proprietors had spent a further £7000, was filled again with the noise of rioting crowds, for Kemble had defied the Crown and Anchor Treaty. In an attempt to minimize the financial loss incurred by surrender to the OP campaign, he had maintained some private boxes, the last few bones of theatrical contention; and the nightly hubbub was still in full swing when Joe Grimaldi returned in *Mother Goose* on 17th September (with a new Pantaloon — Richard Norman.) A week later, however, the OP dispute was ended for ever when the private boxes were opened to the public, and the royal theatre of Covent Garden entered a new decade of peace and prosperity, for which its Clown could take a large share of the credit. It was the decade of Grimaldi's kingship, better known to historians as the Regency.

At Christmas the pantomime of *Harlequin and Asmodeus: or Cupid on Crutches*, inspired by recent campaigns on the Continent, was dressed up in pseudo-Spanish finery, and Grimaldi appeared in the 'opening' as an Old Duenna; but the production was chiefly renowned in the print-shops for the way that Joe, in one of his most characteristic and memorable transformations, created a Vegetable Man from the produce of Covent Garden market — a greengrocer's nightmare with a melon-head, turnip hands and carrot-fingers, which fought its clownish creator, 'Joe Franken-stein', upon the stage. This proved to be the first of the Regency pantomimes, for a week before its production the Regency Bill was introduced in the House of Commons. After the death of his daughter Princess Amelia on 2nd November, the old King had plunged into a complete insanity from which he was never to recover, and his dissolute son and enemy, once known as the First Gentleman of Europe, became the nominal ruler of England.

Whatever his shortcomings as the leader of a nation, 'Prinny' was perfectly cast as the monarch of a golden age of pantomime; and he was for some years the central figure in a series of royal harlequinades that his absurd, uproarious family presented to the British public, which paid heavily for the privilege. While the old, mad Pantaloon-King lived out his dreams at Windsor under lock and key, ruling his shadowy court of doctors and warders, his sons, their wives and their mistresses engaged in farcical campaigns of civil war. The Regent himself, royal Harlequin, swelled out like a pantomime joke into a huge balloon of a man; his brothers York and Clarence, whose private life was public property, were booby warriors in the comic chase; the Duke of Cumberland was in the background as a kind of Demon King; and the crowning touch of fantasy was lent by Prinny's wife Caroline, for this 'pantomime source of ribaldry and indecorum' — as Sir Arthur Bryant describes her[1] — was for years the tragi-comic Columbine in the Hanoverian harlequinade. The Pavilion at Brighton seems an appropriate setting for Grimaldi's Chinese Clown, or for one of those Grand Oriental Marriages which were once so popular a consummation of London pantomimes; while at Carlton House the Regent exercised his talent for stage management, exotic spectacle and amorous intrigue, conjuring the money for his experiments out of the wartime treasury. There was one substantial difference, however, between Regency pantomime at court and on the stage: vices which were applauded in the King of Clowns won less honour in the future King of England. Joe Grimaldi won love and respect from the people for whom he made himself a standing joke, but the royal buffoon demanded to be taken seriously . . . and became the country's laughing stock.

*   *   *

Was Grimaldi, specifically, a Regency Clown? According to Mr D.L.Murray,

> his whole conception of the Clown reflects that period of genteel blackguardism, pugilism and practical jokes. The 'grimacing, filching, irresistible Clown', his white face larded with red like a schoolboy's that has been dipped in a surreptitious jam-pot, is a plebeian successor of the mohocks, a companion of Jerry Hawthorn and Corinthian Tom, whose recreations are breaking windows, tripping up old women and assaulting the constables.[2]

These were days, in the words of Sir Arthur Bryant, when a heartless disregard for the feelings of others was the hallmark of the 'blood'. It was considered a joke to throw a drunk in a dunghill, drop a live coal on a sleeper's head, rob a blind man of his dog and swear in the presence of ladies and clergymen.[3] And it is certainly true that the violence of the times was reflected in the harlequinades.

Their brutalities were satirized in Tom Dibdin's popular *Harlequin Hoax*, first staged at the Lyceum in August, 1814, with Liston as Harlequin and Fanny Kelly as his Columbine. In this piece the author of the pantomime introduces himself as 'Peter Patch of Pimlico, Poet, Painter, Prompter and Performer: principally proud of the province of Pantomime, my whole family bred to the boards, my mother was a mute, and my daddy a dumby; I was the original Goose in the Golden Egg, and work'd the wire whiskers of the White Cat, and have so much Pantomime fire about me, that I'll undertake, on the most reasonable terms, to blow up your whole House, like the Miller and his Men; or burn you, like brushwood, on the Woodman's Hut.' This prodigy hands his Harlequin-to-be a synopsis of his scenes — 'you have some of the most delicious situations: read, Sir, read' — and Liston reads out a revealing commentary on the taste of the time.

LISTON: 'Harlequin is carried up by the tail of a kite, and when at the top of the theatre, drops through a trap at the bottom and returns enveloped in flames, as if shot from the crater of a volcano; then thrown into a cascade of real water — with sufficient force to let the splash convince the audience that the element is genuine.' — So I'm to make a splash in real water, after broiling in the crater of a volcano!

PATCH: Yes, but that's nothing — I've engaged a skilful juggler, who will run you through the body with a true toledo, lodge a musquet-ball in your left eye, and after breaking every bone in your skin, put you right by a galvanic experiment, which shall make you roar like a town bull to the great amusement of a brilliant and overflowing audience. — Proceed, sir.

LISTON: 'To meet Columbine at the street door, Harlequin throws himself out of a three-pair of stairs window, and is caught with his head in a lamp-iron: the lamplighter pours a gallon of oil down his throat' (a gallon of oil! I'll not take that, by Jupiter!) 'sticks a lighted wick in his mouth, and a set of drunken bucks, having no better business on earth than to break lamps, knock his nob to shivers, and all go to the watch-house together'. Upon my honour, I'm much beholden to you.

This parade of absurdities is not too far removed from the mimic tortures applied to Regency buffoons; and, indeed, the agonies were often all too real. Broken bones, wrenched muscles, wounds with swords and pistols were all endured by Grimaldi and his colleagues in the cause of fun: Jack Bologna broke a collarbone, the elder Follet lost a leg, James Parsloe was blinded in one eye. Although Joe's own style became quieter with the years, he was singled out by *The Times* for his successful masochism in the Covent Garden pantomime of 1812–3, *Harlequin and the Red Dwarf*:

Grimaldi is the most assiduous of all imaginable buffoons, and it is absolutely surprising that any human head or hide can resist the rough trials which he volunteers. Serious tumbles from serious heights, innumerable kicks, and incessant beatings, come on him as matters of common occurrence, and leave him every night fresh and free for the next night's flagellation.

At one time or another, Grimaldi once said, almost every bone in his body had been broken or seriously injured.

In this respect, then, Grimaldi reflected the manners of the Regency; and he himself, in clowning, played havoc with the watch, tripped up old women, assaulted Pantaloon, and committed every kind of felony with infectious zest and perfect licence; yet it must be remembered that, compared with his contemporaries, Grimaldi was a gentle, good-humoured Clown, and that this kind of horseplay was only one facet of his comic genius. The violence that he expressed, moreover, far from being peculiar to the ten years of the Regency, lies at the heart of all clowning, although the forms may change. Said *The Times* in 1823:

A pun tells only once — but it is not so with a poke in the eye. There will always be a certain comicality about a man's breaking his shins, or having his toes trodden upon — or in an old woman's firing off a gun, and being knocked down by the report — and with a fit of the colic, in male or female, we could commune for ever. These things have all been jokes in the last century, and will be so six centuries to come.

An off-stage glimpse of Joey in an 1812 print by H. Brown

Above. Grimaldi, Norman and the Alpaca, in *Harlequin and the Red Dwarf* (1812). *From the British Theatre Museum*
Below. Grimaldi and the Vegetable Man, in *Harlequin and Asmodeus* (1810). *From the British Theatre Museum*

Above. Grimaldi and Norman, the Pantaloon, in the Epping Hunt scene from *Harlequin and the Red Dwarf* (1812)
Below. Grimaldi plays leapfrog, in *Harlequin and Padmanaba* (1811), or, as it was more popularly known, 'The Golden Fish'. *From the British Theatre Museum*

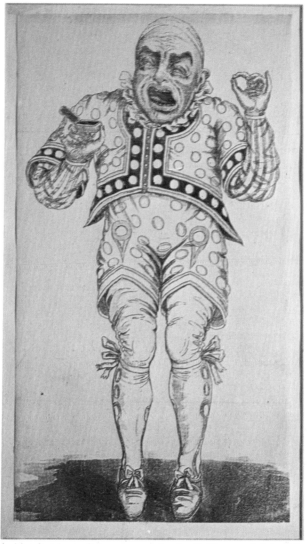

This primitive but immediate representation by T. Turner of Grimaldi singing 'Typitywitchet', now in the Kay Robertson collection, has been described as the only contemporary painting of the Clown — in costume and in action. It formerly belonged to Maurice Willson Disher

That was a dangerous prophecy, for these jokes have long ago lost their savour; nor is a modern audience likely to sympathize with Andrew Halliday's rhetorical question, posed forty years later, 'Where is the witticism that can compete with sitting on a baby, and flattening it to the shape of a pancake?'[4] Yet though manners have become superficially milder (and mime has almost disappeared) the savagery of clowning — and, in particular, its self-punishment — endures in the verbalised buffoonery of many entertainers who thrive on insult and humiliation, in the tradition of cruelty transformed by art.

Although Mr D.L.Murray exaggerates Grimaldi's debt to his time, he was in other ways an unmistakable Regency clown — as a satirist upon society. 'Other performers of the art,' as one critic observed, 'may be droll in their generation; but which of them can for a moment compete with the Covent Garden hero in acute observation upon the foibles and absurdities of society, and his happy talent of holding them up to ridicule. He is the finest practical satirist that ever existed.' Moreover, 'his style of humour had always a satirical relation to our everyday emotions.' This 'practical satire' found many targets, in many pantomimes, although it is a mistake to assume that his basic costume was invented as a parody of fashionable dress.

There was a sufficiency of folly in Regency England for the Clown to snipe at fashionable society, without overstepping the mark; this was no Jaques, eager to 'cleanse the foul body of th' infected world', but plump-faced, smiling Joey, mocking the ballerinas and boxers of the day, pouring fun on duelling and dandyism, burlesquing the latest fashions. Sometimes he turned his attention to the theatre, 'sending up' Indian jugglers, sword-swallowers, or such stars as Mrs Charles Kemble. In *Harlequin Gulliver: or The Flying Island* he burlesqued a famous duet in that popular operetta, *The Padlock*, by singing a comic duet with a Brobdingnagian canary which he described as a 'Casso-wa-ry':

> *Say little, foolish, fluttering thing,*
> *If you're a cock bird, why not sing?*

'he being all the time quietly seated on a Brobdingnagian quartern loaf, into which he might have eaten his way like a mouse into a cheese.'[5] Sometimes Grimaldi ridiculed women's dress, as in the same pantomime of *Harlequin Gulliver*:

A long plum dumpling placed on his back beneath a gown supplies the hump which has now become necessary to female symmetry. A coal skuttle [*sic*] furnishes the bonnet, to which an iron stove pipe furnishes a fashionably high crown, and a dealer in flowers makes his appearance in time to contribute the ornament which is to surmount the whole. A front adorns his brow, a scarf is thrown over his shoulders: and thus altered, he waltzes divinely, and faints at last from exertion with inconceivable grace.

In another caricature of the 'dandizette', or female dandy, he used a cabbage net for a veil, a mushroom for a parasol, a fruit basket as his bonnet, and a rush-basket as his reticule.

It was not only women who suffered ridicule, however, in the pantomimes at Covent Garden and Sadler's Wells. Grimaldi often caricatured male fashions, in an era when dandyism, under the leadership of the Regent and Beau Brummell, was supreme. 'Starch is the man!' was Brummell's farewell message, before his flight to France: it might well have served as a slogan for the upper set of Regency young men about town; and it was Grimaldi's privilege to take some of the starch out of this overdressed generation, at a time when, to quote Sir Arthur Bryant, 'class feeling was turning into a religion'. In one scene the Clown turned a chimney-pot into a hat, a miller's sack into white ducks, a girl's shawl into a fancy waistcoat, and a cellar-door iron ring into a fop's eyeglass; in another he wore a travesty of the fashionable huntsman's rig; but it was the dandy officers, above all, of whom Grimaldi made a butt, and the most spectacular demonstration was in *Harlequin and the Red Dwarf*, when he burlesqued the Hussars.

The scene changed to a street, with a farrier's shop beside a blacksmith's. A Hussar officer, in all the extravagant and foolish finery of the corps, passed thundering by. The spirit of imitation instantly took possession of the Clown, and, not unwisely judging that the secret lay in the dress, he determined to be a hero and a Hussar in his own person. A pair of red pantaloons, which he put on before the audience with the happiest play of blushing modesty, was the only thing which he condescended to borrow of his model; two black varnished coal-scuttles formed his boots, two real horseshoes shod the heels, and with jack-chains and the help of large brass dishes or candlesticks or spurs, equipped his legs in an uniform almost as clattering, unwieldy, and absurd, as the most irresistible of our whiskered propugnatores. A white bear-skin formed his pelisse, a muff his cap, and a black tippet finished his toilet, by giving him a beard, whiskers and pendent moustaches. The whole house, in the spirit of the general contempt of these miserable imitations of foreign foppery, roared with laughter, as they saw the buffoon of a Theatre turn the favourite invention of the mighty, and the wise, and the warlike, into merited ridicule. The satire was even more pointed, and more intelligible, by the presence of *genuine* Hussar Officers in the stage box, covered *de cap a pied* with chains and catskins.[6]

The dress of the Hussars — thus held up to ridicule at Covent Garden — was the particular preoccupation for many years of the Prince Regent himself: 'his whole soul,' said a friend, 'is wrapped up in Hussar saddles, caps, cuirasses and sword belts!' Yet Grimaldi was unchecked. On another occasion, however, 'he "commanded a regiment" with such an air of hauteur, and in such unintelligible tones, that a private message was sent from the mess-room of the Horse Guards to the manager of Covent Garden, threatening the withdrawal of patronage if Mr Grimaldi was permitted to continue "his infernal stupid foolery".'[7] This may have started at Sadler's Wells in 1809, when he reviewed an 'awkward squad' in *Fashion's Fools* — a time-honoured comic routine which dates from the seventeenth century and still graces the English music-hall; or when the Clown, sitting in an alehouse garden, transformed the butts, pots and barrels into soldiers, whom he reviewed astride a barrel with a saw as its neck and a funnel as its tail, brandishing a butcher's knife, and wearing a bowl as his helmet.

Grimaldi practised a similar equestrian burlesque in the 1811 panto at Covent Garden, *Harlequin and Padmanaba: or The Golden Fish*, when, having begun the evening as a Persian Cook, Cayfacattadhri, he introduced two comic scenes which soon featured in all the London print-shops and were frequently repeated in later pantomimes. In one of these the Clown played leap-frog with a man-size frog, who afterwards appeared in an opera hat, ruffles and other fashionable accessories; and in another he created a coach, pulled by dogs, out of a cradle, four cheeses and a fender. Grimaldi, who wore a basin on his head, blew a toy trumpet and brandished a ribboned stick, was burlesquing the notorious curricle of Romeo Coates, an ostentatiously rich eccentric from the West Indies who had an extravagant passion for the theatre, high society and self-advertisement.

*   *   *

The star attraction of this pantomime, however, was not the Clown but Chuny, and this leads us into a zoological digression: for Chuny, whom Henry Harris is said to have bought for 900 guineas, was the largest elephant ever seen in England, and the first to tread the stage of Covent Garden. Animals were not unknown in this temple of the drama, for in the previous February a sensational revival of *Bluebeard* introduced sixteen horses, mounted by 'Spahis', and the Rev. John Genest noted that 'in the first row of the pit the stench was so abominable that one might as well have sitten in a stable.'[8] But an elephant was then a considerably greater novelty — in a metropolis without a zoo in any way comparable to the modern menageries, and unaccustomed to the annual exhibition of wild animals in the circus ring — and many people visited Covent Garden that Christmas merely in order to see Chuny. Perhaps the elephant later justified his owner's investment, but as a performer on the opening night he was disappointingly intransigent; for he 'took the unparalleled freedom of clearing one part of the stage several times, and appeared somewhat disposed to throw his human incumbrances from his shoulders' — one of these incumbrances being the hapless Columbine, Mrs Parker; and in spite of repeated bribery with boiled rice Chuny '*rumped* the audience repeatedly: but whether this awkward movement arose from the *contempt* or the *modesty* of the animal, was not ascertained.'[9] It is not surprising that he earned the scorn of Johnstone, the Drury Lane machinist, who was 'famous for wicker-work lions, paste-board swans and all the sham birds and beasts appertaining to a theatrical menagerie'. At a night rehearsal at Covent Garden, Johnstone hid in the two-shilling gallery with a friend, in order to watch this threat to the Lane's annual pantomime. When Chuny appeared, his friend whispered:

'This is a bitter bad job for Drury! Why, the elephant's *alive!* — he'll carry all before him, and beat you hollow: what d'ye think on't, eh?'

'Think on't?' said Johnstone, in a tone of the utmost contempt,

— 'I should be very sorry if I couldn't make a much better elephant than *that*, at any time.'[10]

Three years later Harris sold Chuny to the proprietor of Exeter Change, where it was often visited by the tragedian, Charles Young, with whom the elephant had established a close friendship. Chuny's end was tragic, for he went mad in captivity and the Guards were called in to kill him: 152 shots were needed.[11]

In the following year the Covent Garden management persisted in trying to rival the circus by introducing live animals in the pantomime;[12] and in the Epping Forest scene of *Harlequin and the Red Dwarf* an alpaca or llama ('some curious quadruped from Peru') was introduced as a stag-substitute. He disappointed, however, as much as Chuny.

Great preparations were made for him, and two platforms placed to give him an opportunity of making his surprising leaps. He betrayed a total want of confidence in his powers, or rather showed a perfect indifference to all that was doing, and walking over the platforms, seemed only desirous of making his exit.

The hounds, moreover, which had been borrowed from a Member of Parliament, were as totally disinterested in the proceedings as was their hypothetical quarry. 'We cannot but say,' announced *The Times*, 'that we felt no regret at this total failure. The thing itself is equally ridiculous and disgraceful to the British Stage.' Yet Grimaldi now received recognition in its columns for the first time, and the print-shops did a brisk trade in recording *Harlequin and the Red Dwarf* for posterity. In one scene, Grimaldi 'dashed little Boney into the jaws of the Russian bear' — a topical allusion to Napoleon's disastrous invasion of Russia; in another, he created the 'Nondescript', a popular label for pantomime monsters, out of Pantaloon's corpse, which he dressed in the skin of a lion, the head of an ass, eagle's wings, cat's feet, and a fish's tail; and in a third, probably the most popular of all, he rode to the Epping Hunt on a huge cart-horse with an enormous jockey-cap and a long waggoner's whip, while Pantaloon rode ahead on a little toy-size pony. It is worth noting, however, that Covent Garden did not feel that Joe Grimaldi and his comic colleagues were enough to make the pantomime go at Christmas time: in spite of the lessons of *Mother Goose*, which seems to have been regarded as a lucky freak, the management felt obliged to stage spectacular scenes of action, with such zoological novelties as Chuny and the Quadruped from Peru.

* * *

It was not *what* Grimaldi did, however, but *how* he did it, that made him the greatest Clown not only of the Regency but of all English pantomime; and in no aspect is this plainer than in his comic songs, and the patter that survived in print. Charles Dibdin says:

> The Songs which I wrote for Grimaldi were of a singular nature, and, generally speaking, unless sung by the Clown of a Pantomime, in Character, lost half their effect: when writing them I had in view much more his peculiarities of what I may call expression, than any literary fame. Many Songs *sing* well (technically speaking) that would read *ill*. Even Nonsense, in its place, can have a meaning.[13]

One of the most celebrated of these 'singular' songs was *A Typitywitchet: or Pantomimical Paroxysms*, especially composed by Dibdin to enable Grimaldi 'to exhibit several of his peculiarly whimsical characteristics'. It was sung for the first time on 30th July 1811 at Sadler's Wells, in *Bang Up: or Harlequin Prime* (a satire on the contemporary mania for racing).

This very morning handy
  My malady was such,
I in my tea took brandy
  And took a drop too much.
    (Hiccups) *Tol de rol, etc.*

Now I'm quite drowsy growing,
  For this very morn,
I rose while cock was crowing,
  Excuse me if I yawn.
    (Yawns)

But stop, I mustn't mag hard,
  My head aches — if you please,
One pinch of Irish blackguard
  I'll take to give me ease.
    (Sneezes)

I'm not in cue for frolic,
  Can't up my spirits keep,
Love's a windy colic,
  'Tis that makes me weep.
    (Cries)

I'm not in mood for crying,
  Care's a silly calf,
If to get fat you're trying,
  The only way's to laugh.

146

The only way's to laugh: perhaps we can see the Clown of Sadler's Wells, with feet turned in and arms akimbo, sneezing and hiccoughing and crying while the customers roar with delight, until he gives his celebrated, screeching peals of laughter that echo and re-echo round the theatre; perhaps we may understand, if we look at that grinning mask of fun, the reasons why so infantile a ditty was one of the most popular songs on the Regency lighter stage. Sneezing songs were not invented by Dibdin — an Italian burletta in John Rich's time featured a sneezing duet — and laughing songs, too, have a long pedigree; yet until Grimaldi's time no one had touched these buffooneries with art and, once he was dead, no one could give his own nonsense life again.

By no means all Joe's songs were nonsense songs, yet it was with these that he achieved his greatest success; and the most famous of all was *Hot Codlins*, which he introduced towards the very end of his career — in 1819. *Hot Codlins* was sung on the opening night of the Covent Garden season in *The Talking Bird: or Perizade Columbine*, one of those pantomime 'olios' or anthologies which were then a popular managerial expedient; as Dibdin says,

> those who never heard him cannot be made to understand how words so utterly destitute of humour, and music so entirely guiltless of merit, could have been rendered effective.

Yet this song was 'rendered' so effectively by Grimaldi that it became, in effect, the anthem of the English Clowns, and long after Joe's retirement it was demanded by the gallery every Christmas as an inalienable right and glorious tradition. Here are the words: codlins, it should be explained, are apples.

> *A little old woman her living got*
> *By selling codlins, hot, hot, hot;*
> *And this little woman, who codlins sold,*
> *Tho' her codlins were hot, she felt herself cold.*
> *So to keep herself warm, she thought it no sin*
> *To fetch for herself a quartern of . . .*

and here the pit and gallery roared out the rhyme of 'Gin'. Grimaldi cried 'Oh, for shame!' and sang a chorus, in which the whole audience joined, of 'Ri tol iddy, iddy, iddy, Ri tol iddy, iddy, Ri tol lay'. This was repeated at the end of each verse, after the appropriate final rhyme, as follows:

This little old woman set off in a trot,
To fetch her quartern of hot, hot, hot!
She swallowed one glass, and it was so nice,
She tipped off another in a trice;
The glass she filled till the bottle shrunk,
And this little woman they say got . . .

This little old woman, while muzzy she got,
Some boys stole her codlins, hot, hot, hot.
Powder under her pan put, and in it round stones:
Says the little old woman: 'These apples have bones!'
The powder the pan in her face did send,
Which sent the old woman on her latter . . .

The little old woman then up she got,
All in a fury, hot, hot, hot.
Says she, 'Such boys, sure, never were known;
They never will let an old woman alone'.
Now here is a moral, round let it buz —
If you mean to sell codlins, never get . . .

Only a Regency audience, perhaps — or at least a pre-Victorian audience — could appreciate the rich humour of such Corinthian pleasures; but it was not so much the crudity of the song that brought it such success as the ephemeral genius of its first singer.

* * *

If it is difficult for twentieth century readers to understand the popularity of Grimaldi's songs, it is not much easier to detect comic genius in his patter, as recorded in surviving texts; yet the examples reproduced below illustrate, in various ways, the groundwork of buffoonery on which the speaking Grimaldi built his grotesque palaces of laughter. Here is an extract from a pantomime in 1811, at Sadler's Wells, with a preliminary verse:

Mrs Mag, mantua-maker, ask'd ladies to tea,
They came all figg'd out as customaree,
All talking at once and as near as may be.
> *Hurrah, whurrah, click, clack.*
But all entertaining and innocent chat,
Now and then rather candid when purpose was pat,
A little like scandal but — never mind that.

Then, 'in different voices', Joe began his patter:

Pray ladies, is your tea to your liking? — Dear Mrs Mag, you've made mine too sweet — La, mem, you're not like Miss Muzzlemump fond of the grocer — yes, and if report speaks true there's no love lost between 'em — he! he! he! I *protest* Miss, you're quite scandalous — pray ladies how long has the *invisible girl* opened shop? — dear me, Miss, that's a queer question — I suppose the lady deludes to the advertisement about *invisible* petticoats — Dear me, aye — *Mrs Roundabout* bought one — she'd no occasion, her petticoats were always *invisible* — Bless me, Mrs Crump, you're quite shocking — *delicacy*, I say, is the honour of our *sect* — suppose *ve* elect that lady of petticoat government — Fye, ladies, if you go on so — 'What'll Mrs Grundy say?' ...

This kind of Dame-work, mixing Mrs Malaprop and Mrs Harris, has been a feature of music-hall humour until our own times.

In another Sadler's Wells pantomime — *Fairlop Fair: or The Genie of the Oak* in 1812 — Grimaldi sang a satirical song about the popularity of antiquarian pursuits, delivered outside Bullock's Museum, and he included among his patter an oblique prophecy of his own future fame:

> *Antiquaries, what creatures to please!*
> *Their fancies are cast in a droll die:*
> *Their standard for everything's Cheese,*
> *The better it grows the more mouldy ...*

As if a bright picture of King George, heaven bless him, wasn't better than all the old worm-eaten coins of all the outlandish Emperors of the world: but as times go, I may be an Emperor, my comical phiz stuck on a farthing, and somebody be fool enough to give a ha'penny for it.

> *For folk curiosities love to see,*
> *And, as I'm a curiosity, come to see me ...*

'As times go, I may be an Emperor ...' What wouldn't we give today for a good picture of that 'comical phiz', on and off the stage — in the garden at Baynes Row, with Mary and young Joe; directing rehearsals of the harlequinade; or in his full war-paint as the Clown?

149

Everyone at the Wells, of course, knew Joey the Clown, even if they had little information about the private life of Mr Grimaldi; for in any situation, and in any disguise, the Clown was always recognizable, always the same Joey; and this standing joke of personality underlay the apparently arid banter of the scripts. Here is an extract from the first scene of *The Astrologer: or Harlequin and Moore's Almanack*, which opened the Sadler's Wells season of 1810:

MOORE: Well, I've dispersed my Myrmidons, and now to study. Hey, what's here? — Old woman, rise.

CLOWN: Old woman! Why, it's I.

MOORE: Thou art a strange thing! Will't my servant be?

CLOWN: Oh, yes: provided I've *good wages, no work,* and the privilege of the pantry: then you'll find me quite docile and *dogmatical*: and, as the immortal Packwood says, 'No grumbling'.

MOORE: I like thee, and now will cast thy nativity (writes).

CLOWN: Oh, he's going to tell my fortune (looks at the horoscope). What pothooks and hangers!

MOORE: Thou wert born under the light planet Mercury, Therefore by disposition thou'rt a *Thief!*

CLOWN: Who do you call *Thief!*

MOORE: Thou wert not in the sign of Taurus born: Leo, Virgo, nor Libra:

CLOWN: Go to the library?

MOORE: No, Pisces, Aquarius, Capricorn disown thee Scorpio, Sagittarius —

CLOWN: Sassages! O, I likes 'em!

Such lines, of course, are only the skeleton of fun; but before Grimaldi's Clown ever appeared on the scene, the audience knew his violent appetite for 'sassages', for thieving, and for knavery in general. How irresistibly comic, in such a star, must have seemed that indignant entrance line of 'Old Woman! Why, it's I!' Moreover, like all great buffoons Grimaldi always did more than was set down for him. Scripted dialogue did not play an important part in the clowning of such a confirmed ad-libber, who relied to a great extent on business and allowed his own personality to be the cause of laughter — in silence. Joe did not need to speak: he chuckled, he squeaked, he *was* ... and that was enough.

Fourteen

*To tell a good clown from a bad one is easy: either you are
amused or you are not. But to distinguish a great clown from
a good one is more difficult. A great clown will never give
anyone the impression that he is playing a part. He never
appears to have learnt his lines or studied his gestures. He
seems to be a fathomless source of perfect improvization.
One is conscious of a power which appears limitless because
it overturns our preconceived ideas...—*ANTONY HIPPISLEY
COXE

'HE THAT DOES ANY ONE THING BETTER than all the rest of the world,
is a genius. Grimaldi has done this,' said one of his admirers during
his lifetime. But what was the secret of this superiority? How did
he make people laugh? To those vast questions the reader may
already have gathered several clues from the preceding chapters,
and a more detailed attempt to describe Grimaldi's Clownship is
made in the following pages. Yet at the last those questions are,
of course, unanswerable, for once a clown is dead all explanations
are only guesswork. Even when he is alive the ultimate cause of
his distinctive funniness remains an enigma, like the ultimate cause
of laughter itself in all its kinds, despite the Everest of theory
heaped up by philosophical and psychological analysts. The
clowns themselves don't know or can't tell, though some may
reveal their own trade secrets and others may join in the theorizing.
In Chaplin's words, 'I laugh because I laugh, and to laugh is
sufficient reason for existence, and there is no limit to our laughter.'[1]
As Christopher Fry says, 'laughter is a great mystery of the flesh'.[2]
In Fry's play *The Lady's Not for Burning* Thomas Mendip asks,
'For God's sake, shall we laugh?'; and Jennet Jourdemayn replies,
'For what reason?' Mendip answers:

> *For the reason of laughter, since laughter is surely
> The surest touch of genius in creation.*[3]

Ultimately, the audiences of Covent Garden and Sadler's Wells
and all those provincial towns which Grimaldi visited towards the
end of his stage career laughed at the Clown 'for the reason of
laughter'; yet there is a number of more specifically material

reasons for his especial status in the Regency theatre. First of all, the creature to which he gave his name — Joey — was a new and endearing character, who immediately staked his claim to be admitted to that exclusive gathering of immortals which now includes Charlie and Auguste, besides such founder-members as Harlequin, Punch, Pierrot and Pantaloon. In summing up the early nineteenth-century English theatre, the great French historian Halévy wrote: 'Kemble and Kean were content to "revive" Shakespeare, but Grimaldi created an original type, the English clown';[5] and though this exaggerates Joe's achievement — for no stage character is ever perfectly original, or the creation of one man alone — it puts his genius in perspective as no English historian has done.

Joey's pedigree may be traced back to the fools of folk ritual, and some elements in his costume — the crested wig and the red-hot poker — have a very ancient history; but his more immediate ancestors included the *zanni*, or comic servants, of the Commèdia dell'Arte. There were often two *zanni* in the comedy — one simple and the other shrewd, one the butt and the other the rogue — much as in Roman farce the secondary mime or *stupidus*, with the traditional bald or shaven head of the Attic fools, had mimicked the first mime and had been beaten for his pains. Laurel and Hardy, and Abbott and Costello, have many centuries of fooling behind their comic opposition of character; audiences in every age like to laugh at the wise fool, the idiot and the jester, but there must always be a victim — 'he who gets slapped'. In time, however, the butt turns the tables, and the simpleton becomes a rogue. Thus Arlecchino, originally a country booby from Bergamo, was transformed by stages into a rascally servant, a spirit of mischief, and a romantic magician-lover, and he found new butts in Pedrolino (Pierrot) and other Italianate characters of the Commèdia, as it was naturalized in various parts of Europe. Long after they left the village fairs, however, both *zanni*, as Professor Allardyce Nicoll remarks, were coloured by popular conceptions of the peasant; and that rural tradition influenced the English Joey of Grimaldi.

In the English pantomime of the eighteenth century, which was derived from the Gallicized Commèdia dell'Arte, Harlequin had as his butts old Pantaloon, or Pantaloon's servant, or a country yokel. Sometimes the servant was Pierrot, sometimes he was himself a rustic bumpkin. But all Harlequin's partners — Pierrots and Pantaloons alike — were indiscriminately described as clowns, which was regarded as a synonym for a pantomime buffoon, though the name belonged by right to the rural *stupidus*. (Skeat defines 'clown' as 'a clumsy lout, rustic, buffoon,' and links it with the Anglo-Saxon *clyne* [mass, or lump] and the Icelandic *klunni* [clumsy boor]: the term was employed for many years in a non-pejorative sense, as by Macaulay in describing the rebel army of Sedgemoor.) As late as 1802, two years after Grimaldi's début in the new role, the *Theatrical Recorder* supplied its readers with the following definition:

CLOWNS: Rustic appearance, vacant or gazing eyes, an open mouth, arms dangling, yet the shoulders raised, the toes turned inwards, a shambling gait with a heavy step, great slowness of conception, and apparent stupidity of mind and manner, characterize the absolute clown. The varieties of this class ... are interesting objects of study for the stage; but are too frequently misunderstood. Vary the portrait by red ribbands, yellow petticoats, timidity, and maudlin freaks, and his counter part is seen.[6]

This was the family background of the first Joey and from this rustic stereotype, it seems, Grimaldi took the 'toes turned inwards', the 'great slowness of conception', and, on occasions, the 'apparent stupidity of mind and manner', while he introduced other colourful variations into the dress beyond the 'red ribbands and yellow petticoats' of the country wench; but in so doing he drew on other sources, and transformed the traditional stage yokel.

The rustic clown of pre-Grimaldi pantomime was cast as the stooge in the comic scenes, the 'feed' who got the rough end of the knockabout, the pre-ordained butt, victim and second *zanno*; under the name of Dulman, Blunder, Simon, Clodpate or Clodpoll, he was usually played by a member of the acting company, not by a pantomimist; and until Signor Grimaldi first assumed the role in 1779, it was played at Drury Lane by Clough, Ackman and Carpenter, all legitimate actors with parts in the dramatic repertory, who did not distinguish the pantomime clown from the clown of 'straight' comedy. Clodpoll was usually dressed in a plain smock and trousers, in a recognizably bucolic *couture*, and the traditional red wig of the countryman: Dubois himself, Grimaldi's predecessor at the Wells and the Lane, 'never dressed himself otherwise than as a rustic booby, with red hair'.[7]

A more important character in the harlequinade, however, was Pierrot, to whom Grimaldi was also in debt for the creation of his English clown. Pierrot was the descendant of Pedrolino, one of the original *zanni*, a kind of idiot Pulcinello from Naples. Gallicized by Giaratoni in the 1660s, he appeared in a stylized rural costume — a white smock with a wide collar; long, white, loose trousers; a soft, flat, white hat, under which he wore a skull cap — itself a version of the traditional bald head; and instead of being masked, like the other Italian characters, he powdered his face with white. The main features of this costume persisted in English pantomime until the end of the eighteenth century, but the simple servant was gradually transformed, like Harlequin before him, into a sly and artful rogue.

Pierrot and Clodpoll, the French valet and the English booby, were combined in Grimaldi's Clown: but Joey was also closely related to the fools of the fair, the merry andrews and jack puddings, the clowns to the rope, clowns to the horsemanship, and other shadowy buffoons of that 'variety' world which then, as now, was so near to the realm of pantomime. The influence of their feathered hats, flat ruffs, gaily coloured breeches, clocked stockings, rosetted shoes and belted jackets is clearly reflected in Joey's own costume; and, as Mr Willson Disher suggests, he may also have been influenced, through local traditions of business and technique, by a famous predecessor at the Wells, Jemmy Warner, a fat buffoon who for some thirty years wore the merry andrew's ruff and breeches at Islington. Yet although Grimaldi's 'new school for clowns' was enriched by centuries of theatrical tradition and experience — his later baggy breeches may be compared with the Elizabethan, Dick Tarleton ('*Clowns* knew the clowne by his great clownish *sloppe*'); although Joey was, in some degree, a collective creation; in the last resort it was Grimaldi's comic genius which inspired this novel character with immortal life.

*   *   *

Joey was born just at the right time in the history of pantomime: he was, indeed, the answer to the manager's prayer. During the last twenty years of the eighteenth century various experiments were made to find a new balance of power within the harlequinade, for Harlequin himself was losing ground, and most of these were concerned with the fourth member of the quartet — the ancestor of the Clown — in the search for laughter. In the time of Grimaldi's father, pantomime comedy had been tinged with the melancholy and macabre: 'like most modern entertainments of the same species,' observed a critic of the 1784 pantomime at Covent Garden, 'it consisted too much of the calamities of the Clown, and the dire disasters that Knight of the Woeful Countenance is destined to encounter.' But the new audiences of an expanding London demanded lighter entertainment, and the managers looked for new merrymen — or new characters. Thus, Punch took a brief lease of life upon the stage (as in Grimaldi's own *Harlequin Amulet*) and it is worth noting that a famous 'straight' comedian, John Edwin, was engaged for this role at Covent Garden in the 1780s because there was 'no other individual competent'.[8] Sometimes the management attempted to ensure the laughs by duplication: when Dubois made his début at Drury Lane in 1789, one critic complained that

as if one clown was not sufficient, a lover's servant was made to bear his part: and, between the two, there was such an incessant display of knocking each other about, that even the Holiday Gods at length grew disgusted.

Sometimes the traditional plot was altered: in *The Ceinture* at the Wells in 1790,

the old and hackneyed tale of Harlequin's being pursued by Pantaloon and his suite is avoided, by fixing the fair Columbine's affections on her father's clownish serving man, and thence striking into a track of Pantomime business truly whimsical.

Sometimes variations in character were introduced: Dubois played Hunchback Clown, a Dutch Clown, a Jewish Clown and other novelties at the Wells. And sometimes there were innovations in costume: at Drury Lane in 1796 Dubois appeared in a 'gold-laced jacket', a dress which, one shocked traditionalist observed, 'we conceive to be too extravagant an idea even for a pantomime.'

All these experiments were straws in the wind — signs of the need for a new funny man, in a new kind of pantomime; and Grimaldi met the need with an urban, English clown, neither butt nor yokel, no foreigner but a true John Bull. There have been several explanations of Grimaldi's costume: one of the most popular — and, I think, the most misleading — is that

> he made himself up to represent a great lubberly loutish boy... His trousers, large and baggy, and well defined by the aid of stuffing in the posterior quarter, were buttoned on to his jacket; and round his neck he wore a schoolboy's frill. He did not chalk and paint his face in the elaborate manner now adopted... but put on some patches of red, so as to give the notion of a greedy boy who had smeared himself with jam in robbing a cupboard.[9]

With as much accuracy, those red patches on Grimaldi's face have been solemnly explained as the insignia of a nation of gin-drinkers, a satire on the fashionable 'beauty spot', and a counterpart of the 'warts' on devils' masks in medieval mysteries and Atellane *terra cottas*. A more reasonable explanation, perhaps, is that they represent a formalized expression of the 'florid colour' of the country Clodpoll,[10] just as the blue wig may be a parody of the traditional stage yokel's red hair (the crest may be a gibe at the Household Cavalry) and the motley is a fancy-dress version of a servant's livery, now a forgotten form of social disguise. It also seems likely that, as Dr David Mayer has suggested, Grimaldi's make-up was designed to solve the difficulty of projecting expressions in candlelight across so vast an auditorium as Covent Garden (where gas was not installed until 1817). Grimaldi evolved his method of painting red triangles on his cheeks, together with exaggeratedly expressive eyebrows and extensive, scarlet mouth, so as to transmit facial nuances to the back of the house. This extravagant make-up helped to give his 'oven-mouth', big by nature, the appearance of being exceptionally wide. The Clown's breeches, for instance, were not always large and baggy: for although they expanded in the later years of his buffoonery they were apparently of normal capacity in the first decade of Joe's Clownship. He did not, moreover, wear the same costume in every harlequinade: his wigs included a shock-headed bristle, a bald-head with two antennae, one with a cockscomb, and another with three tufts or cockles — and the design of his jackets, waistcoats, shirts and breeches varied from pantomime to pantomime. The variety of his shoes and wigs is illustrated in a drawing in the Harry Beard Collection, now in the British Theatre

Museum. According to one actor's recollection Grimaldi would often wear two or three different wigs during the evening: his 'cock-a-doodle-doo', as he used to call it, in the first part, and 'a great shock of red hair, that he put on when singing comic songs'. The 'schoolboy's frill' was a combination of the traditional fool's bib and the Italian ruff, and was not invariably part of the Clown's costume. It is quite untrue that he did not use an elaborate make-up, for William Robson tells us that he had 'scarcely less make-up than Munden had', and Munden 'could make copious use of colours, and give his whole countenance the most grotesque appearance'.[11]

In the last resort, of course, Grimaldi dressed and painted as he did because it looked right in the mirror. He did the things he did because they made people laugh, not because he had studied the records of the Atellane farces, the medieval merry andrews or the Restoration fairs; but the Clown that he created has obvious roots in theatrical tradition, and in the life of Georgian England. It is not altogether a coincidence that the disappearance of the comic Clodpoll from pantomime took place during a period of land enclosure which drove labourers from the country to the new industrial slums. During the last sixty years of the eighteenth century nearly three million acres were enclosed, and Grimaldi's transformation of the rustic booby into the metropolitan Clown seems, in one sense, to mirror the wider transformations of country life. Moreover, at this time 'man in England was a tool-making animal', as Sir Arthur Bryant says, and Grimaldi's home-land was a 'seed-plot for invention'.[12] It was the age not only of the Cromptons, Stephensons and Rennies, but also of such gadgets as waterproof hats, patent folding carriage-steps and chairs that sprang out of walking-sticks — trick transformations that might have come out of a Regency harlequinade. Joe Grimaldi, too, was a great inventor, endlessly improvising new materials, devising a world of gadgets in which anything could be made to serve his comic ends, to which all objects seemed interchangeable. At his command buckets turned into boots, vegetables took on human shape, alehouse barrels were transformed into soldiers. Harlequin achieved his transformations with a magic wand: Joey did it all by thinking it out for himself, rearranging Creation in bouts of inventive absurdity. As *The Times* observed (in 1828):

He was a sort of Shakespeare in his way — he exhausted

natural monsters, and then 'imagined new.' Frankenstein was nothing to him. Place him in any warehouse, and he soon produced a creation that you would have sworn was indigenous to the soil. Again, what various uses did he not make of the passing fashions and propensities of the day? When he turned one of them into ridicule, he became a living epigram, so terse and pointed, as to set translation entirely at defiance.

Under the Lord Chamberlain's stage censorship the Regency pantomime was, Leigh Hunt declared, 'the best medium of dramatic satire': a claim substantiated in David Mayer's *Harlequin in his Element*, although it is one, as he says, that 'promises more than most historians of the theatre are willing to concede'. Although the censor might castrate a text and inhibit verbal satires, the non-verbal harlequinade offered the chance of 'a tentative and general satire on follies and issues'. As *The Times* asserted, after Grimaldi's retirement, 'a good pantomime should be a running commentary...upon the whims and speculations of the year...it forms a powerful engine — though sometimes a fantastical one — for striking, sharply and rapidly, at the monstrosities of the time'. The tricks in which Joe delighted seemed indispensable to this 'engine': 'a good pantomime trick', to quote *The Times* again, 'should be an epigram in two lines — the object presented should be the first — the change (constituting the commentary) the second'. With their help Grimaldi was acclaimed, posthumously, as 'Hogarth in action' (in the *New Monthly Magazine*).

The Clown himself was, in some respects, a satirical mirror of the times: his guzzling, for instance, was a parody of Georgian greed — a further reason why audiences found him so wildly funny. 'There seemed so much to eat that many found it hard to stop eating,' wrote Sir Arthur Bryant. 'A Yorkshire squire at a single sitting absorbed a plateful of haddock, another of veal, two of tongue, three of mutton, two of roast pig, a wing of duck and half the tail of a lobster...Statesmen, judges, merchants, poets, all engaged in the national vice of stuffing.'[13] Not all the patrons of Sadler's Wells and Covent Garden could afford to eat in such quantities; and guzzling was a traditional accomplishment of clowns ancient and modern. Thus the *Tatler*'s ironic discrimination in 1710: 'Penkethman devours a cold chick with great applause; Bullock's talent lies chiefly in asparagus'. But when Joey gulped down a tray of tarts, or made a Gargantuan meal of pies, or crammed more food into his capacious pockets, he was satirizing — with wild extravagance — the everyday habits of the people. At the exaggeration of our normal appetites, the extreme satisfaction of our desires, we laugh in gratitude and contempt — as we laugh today at Harpo Marx's demented, eternal scamper after girls: but sex played little part in Grimaldi's buffoonery. 'If the English clown was brutal, he was not obscene', says Halévy;[14] or in the words of a contemporary, 'he can please the galleries without offending the boxes, for, though he abounds in humour, he never departs from decency'.[15] The starvation reflected in his guzzling comedy was somewhat less hysterical than our own, different hungers.

Joey was also a specialist in stealing:

He was the very *beau ideal* of thieves — robbery became a science in his hands — you forgave the larceny, for the humour with which it was perpetrated. He abstracted a leg of mutton from a butcher's tray with such a delightful assumption of nonchalance — he threw such plump stupidity into his countenance, whilst the slyness of observation lurked in his half-closed eyes — he extracted a watch, or a handkerchief, with such a bewitching eagerness — with such a devotion to the task — and yet kept his wary eye upon the victim of his trickery — he seemed so imbued with the spirit of peculation that you saw it in him, merely as a portion of his nature, and for which he was neither blamable nor accountable.[16]

Apart from his own artistry in performance, the comedy of stealing seemed considerably funnier in an age when a guide book to London could say that 'a man who saunters about the capital with pockets on the outside of his coat deserves no pity':[17] everyone laughed at Clown, the master-thief, when petty larceny was punishable by death. The greater the danger, the better the joke.

Joey's genius for theft was, of course, only one aspect of his villainous character: he had taken from Rich's Harlequin the role of licensed anarchist, but without the romantic glamour that Rich cast over Harlequin's rascality. Clown — considered objectively — was cruel, greedy, cowardly, treacherous, and criminal; yet

we were quite blind to the moral delinquency of Mons. Clown's habits: he was a thief — we loved him nevertheless;

a coward, a most detestable coward — still we loved him; he was cruel, treacherous, unmanly, ungenerous, greedy and the truth was not in him — yet, for all this, multiplied up to murder, if you would, we loved him, and rejoiced in his successes.[18]

His delight in his own roguery was irresistible: 'he is made of sweet oil,' said *The Champion* (1816). 'He trickles over our senses, and makes them supple. He is as good as a half-holiday. He is a red-letter day to the spirits.' As another enthusiast wrote, 'If he took up a red-hot poker to anybody, we could never interfere — though it had been to save our own father — and when he stole apples, we really doubted whether common honesty was not a kind of prejudice.'[19] This gleeful buffoon, who radiated great friendliness and great mischief, exuded 'a fine, frank, confiding jollity...which at once made friends, and not mere spectators, of the audience'. He was a Cockney incarnation of the saturnalian spirit; a beloved criminal free from guilt, shame, compunction or reverence for age, class or property. That was Joey: Mr Grimaldi was quite different.

*   *   *

The question still remains unanswered: why was Joey so especially funny? If his contemporaries despaired of putting his secret into words —

> An attempt to describe Mr Grimaldi's Clown has always proved a failure: his humour could not be tied down to pen, ink and paper: it was an essence too subtle to yield to mere phraseology —[20]

how slender is our hope of discovering today the complete Joey! All clowns, as A. B. Walkley said of Grock, defy description: 'they proudly confront a universe which delights in them but cannot describe them.' Yet certain distinctive qualities may be assumed, from the evidence of 'mere phraseology' and contemporary prints and pictures. On stage Grimaldi obviously had the eloquent features of the true clown. 'His eyes, large, globular and sparkling, rolled in a riot of joy':[21] these 'winking, reeling, *drunken* eyes'[22] were so expressive that 'he did more by one look than his rivals could effect by the most injurious and elaborate transformations.' It was not so much the ingenuity of his own comic changes that amused his public so greatly as 'the style in which he joined and subjoined them — looked, studied (what a brown study was his!) — and then rushed, in triumphant joy, when a new idea flashed over his extent of countenance!'.[23] No less remarkable than his eyes were his hands. 'Grimaldi and Coleridge are the best pantomime players in the world', said one critic.[24]

Joey's nose, too, was an active contributor to the Regency fun: it was a vivacious excrescence capable of exhibiting disdain, fear, anger, even joy. We think we see him now screwing it on one side; his eyes, nearly closed, but twinkling forth his rapture; and his tongue a little extended in the fulness of his enjoyment; his chin he had a power of lowering, we will not say to what button of his waistcoat, but certainly the drop was an alarming one. It always appeared to us that Grimaldi *moved his ears*; and this, anatomically speaking, is not an impossibility. Be it as it may, the way in which he drew down his lower jaw on any sudden surprise gave this effect to the auricular organs. Speech would have been thrown away in his performance of Clown: every limb of him had a language.[25]

A critic in *The Champion* paid tribute to the Clown's face in these words (in 1815):

> The face of Grimaldi is a source of laughter, night after night, to many hundreds of people; it is a living jest-book, in which may be read all the whimsical notions which owe their birth to his prolific fancy. There is not, perhaps, a more perfect *figure of fun* to be found in existence. ... We look upon Grimaldi, in his way, to be as excellent as Kean. He is as facile in expression as that gentleman, and his eye as fully seconds his thoughts; — we think, also, that he is as energetic, and perhaps even excels the tragedian in trick and activity. Of this we are certain — the audience appear extremely fond of his presence, and are always ready to surrender themselves up to his inimitable buffoonery. It is not a little amusing, to look round the house, when Grimaldi has played off some pleasant practical joke, or accomplished any particular feat of agility; all parties seem convulsed with laughter, and their arms, shoulders, features and whole bodies are at once set bustling with delight. In the pit, there immediately appears a sea of pleasure; and the people roll backwards and forwards like waves.

Grimaldi was a mute Clown by modern standards: he spoke

only, so it seemed, 'when an overwhelming sensation forces the words out of his mouth.'[26] As Leigh Hunt wrote,

when Grimaldi used to say "Don't!" to some fellow putting him to a horrible torture; or "Nice!" when eating gingerbread; or "Nice moon!" after sentimentally contemplating the moon-light, the necessity with which he was delivered of his exclamation was made apparent to everybody, and contained a world of concentration.[27]

That concentration — in a thoughtful silence — was one of Grimaldi's most celebrated effects. 'The hopelessness of one who knows not what to do next, he hits to a nicety — he always appeared to us to represent a grown child, waking to perception, but wondering at every object he beholds.'[28]

When Joey spoke, however, it was in a voice which 'seemed husky with constant laughing, and from repetition of odd cries and utterances to alarm and hoax the pantaloon and the trades-people, who so readily allowed themselves to be imposed upon and defrauded of all their wares;'[29] or, as William Robson des-cribed it, 'richly thick and chuckling, like the utterance of a boy laughing, talking and eating custard, all at once; or a gin voice, heaved from the very bottom of the chest; or, most notoriously, a tone compounded of laugh, scream and speech'.[30] His laugh, on 'an odd descending scale of merry notes', was 'a comedy of itself'; 'the whole house laughed with him — laughed until they cried, again.'[31] To Leigh Hunt 'his short and deep snatches of laughter' were 'like what we read in the poets of Robin Good-fellow.'[32]

Then, his exuberance of animal spirits was really miraculous ... the self-approving chuckles, and the contemptuous look, half pity, half derision, that he gave to the dupe of his artifice — his incessant annoyance with Pantaloon — and his feigned condolence for the very misfortunes of which he was the author — his amazement and awe of Harlequin — his amorous glances at Columbine ... his braggadocio blustering — his cautious escapes from detection ... were all his, and HIS ALONE.[33]

In his art of grimacing or mug-cutting, Grimaldi resembled Munden — 'The roll of the eye — the drop of the chin — the elongated respiration — were peculiar to both';[34] and it was asked of Munden, 'what is he, indeed, but a speaking Grimaldi?';

yet Joe had no Lamb to chronicle his 'battery of looks'. Lamb's celebrated description of Munden's genius for transforming the objects of everyday life might well be applied to Grimaldi, 'wondering at every object he beholds':

A tub of butter, contemplated by him, amounts to a Platonic idea. He understands a leg of mutton in its quiddity. He stands wondering, amid the common-place materials of life, like primæval man with the sun and stars about him.[35]

Both men, as face-makers, were in the great tradition of English popular art. 'To untefined and uneducated minds,' says Thomas Wright, a historian of caricature, 'no object conveys so perfect a notion of mirth as an ugly and distorted face. Hence it is that among the common peasantry at a country fair few exhibitions are more satisfactory than that of grinning through a horse-collar."[36] The 'oven mouth' of Joey all agrin reminds one of the distended masks and gargoyles of medieval designers, or the masks of the ancient Roman pantomimes.

Yet there was one substantial difference between these two great artists, which is in part the difference between the clown and the comedian. Of Munden, Lamb wrote: 'He is not one, but legion. Not so much a comedian, as a company. If his name could be multiplied like his countenance, it might fill a play-bill.'[37] But Grimaldi, in his character of Clown, was always the same Joey: that was the essence of his success.

Instead of representing a comic character he had to be himself in spite of his disguise. His familiar manner made his everyday reality known to the audience; his fantastic face made him a creature of the imagination. He was thus in himself a standing joke.[38]

Unlike Munden, moreover, Grimaldi was almost as eloquent in the legs as in the face: as E.E.Cummings says, a clown's expression is chiefly to be seen in his knees, and Joey's were notorious. Trained as a dancer and an acrobat, he strode across the stage in four paces; leaped, capered and bounced into the air with agility and grace; and in his younger days, tumbled and fell with 'a free and easy body without a bone in it, or apparently any centre of gravity'. As another critic put it: 'his action is the very summit of grace, yet ridicule as well — and his eye speaks more than his tongue could;' yet he did not rely upon his acrobatic skill for his effect, especially in his later, 'sleepier' style. Dutton Cook remembers that 'he fell down once or twice, and affected to slip and slide about upon occasions; but he was not a tumbling clown of the modern school. .... This clown took things more easily and quietly: he amused by glances and gestures, by the drollery of his grimaces, by a certain innocent heartiness which marked his every movement. ...'[39] He could, indeed, 'produce the strongest effects by minute touches of quiet humour, attainable only by peculiar genius.'

In face and body, gait and manner, laugh and gesture, Grimaldi was equipped with the rare and dangerous gift of turning life into a joke. Everything he did seemed funny when he was at the height of his power. At his retirement, Thomas Hood wrote:

> Oh, who like thee could ever drink,
> Or eat — swill, swallow — bolt — and choke!
> Nod, weep and hiccup — sneeze and wink? —
> Thy very yawn was quite a joke![40]

The novelty of Joe's transformations, the topicality of his satire, the originality of his costume were, in the last resort, irrelevant: 'it was all what we had an hundred times seen, without the innate ridiculousness of things being made apparent to us. Grimaldi had looked on the follies of humanity, and fairly turned the seamy side without.'[41] He was often described as an 'intellectual' clown, but this was not — as in the critical cant of today — intended to imply that he was, in some way, inferior to the non-intellectual performer. The quality recognized in this term was expressed by the younger Charles Dibdin, who wrote:

> I never saw any one to equal him — there was so much *mind* in everything that he did. It was said of Garrick, that when he played a Drunken Man, he was 'all over drunk'. — Grimaldi was 'all over Clown'.[42]

To sum up, there is no better witness than William Robson, who said that Grimaldi was the only clown he ever saw with pleasure, and who tried to analyse the reasons in *The Old Play-Goer*:

> Grimaldi was not only the prince of clowns, he was the only one that I ever saw who knew his business: he was not the jumper, tumbler and face-maker; his pantomime was such

that you could fancy he would have been the Pulcinello of the Italians, the Arlequin of the French — that he could have exchanged quips with Salvator Rosa, or returned a smart repartee upon Carlin. His motions, eccentric as they were, were evidently not a mere lesson from the gymnasium of limbs and muscles; there was a will, a mind overflowing with, nay living upon, and having their existence in *fun*, real *fun!* Nobody ever saw a practical joke of Grimaldi's miss fire — a common repeater of tricks might be out — but he who entered heart and soul into the mischief afloat, and enjoyed it as much as did the youngest of his spectators, could never be at a loss.[43]

*   *   *

It was not only as a merryman, of course, that Grimaldi made his name in the Regency theatre: like all great artists of the lighter stage, he could not only make 'em laugh but also make 'em cry, and it was as that traditional stimulant of paleface sentiment — the Black with the Heart of Gold — that he made some of his biggest successes. The Noble Savage and the Wild Man were popular institutions of British melodrama during the Napoleonic wars, and Grimaldi was one of their most popular incarnations, for as Friday in *Robinson Crusoe*, Kanko in *La Pérouse*, the Indian Ravin in *Ko and Zoa*, and Orson in *Valentine and Orson* he inherited and improved the business of athletic blackface and barbarity, and mimed his way through the dumbshows of primitive virtue and savage innocence. It was at Sadler's Wells in 1809 that he created what was probably his outstanding role in this line. Charles Dibdin wrote a new aquadrama called *The Wild Man: or Water Pageant*, with a subplot about some fictitious adventures of Don Quixote, and he cast Joe as the eponymous hero.

Dibdin wrote in his autobiography:

In order to give his talents full scope I wrote a scene representing the powerful influence of Music over even the Savage Mind, which, as the fluteplayer varied his measure, drew from Grimaldi, a very impressive exhibition, in action, of all the various passions of the natural mind; and so popular did this Scene become, that the incident, as a Scena, has been perpetually introduced as an attractive feature on Benefit nights, at almost every Theatre in Town, and many in the country, under the title of 'The Power of Music'.

It seems to have been this 'Scena' which William Robson described forty years later in *The Old Play-Goer*,[44] a description which supplies further evidence of Grimaldi's distinction from the Bradburys, Montgomerys and Laurents of the day, and provides another clue to the secret of his genius.

Robson wrote:

His jealous savage in 'Pérouse', and his *wild man* in an entertainment, I believe, of the same name, I shall never forget. In the former the picture of the passion in the wild uncultivated *man* was astonishing, frightful, but truthful; but the very height of pantomime action was displayed in the latter. As a wild man, of the Orson kind, he is about to tear a child to pieces, whose father, destitute of other means of conquering him, tries the power of music. The first fierce glance and start, as the sound struck upon his ear, were natural and fine — the hands hung as if arrested, the purpose was at pause. As the plaintive air of the flageolet continued, it was really wonderful to watch that which you felt was the natural effect of the music upon such a being — and when, at length, the savage heart became so softened that his whole frame shook convulsively, and he clasped his hands to his face in an agony of tears, he never failed to elicit the proudest triumph of the actor's art — the sympathizing drops from the eye of every spectator. And, when the measure was changed to a livelier strain, the picture became almost frightful, for his mirth was in as great an extreme as his grief — he danced like a fury! I have seen him play this a dozen times at least, and was as much affected by the last exhibition as the first.

This demonic, *possessed* quality in Grimaldi's miming is something which he shared with all great clowns, whose bodies are, like a Danish actor described by Kierkegaard, 'the home of the crack-brained, insane devil of comedy, a devil who will break out of his chains at any moment, and destroy everything in berserk fury;'[45] and English pantomimists of the nineteenth century had, according to Baudelaire, a particular talent for hyperbole.[46] Only the clown can dare to go to these extremes, to risk toppling over the edge: this fury marks him off from the mere comedian. 'The good comedian,' said Riccoboni, 'marches in the middle of the road. The great comedian wanders along the edge of a

166

precipice'; or, in the words of Chaplin, 'the clown is so close to death that only a knife-edge separates him from it, and sometimes he goes over the border, but always he returns again.'[47]

More specifically, such characters as the Wild Man illustrated Grimaldi's talent as an actor; for it must be emphasized that he was a great clown in part because he was a good, if not a great, actor. 'Say what you will,' wrote William Robson, 'from tragedy to pantomime, good understanding and good feeling are inseparable from good acting; and even Joe Grimaldi would never have played off the broadest of all possible humour half so well, if he had not sense and feeling enough to perform serious pantomime in the beautiful manner he did.'[48] As *The Times* observed, 'the faculty of representing every passion by mute gesticulation was one of Grimaldi's great qualities': that was one reason why his father's skeleton scene was repeated in so many of his pantomimes, because of the way he presented 'intense terror' in silence.[49] As one actor recalled, 'What a face he used to make in his fright! He would drop his jaw to such an extent that it seemed to go right into his stomach.'[50] And his mimetic talent gave a unique aura to his one Shakespearian turn. 'I once saw Grimaldi, on a benefit night, give the dagger scene in *Macbeth*,' R. H. Horne recalled. 'It was a darkened scene introduced in a pantomime, and he was in his clown's dress. Notwithstanding which, and that he only made audible a few elocutionary sounds of some of the words, a dead silence pervaded the whole house, and I was not the only boy that trembled. Young and old seemed to vibrate with the effect upon the imagination. This may now seem incredible; but my friends Mr [Samuel] Phelps and Mr [J. R.] Planché, among others, will remember it.'[51] More succinctly, an actor looking back at the same scene remembered Joe as being 'just like the great tragedians'.

*　　*　　*

What a Caliban he would have made! When Hazlitt saw Emery in the part in 1815, he complained that 'he has nothing romantic, grotesque or imaginary about him. Mr Emery had nothing of Caliban but his gaberdine, which did not become him. (We liked Mr Grimaldi's Orson much better, which we saw afterwards in the pantomime.)'[52] Why was Grimaldi never given the opportunity to play the Shakespearian drolls and grotesques, all too often presented as negations of the comic spirit by earnestly unfunny actors? Was it because of the theatrical caste system that he was excluded? Was it because such star comedians as Munden, Liston and Emery were already in occupation, with Fawcett, Farley and Simmons in reserve? Or was it, simply, that Grimaldi was a bad study, an inveterate ad-libber, and was unwilling to risk his reputation in a new field? Whatever the reason, it is tantalizing to think of what he might have done with Gobbo, Pompey, Dogberry and other parts which were written for clowns but are all too seldom played by them, parts in which the saying matters less than the doing. Grimaldi, it is conceivable, might have done for Shakespeare's comics what Kean did for Shakespeare's villains. But the first and last time that he appeared as a Shakespearian character — apart from the Second Gravedigger in *Hamlet* — seems to have been in April 1816, and even then it was not in a Shakespearian play. Garrick's *Jubilee*, revived for the Birthday Celebrations of that year, included Fawcett as Falstaff, Liston as Bottom, Emery as Sir Toby, Simmons as Pistol, Farley as Caius ...and Grimaldi as Sir Hugh Evans. For four nights only the great Clown walked in procession under the banner of the Bard, with never a word to say.

Yet Grimaldi was, in a sense, the Regency's substitute for Shakespeare. The early nineteenth century lacked dramatists to meet the challenge of the time, to create enduring characters out of that changing, turbulent England. 'Such a society,' says James L. Lynch, 'was in the mood to welcome drama that was contemporary, vital and organic. But no dramatist came along who found the means to translate the melancholy Dane or the fat knight of the Boar's Head Tavern into the universal man who might walk the streets of Georgian London. Since the dramatist failed, the destiny of the theatre depended largely, upon the factor and the stock piece.'[53] The Keans and Kembles never succeeded in discovering the Georgian equivalent of Hamlet, but only in bringing parts of the Shakespearian characters up to date. It was Grimaldi who, above all others, supplied 'the universal man who might walk the streets of Georgian London' — in caricature.

Fifteen

Clowning gets in your blood, your looks and your ways, and when people know you are a clown they will never take you seriously again.—BUTCH REYNOLDS (Broken-Hearted Clown, 1955)

FOR THE AUDIENCES OF REGENCY ENGLAND, Joey the Clown and Joe the man were inseparable personalities, and Grimaldi's private life — which was never illuminated, until after its end, by the publicity which shone upon the leading players of the legitimate stage — was regarded as little more than a laughing matter; a man so irresistibly comic in the theatre, so little dependent upon the book of words, so uniquely and unchangeably clownish from panto-mime to pantomine, was clearly expressing his natural buffoonery. A clown so rich in laughter must be a singularly happy man. A later age, clinging to fallacies of a different kind, has seen Grimaldi wandering, between performances, in a dark night of the soul: a personality summed up in his legendary pun — 'I am Grim all day, but I make you laugh at night '(although the pun had inevitably been made about his father before him). This belief in the broken-hearted clown, which seems almost as old as clowning itself, is expressed in the celebrated story of Grimaldi's visit to the doctor, towards the end of his working life, when he was in constant pain. He assumed a different name, and as soon as the doctor saw him he said: 'There's only one cure for you, sir. You must go to see Grimaldi the Clown.' That simple story, however, has been told for generations before and after Joe's death — about Dominique, Carlin, Munden and Little Tich, among others; and it will be told, no doubt, about Grock, Chaplin and all their heirs in clownship, for it echoes the perennial feeling that the clown is a physician who cannot heal himself. Chaplin himself, according to Robert Payne, believed that the story is true, and that it is 'the best of all the stories ever told of clowns'.[1] Perhaps, as I have written elsewhere, it reflects a vengeful social requirement that the professionally happy man should be outside the reach of laughter: for his hubris in joking at life, he should be denied the consolations of comedy.

The truth about Grimaldi the man lies between these two extremes, and it is time to take stock of the Clown's private character, to answer as best we can the question — what was he like, off the stage, at the height of his career? In the 1830s, ill and lonely as he was, Joe exaggerated the hazards and miseries of his life when he compiled his reminiscences; and the darker underside was perhaps emphasized in editing because it made better copy than the chronicle of contented years. True, his life was marred by many private sorrows, some of which have already been described; he was the heir to a family melancholia; his career ended prematurely and in relative poverty. Yet his misfortunes were by no means unbroken. For many years, indeed, he was an apparently happy and successful man, enjoying a prestige, prosperity and continuity of employment which were unknown to most of his profession.

*   *   *

In appearance Joe was short, dark and muscular. His lips were full, his eyes large, his eyebrows well-arched, and the lines around his capacious mouth were etched by years of grinning. 'If in the street he came in contact with any who recognized him, or with the good humour of whose countenance he felt any masonic sympathy,' wrote William Robson, 'you might see by the working of the muscles of his face, that it was a struggle with him to repress a joke, and it was ten to one that he indulged in such a grin as never distorted other features.'[2] Versatile and practical, he was an experienced carpenter and shoemaker; and he loved to play the fiddle, write verse, make models of scenery and tricks, and go shooting. Although not, like Bradbury and some other clowns, a flashy dresser, he was sartorially 'very particular...most careful to have everything correct and neat'.

Grimaldi was, in one respect, like Joey, and like his father too: he was a gluttonous feeder. It was indeed stated by one obituary (echoing the Signor's false alarm) that he died from eating two suppers in one night. But he does not appear to have been, as several papers said, a heavy drinker. 'Those who have been his constant companions for over thirty years aver that they never beheld him under the influence of wine,' declared another obituarist; on convivial occasions, said *Oxberry's Dramatic Biography*, Joe 'never outsported discretion himself, but...was the first to check such a disposition in any of his associates'.[3] This was all the more surprising because, as one theatrical paper observed, 'if any persons have an excuse for indulging at the

This picture of Grimaldi — published in 1807 — accompanies the words of 'How I Love to Laugh, or The Yawner', which he sang in *Harlequin and the Water Kelp* at Sadler's Wells

1

How I love to laugh!
   Never was a weeper;
Though, like a lazy calf,
   Have been a mighty sleeper;
Once I got a place,
   But lost it in the morning,
'Cause in my patron's face
   I somehow fell a yawning.
      Yea, au, au, tol, tol, yea, au, au.

2

Then I fell in love,
   Hoping to get married;
Tried my nymph to move,
   And near my point had carried;
But I lost her in a pet,
   'Cause going to kiss one morning,
Just as our lips had met,
   Some devil set me yawning.
      Yea, au, au, etc.

3

Now comes the worst mishap.
   Once being shaved so nice, Sir;
I gaped, and Mr Strap
   He gave me such a slicer: —
But all my griefs to tell
   Would take a summer's morning,
So mum would be as well,
   Least I should set you yawning.
      Yea, au, au, etc.

Above. Grimaldi as the Bold Dragoon, with Norman the Pantaloon, in *Harlequin and the Red Dwarf* (1812)
Below. Grimaldi's tandem, from *Harlequin and the Padmanaba* (1811)

shrine of Bacchus, it is those who are engaged in pantomime; the exertions they are compelled to make, require that they should resort to the use of stimulants.'[4] Such abnormal demands upon their energy accounted for the gluttony of Grimaldi and his colleagues, one of whom, it is said, used to eat twenty eggs for breakfast when on tour.

Apart from this clownish appetite, however, the private Joe appears to have been an almost perfect contradiction of the public Joey. His stage persona was a creature of wild extremes, but moderation in all things, except, perhaps, in melancholy, was the keynote of his offstage character. On the stage he 'possessed every vice imaginable', but 'there is no virtue that could not be found in the everyday Grimaldi.'[5] Kindly, conscientious and hard-working, he was, according to Thomas Hood, 'a simple, warm-hearted being — a Joseph after Parson Adams's own heart'; and he had a natural dignity, which was always respected by the audience. ('He has occasionally had to step forward, to apologise, in a case of accident, and the instant he spoke, all remembrance of the Clown was lost, and the man only was listened to.'[6]) In the peroration to the *Memoirs*, the author wrote: 'That he was a man of the kindest heart, and the most child-like simplicity, nobody who has read the foregoing pages can for a moment deny. He was innocent of all caution in worldly matters, and he has been known, on the seller's warranty, to give forty guineas for a gold watch, which, as it subsequently turned out, would have been dear at ten. Among many private acts of goodness may be mentioned — although he shrunk from the slightest allusion to the story — his release of a brother actor from Lancaster jail, under circumstances which showed a pure benevolence of heart, and delicacy of feeling, that would have done honour to a prince.' That kindliness and simplicity seem, indeed, to have been the outstanding quality of Grimaldi's nature, and it is confirmed in stories such as this, recorded by Alice Hoffmann, the daughter of a theatre musician.[7] One morning, at the age of seven, she was singing to herself in her Drury Lane lodgings, when

the door opened slowly and softly, and a gentleman looked in.

'Go on, my dear,' said he with the kindest smile in the world, 'go on, and sing that pretty tune for me.' I was silent.

'What? quite dumb?' said he, coming over and taking a seat opposite to me. 'Well, if you will not sing, tell me your name.

The gentleman's eyes and voice were so pleasant, that I contrived to stammer, 'Alice Hoffmann' . . . he took me on his knee, and kissed my cheek, and showed me his watch. and so winning my confidence with gentle words, persuaded me to sing to him again.

'Thank you, Alice,' he said, at the close of my second performance. 'You are a good child, and now I will sing you a song in return.' And instantly the gentleman assumed the most comical expression I have ever seen, placed his hands on his knees, and began to sing. I have now no recollection of the words or the air, but I remember dancing and rolling about in ecstasies of mirth. He seemed to tie up every feature into knots, his mouth extended itself from ear to ear, and his words poured forth as if he had a dozen tongues.

It was in this way that Joe Grimaldi entertained the little girl until her father, with whom he had some business, returned home.

At the theatre he was popular not only among his colleagues but among the backstage staff, for he never put on airs and was always ready to give a hand at rehearsals:

when he came into a theatre, he stripped off his coat, clapped on an old jacket, and went to work. So did Farley, And both of these gentlemen did not scruple to lend their assistance to any work, however arduous, that aided the business of the scene.[8]

This easiness of manner and his reputation for generosity stood Grimaldi in good stead, for when pantomimes depended so much upon their trickwork and machinery, the carpenters, scene-men and stage-hands in general levied a peculiar kind of blackmail upon management and performers alike. Sometimes, in one night, all the strings were cut, the drums were sliced open, the trick-changes broken, because of some backstage quarrel among the machinists, and often reprisals were impossible, even if the culprits were known, because they might endanger the whole production. Sometimes the men would take a brutal revenge upon panto-mimists who did not give them sufficiently large or regular tips: this happened to Tom Ellar, the famous Harlequin, who broke his hand in taking a leap through a stage clock because the men supposed to catch him on the other side had deliberately moved out of reach, wanting more 'catch money'. No such tricks, it seems, were played on Grimaldi, although he had his fill of accidents.

In spite of Grimaldi's kindliness, however, he was 'always nervous' at the theatre, even in the heyday of his fame.

Mr Grimaldi was petulant, and suffered under nervous irritation and morbid sensibility: except Mr Matthews, we never met with a performer so nervous: he had no self-reliance until he was in the heart of his mystery, and then he had no fear.[9]

Moreover, he suffered from a form of 'persecution complex', as we have already seen, and the 'child-like simplicity' extolled by the *Memoirs* was combined with some shrewdness in both private and professional life. 'I was always a Man of Business,' he wrote to his old friend Norman, the Pantaloon, and as a man of business he tried to present his personality to the best advantage.

Everything was grist to his mill, for although a slow study he was always ready for any emergency in his own line of business. One night, at Covent Garden,

the prompter in dismay informed the great mime that certain tricks were not ready, nor would be so for at least five minutes. Grimaldi reflected a moment, looked round, saw a pot of porter in the prompter's box. 'All right,' said he, 'send on a boy with that tipple.' On went the Clown, and following him the boy. Grimaldi soon stole the liquor, and despatched the bearer. He proposed to drink it. Conscience arrested him. A discussion ensued in gesture between him and Conscience. The discussion grew hot. They quarrelled. He proposed to fight Conscience for the porter. Down he put the pot on one side, and the fight began. At the end of the second round, he took a pull at the liquor. At the end of the third, another refresher. Conscience put in 'a nasty one' in the wind. He recovered himself by another application, and so on, until when at last Conscience was declared winner, the pot had been emptied. By this time, the prompter signalled that the next scene was ready, and Grimaldi limped out of sight, drunk, but repentant.[10]

Even in illness, Grimaldi found comic possibilities all around. He wrote to Norman in 1821, 'I am taking the Medicinal Gas — and I cannot describe the good it has done me — Oh! what a scene would it make for a Comic Pantomime — but more of that *Anon.*' And in the Covent Garden pantomime of that year Joe turned the 'medicinal gas' into a comic trick, in which he was inflated to Falstaffian size by inhaling gas from Aldgate Pump.

At the theatre, Joe often diverted the company with his good-humoured wit, especially in puns and malapropisms. A woman dramatist recalls that on the ninth performance of her comedy at Covent Garden, she ordered a dinner for the whole company and staff of the theatre: Grimaldi was among the guests, and

noticing him eating, with uncommon gusto, some fine asparagus, I could not help observing the fact, and asked him what sort of vegetables he liked best. 'Oh!, replied the motley hero, smacking his lips, 'vegetables I likes, but of all vegetables in the world give me a leg of boiled mutton and a jowl of salmon.'

Joe was clearly addicted to assuming his stage character in public, but his mistakes were not always intentional.

On another occasion he boasted of certain overtures which he had received from the rival house. 'Sir,' said he to Mr Kemble, 'they wants to inviggle me. They say they will give me a couple of guineas a week more and a bonassus of £20 to leave the old shop.'

'And are you not tempted to improve your fortune by such an offer, Mr Grimaldi?'

'Not I, indeed, Mr Kemble. As I have lived with you, I wish to die with you, and if ever I go over to the other house, I hope I may perspire that very minute.'[12]

During the pantomime, one night, he was overheard in angry expostulation with the producer, Farley. Farley was reprimanding Grimaldi for failing to answer the summons of Harlequin's wand, when he was meant to rush on the stage and carry off a figure which was supposed to be petrified.

'Go on, go on,' said Farley. 'It is not yet time, sir,' said Grimaldi. 'I am not wanted till Mr Simmons is putrified.'

Farley, a little man with a large red nose, was a heavy drinker, and he was once welcomed by Joe to his country cottage with: 'Oh! Mr Farley, I am right glad you are come, my peaches are very backward: do, for goodness sake, hold your nose over them for two or three hours.'[13]

Grimaldi, although a star in his own right, had to observe the proper deference towards Farley in the theatre; and, as a buffoon, he was still regarded by the management as a social inferior. It was a notable innovation — and a mark of his polite manners — when he was made a steward of the Royal Theatrical Fund, in company with some of the leading players of the day. But it is significant that twenty-six years after he first worked with Farley he was signing himself 'Yours respectfully' to him. This letter (in the Kay Robertson collection) recommended an out-of-work actor from the Wells as a good Pantaloon. 'This is the first time I have had the pleasure of addressing you since I quitted the profession although I many times had it in contemplation to send for an order, yet always felt a diffidence in so doing for fear of a refusal.' In other words, he had no contact for ten years with one of his closest Covent Garden colleagues, and was afraid to ask him for a free seat. Yet, although Joe knew his place, and for all his simplicity, he learned in time to protect himself where his purse was concerned. 'If I work I must be paid,' he wrote peremptorily to Elliston at Birmingham, insisting on his own terms for an engagement in 1817. Care in such matters was all the more necessary because both the Grimaldis were heavy spenders, and on one occasion at least — in 1811–12 — they were deeply in debt and in trouble. That should have been a good year for the Clown. By his own account he earned at least £700 from one benefit at the Wells and some provincial dates, and there was also a second Wells benefit, a Covent Garden benefit, and his regular salary at two theatres (£8 a week at the Garden and about 12 guineas at the Wells). Yet in spite of his unparalleled earning power among clowns he was in serious financial straits in mid-career. The expense of bringing up young Joe in a style to which he himself had never been accustomed; the cost of running 'Tippity Cottage' in Finchley and a house in Islington, with servants and a gig; his own generosity and improvidence, and the extravagance of Mary Grimaldi, who had 'a love of dress which almost amounted to mania'[14] — all these uncomfortable facts obliged Joe to let his cottage, sell his horse and gig, discharge his groom, and put his affairs in the hands of a solicitor. Within a year, according to the *Memoirs*, all his creditors had been paid in full; but it was probably at this stage in his life that William Bestow, a fellow-actor, smuggled the Clown out of Sadler's Wells in a sack, because the bailiffs were after him.[15] His attitude to money was, as Bestow said, notorious, and this augured ill for the years when Joe could no longer command so high a salary and so rich a life-style. For rich it was, by the standards of most of Joe's fellow-countrymen. When in acute financial difficulties, before and after this crisis, he would sometimes 'raise the wind' by pledging himself to a pawnbroker. As one admirer recalled, at the time of Joe's death, 'he would proceed, about six o'clock, to the shop of Mr Crouch, a pawnbroker in Ray Street, Clerkenwell, state the sum required, which was immediately paid, wait with the greatest patience till a messenger from Sadler's Wells, who always knew where to find him, made his appearance to redeem him, and then proceed to the theatre.' A similar story was told about a jeweller's business elsewhere in Islington: the correspondent (whose recollection is preserved in the Finsbury Library collection) was once shown the 'very slab, or shelf' on which Joe sat till he was redeemed.

The fact that neither Joe nor Mary was a good 'manager', financially, may well have led to marital friction. But the only published indication of that occurs in a story quoted in Blanchard Jerrold's life of George Cruikshank. According to Cruikshank Joe and his 'much better half' resolved to settle all differences of opinion forever by taking poison one evening.

But not taking enough, and forgetting the oft-quoted maxim, now travestied, 'Drink deep, or taste not any poisonous thing,' the feeble dose merely kept them awake and talkative, and lying in the same room, with a slight partition between them, sensations became unpleasant; and so they held a colloquy in their fears as follows:

'Joey, are you dead?'
'No, Mary — are you?'
'No.'

And then they altered their minds, and felt disposed to live a little longer, arose, had a good supper and something warm and comfortable as a sedative and antidote, and then jogged on a little more in unison.

Backstage at the Wells Grimaldi was a much more important person than he was at Covent Garden. Here he enjoyed not only popularity but also prestige; and it is an indication of both — and of life behind the scenes in Islington — that in 1813 he was elected Chief Judge and Treasurer of the Court of Rectitude, a self-governing body of performers which acted as an unofficial tribunal of morals and conduct. The Wells company elected two judges, two counsellors (for the court and the defendant), a clerk and a treasurer. The clerk's duties were to collect the fines, pay them to the treasurer every Saturday, and post an account of

them in the green room every week: the treasurer's job was to
keep the money 'till the company thinks fit to appoint a time for
a dinner'. Among the 'causes and fines', which the Court of
Rectitude listed under Joe's judicial eye, are:

ANY PERSON making use of profane language shall be fined for
each offence 1d.

ANY PERSON calling another a b–g–r, shall be brought to trial.

IF ANY PERSON takes the liberty of taking another's property from
his pocket (which has been the case) though in a joke, he shall
be brought to trial.

ANY PERSON coming drunk, and disturbing the company, shall
be brought to trial.

IF ANY PERSON brakes wind in the room he shall be fined 1d.
for the first offence, and 2d. for the second.

Here was a Court fit for a Clown to rule! And it must be
remembered that for all Grimaldi's gentle manners, natural
courtesy, and kindly heart, he was, by the rigid standards of the
day, a member of the lower orders, a vulgarian: his class was
revealed in his voice, his dress, his appearance: he was,
incontrovertibly, *common*. That was part of his greatness.

As a peculiarly gifted, gentlemanly commoner, however,
Grimaldi could be tolerated and entertained by his social superiors;
and it was on these terms, no doubt, that he made the acquaintance
of Lord Byron. It was about 1808–9 that Joe was first patronized
by the poet, who also honoured with his notice those other stars
of the sporting and dramatic, Jackson the prize-fighter and
D'Egville the ballet-master; and it was a great day for the Clown
when he received a letter from Byron, informing him that he had
seen him in a pantomime — *Mother Goose?* — and requesting him
to forward a box ticket whenever he took his benefit. From that
time onward, Byron was a regular patron, to the tune of five
guineas a year, though he did not meet Grimaldi until some years
later. The occasion was a hunting party at Berkeley Castle, where
Joe was asked for the day by 'Colonel' William Berkeley, head
of one of the oldest families in England.

With his brothers the Hon. Frederick and the Hon. Augustus,
Colonel Berkeley was passionately interested in all departments
of the theatre, not least in the actresses' dressing-rooms, and all
these raffish amateurs themselves acted not only at the Castle but
at the local theatre in Cheltenham. One journalist, in 1825,

noted that 'Colonel Berkeley often previously rendered himself ridiculous by his stage exhibitions, which, however, had the effect of attracting an audience, as Berkeley is a mighty man at Cheltenham.' He was, indeed, known as 'the King of Cheltenham', for he maintained the local hunt entirely out of his own pocket, kept almost open stable and table to his friends, and in spite of his private peccadilloes and his 'extremely violent and abusive language' he was, according to another member of the family, 'regarded almost as a local deity, whose word was law'.[16] This eccentric peer, whose family rent-roll was £180,000 a year, was the principal noble patron of Joe Grimaldi.

Colonel Berkeley had already entertained Joe to dinner in London, and while appearing at the Cheltenham Theatre he was invited for a day's coursing at the Castle, with the manager, John Boles Watson, the father-in-law of Joe's old friend Jack Richer, now retired from the rope. On his arrival, Grimaldi was introduced to Byron: the Clown comes better out of the encounter than the Poet, in his own memories at least, for Byron deliberately set out to make a butt of the professional buffoon, marooned as he was in this hard-riding, hard-drinking, aristocratic set. He greeted Grimaldi with low bows and extravagant hyperbole, but the embarrassed Joe, realizing that the gallant lord was making game of him, returned the bows and the compliments with exaggerated ceremony, and as soon as the introduction was over he

> made a face at Colonel Berkeley, expressive of mingled gratification and suspicion, which threw those around into a roar of laughter; while Byron, who did not see it, looked round for the cause of merriment in a manner which redoubled it at once.[17]

After the coursing was over, the party returned to the Castle for dinner — arranged early, so Colonel Berkeley said, to allow Grimaldi time to reach Gloucester for the night's performance — and Joe was placed between Byron and another young nobleman whom he had seen in the Covent Garden green room. Byron, unabashed by the morning's events, was still determined to make Grimaldi pay for his entertainment, and with the help of the young peer he played an elaborate and unpleasant practical joke upon the unfortunate Clown. Grimaldi's neighbour persuaded him that if he wanted to keep on good terms with Byron, he should eat or drink anything that the poet recommended, and as a result he ate so much that he was 'quite gorged' — for Byron continually pressed him to eat from every dish on the table. The noble poet's joke was not, however, yet exhausted.

Towards the end of his repast his lordship invited him to eat a little apple-tart, which he thought he could manage, the more especially as he was very fond of it; he therefore acquiesced, with many thanks; and the tart being placed before him, commenced operations. Byron looked at him for a moment, and then said, with much seeming surprise —

'Why, Mr Grimaldi, do you not take soy with your tart?'

'Soy, my lord?'

'Yes, soy: it is very good with salmon, therefore it must be nice with apple pie.'

Poor Grimaldi did not see the analogy, and was upon the point of saying so; but . . . he bowed assent to Byron's proposal, and proceeded to pour some of the fish-sauce over the tart. After one or two vain attempts to swallow a mouthful of the vile mess, he addressed Lord Byron with considerable formality, begging him to observe, 'that no one could do more justice than himself to his kindness, but that he really trusted he would forgive his declining to eat the mixture he had recommended; as, however much the confession might savour of bad taste, he really did not relish soy with apple-tart.' He was much relieved by Byron's taking the apology in very good part, and by the rest of the company laughing most heartily — at what, he says, he cannot possibly tell, *unless* it had been determined to put a joke upon him.[17]

The English sense of social humour has, incontrovertibly, changed for the better.

A year or two later, in somewhat less exalted society, Grimaldi was treated to another demonstration of bad manners, which on this occasion he was quick to perceive and resent. During a season at Bath, Grimaldi and Higman, a popular bass, were asked to dine with a clergyman in the city, where they found a large party of guests around the table. As soon as dinner was over, their host requested Higman to sing a song, and although he had only just finished his meal the singer complied, and was warmly applauded. The clergyman then turned to Grimaldi, and made the same peremptory demand. When Joe asked to be excused for the time being, the host exclaimed: 'What, Mr Grimaldi! Not sing, sir! Why, I asked you here, sir, today expressly to sing.' Indignantly, the Clown of the Wells rose from the table. 'Indeed, sir,' he said, 'then I heartily wish you had said so when you gave me the invitation; in which case you would have saved me the inconvenience of coming here today, and prevented my wishing you, as I now beg to do, a very unceremonious good night.' It was an annihilating reply: one hopes that he delivered it.[18]

Such reminders of his inferior social status were, it seems, not infrequent, and this is one reason why Grimaldi insists in the *Memoirs* upon the acquaintance which he later struck up with Byron. The *Memoirs* outline a strange picture of the backstage intimacy between the two men.

It never fell to Grimaldi's lot to hear any person say such severe things as Byron accustomed himself to utter, and they tended not a little to increase the awe with which, upon their first interview, he had been predisposed to regard him. As to Grimaldi himself, Byron invariably acted towards him with much condescension and good humour, frequently conversing with him for hours together; and when the business of the evening called him away, he would wait at the wings for him, and as soon as he came off the stage, recommence the conversation where it had been broken off. Grimaldi rarely contradicted him, fearing to draw down upon himself the sarcasms which he constantly heard fulminated against others; and when they spoke on subjects with Byron's opinions upon which he was unacquainted, he cautiously endeavoured to ascertain them before he ventured to give his own, fearing, as he felt so very warmly upon most questions, that he might chance to dissent from him upon one in which he took great interest.

Such a story — in unedited, muddled, Dickensian prose — may seem open to suspicion, as the testimony of a man who loved a lord and a tall story, but proof of the Byron–Grimaldi relationship has emerged since the first edition of this biography in the recent volumes of Byron's letters and journals edited by Leslie A. Marchand. In February 1808 the poet says in a letter that he is going to a masquerade at the Pantheon with 'Lord Altamont, Grimaldi and a large party'. In August 1814 he wrote to John Jackson, the boxer: 'Dear Jack, Grimaldi has sent me some tickets for his benefit at the Wells which I only received the other day and not in time to go there — Will you pay him five guineas for them and I will settle with you when I come to town...' Before

Byron left for Greece he gave a silver snuff-box to Grimaldi, with the inscription, 'The Gift of Lord Byron to Joseph Grimaldi.' This was bequeathed to Joe's sister-in-law at his death in 1837: who has it now?

The world of Byron's friend and Grimaldi's noble patron, Colonel Berkeley, had a distinctly pantomimic aura. William was the eldest son of the fifth Earl of Berkeley, but his claim to succeed in the Earldom was disallowed by the House of Lords (about the time that he took up Grimaldi) because his mother was widely believed to have lived unmarried with his father for some eleven years before their *recorded* marriage, when William was ten. The Lords did not accept the family story about an *earlier* marriage, of which the record had been destroyed in error by the local vicar. As William's unloving brother Grantley phrased it, in his reminiscences, the Colonel 'was notoriously illegitimate' as well as being a 'worthless profligate'. For twenty years, during the time that Grimaldi knew him, the Colonel tried to get the Lords' decision reversed — his brother Thomas refused to claim the Earldom, though it was his *de jure* — but he had, in the end, to be content with the title of Lord Segrave (in 1831) and later, after Grimaldi's death, Earl Fitzhardinge. Although Colonel Berkeley had an easy command of all the usual social graces, he had 'an inherent dislike to the best society', according to Grantley Berkeley. 'I have often heard him say he hated fine ladies and gentlemen.' He liked to shock them by using the slang of pugilists, pickpockets, highwaymen — and clowns; and the society he enjoyed was that of actors and actresses, 'usually having one of the latter under his protection'. The most celebrated of these during Grimaldi's time was Maria Foote, who had two children by the Colonel.

* * *

Outside this tiny realm of Sporting and Dramatic Life, the war-time backcloths of the European scene were at last changing. The holiday crowds that filled Sadler's Wells for its Easter Monday opening in 1814 — when Tom Ellar made his début there as Harlequin with Grimaldi in *The Rival Genii: or, Harlequin Wild Man* — were in exceptionally boisterous form: they were celebrating the arrival of peace after twenty years of almost uninterrupted war. A few days earlier news had been received in London that Paris had fallen: Boney's power, it seemed, was broken for ever. The last shots were fired on 26th April, and soon Londoners were cheering the Allied commanders. With Blucher and Wellington, the Czar of Russia and the King of Prussia were the surprising heroes of the hour. And the theatres joined in the festivities. Five days after peace was proclaimed *Mother Goose* was revived at Covent Garden for the first time in five years, by desire of Count Platoff, the Cossack Hetman (and for Farley's benefit). The next night Blucher saw the pantomime, which included two of Grimaldi's specialities — the dog cart and the song about the oyster crossed in love. The Czar, the King of Prussia and the Duke of Wellington were less fortunate, for they apparently saw Joey only, if at all, in *Sadak and Kalasrade*, that melodrama full of 'burning palaces, dreary caves, dreadful tempests, blazing volcanoes...and more than a *quantum sufficit* of assassins and murderers among the characters'. For Joe, the wheel had come full circle. This was a piece in which, seventeen years earlier, he had scored one of his first successes at Sadler's Wells, before he had married Maria Hughes or made his début as Clown. Then he had been a penniless, unknown actor. Now the conquerors of Napoleon came to see him.

Their host, the Prince Regent, was in his pantomimic element during that summer of victory, exercising his taste and enterprise in commissioning state pageantry and spectacle that no theatre manager could hope to equal. What could the Royal Aquatic do to rival a royal progress down the Thames, with sixty barges manned by liveried musicians and watermen? Or an aquatic drama on the Serpentine, where Prinny staged a mock Battle of the Nile with miniature three-deckers? To celebrate peace, and the centenary of his family's accession to the English throne, he ordered balloonery, fireworks, stage combats, processions, concerts, and, of course, war. The battles of the Peninsula were fought again in the Green Park. His culminating *coup de théâtre* was timed for midnight, when with a deafening explosion the canvas walls of a mimic fortress in the Park lifted to reveal a Temple of Concord, 'glittering with coloured lamps, while water flowed from the jaws of lions into golden basins, and a detachment of Foot Guards on the roof held aloft the Royal Standard and self-consciously gave three cheers'. It was all a proper pantomime.

Covent Garden did its best to follow the Prince Regent's example that Christmas with Farley's *Harlequin Whittington, Lord Mayor of London*. A balloonist, M. Garnerin, sent his small daughter up in a balloon from the stage. After 'losing itself in those mysterious regions sacred to the magazines of theatric thunder and lightning', the balloon floated low over the heads of the startled pittites and returned to its starting-point. Mlle Garnerin, meanwhile, descended in a parachute — when things went according to plan. A 'celebrated artificer' of fireworks, Signor Ruggieri, helped in an attempt to reproduce the famous 'Illuminations in the Park', and Covent Garden rounded off the pantomime with its own version of Prinny's Temple of Concord. With Ruggieri's aid, from 27th December, a firework display spelt out 'Peace with America' as an unexpected bonus; although when Grimaldi announced that news on Boxing Night, as soon as it came through, he was loudly hissed. It was not clear 'whether the audience did not understand him, or whether they conceived it to be one of the bad jokes of the pantomime'. There was, however, no lack of enthusiasm for Grimaldi's performance as Clown in what seems to have been the first Whittington pantomime. In the opening he played Dame Cicely Suett, ancestor of the modern Sarah or Martha in the same story. During the harlequinade he won especial applause for his walk, with Ellar's Harlequin, along the roof of the stage on their hands; and for his 'transformation' of Pantaloon into a wheelbarrow by forcing a mop-stick through a cheese to make a wheel, pushing it between Pantaloon's hands, and — using the Old 'Un's legs as the barrow handles — trundling him off the stage with a load of other cheeses on his back. Grimaldi's song of the show was 'All the World's in Paris' (sometimes called 'All the World's at Paris') poking fun at the rush of Londoners to the French capital earlier that year. One of the most popular Grimaldi prints was Cruikshank's picture of him singing this hit-number, wearing a huge hat and an overcoat with fur cuffs and collars, in one of his digs at male fashion.

This was another triumph for Joe; yet all was not well with him. Although he was only 37 that Christmas, the hardships of his early life — and perhaps his inheritance from the Signor — now told on him with increasing effect. One sign was that he received the news of a death among friends with a somewhat exaggerated sensibility. A few days before *Harlequin Whittington* began,

Richard Hughes — father of his first wife and for many years his patron and employer — died. Joe had to attend the burial on Boxing Day, in the thick of the last dress rehearsal, and on that first night he was so distressed that he could scarcely finish his performance. The audience's reaction to his announcement of Peace with America did not help his disturbed state of mind.

Sixteen

*With respect to this high and mighty paramount of all
existing and remembered buffoons — this grim Grimaldi! —
his buffoonery is, in its kind (like the philosophy of professor
Kant) transcendant: and positive excellence, of any sort,
even of nonsense or absurdity, indicates something of genius
and originality; and is sure to command — what might be
called respect; if our pride were not unwilling to give it so
respectable a denomination.*—THE CHAMPION, 4th Jan.,
1819

BY 1815, after fifteen years of Clownship, Joe Grimaldi was
recognized as an institution, and it became increasingly respectable
to discuss his art in detail and to hail his genius in print. Hazlitt,
one of his most discerning admirers, wrote in the Christmas of 1815 :

We were glad, right glad, to see Mr Grimaldi again. There
was (some weeks back) an ugly report that Mr Grimaldi was
dead. We would not believe it; we did not like to ask anyone
the question, but we watched the public countenance for the
intimation of an event which 'would have eclipsed the gaiety
of nations'. We looked at the faces we met in the street, but
there were no signs of general sadness: no one stopped his
acquaintance to say, that a man of genius was no more. Here
indeed he is again safe and sound, and as pleasant as ever. As
without the gentleman at St Helena, there is an end of politics
in Europe: so without the clown of Sadler's Wells, there must
be an end of pantomimes in this country !¹

Yet the clown of Sadler's Wells had only five more years to run.
Although the rumour of his death was a false alarm, it had good
foundation: for in the previous October, two days before his
second benefit, Joe had suddenly been taken seriously ill, 'originat-
ing in a most distressing impediment in his breathing. Medical
assistance was immediately called in, and he was bled until nigh
fainting. This slightly relieved him; but shortly afterwards he had
a relapse, and four weeks passed before he recovered sufficiently
to leave the house. There is no doubt,' say the *Memoirs*, 'but that
some radical change had occurred in his constitution, for previously
to this attack he had never been visited with a single day's illness,

while after its occurrence he never had a single day of perfect health.' Allowing for the exaggerations of the *Memoirs*, it seems evident that the tide had turned in Grimaldi's life: the years of overwork were beginning to tell, and his energy was ebbing.

The pantomime in which Hazlitt welcomed his return to the land of the living was *Harlequin and Fortunio: or Shing-Moo and Thun-Ton*, and Joe appeared in the opening as a 'voracious Tartar', Munchikoff, who eats an Everest of bread and drinks a fountain dry in order to defeat the Emperor of China. The story did not linger in China — 'a country, by the bye, [*sic*] which of all others in the world affords least interest, and is least known to an European' — but moved to the more topical spectacles of the Brighton Pavilion and the Plain of Waterloo ('as it appeared the day after the Battle, in which is an exact representation of the Carriage of Buonaparte, taken by permission of Mr Bullock'), and ended in the Realms of Peace, where Mrs Grimaldi found employment as one of the local Spirits. But its principal interest for posterity is the appearance in its cast of Master Joe Grimaldi, the Clown's only son, who had now reached the age of thirteen. It was a great moment for Grimaldi when, after many months of preparation and anticipation, he saw his boy step out on to the stage of Covent Garden for the first time.[2] Not for Master Joe the years of hard apprenticeship as an imp, a cupid or a bear, no struggle for existence against indifference, brutality and hunger, no need to count his pennies or curry favour with the prompter; he came straight from school into a leading role, under his father's protective wing, and took his place in the company as if by right. This was no ordinary case of nepotism, however, for his native quickness, as well as the family name, earned him at once the attention of the press, and he was praised for displaying 'some very extraordinary postures and great agility together with a horse, three donkies, a lamb and some other quadrupeds, who trod the stage with great propriety'. In the opening young Joe played Chittaquae, 'a little-footed Chinese Empress with a Big Body', and appeared as a miniature Clown (Clowny-Chip) in the harlequinade, duplicating his father's make-up and mimicry, just as thirty years before his father had appeared as a replica of the old Signor. Success came easily to Master Joe; his father saw to that. But was it enough for him to be a mirror of the Clown?

Young Grimaldi's next big role was in the following year's

pantomime of *Harlequin and the Sylph of the Oak: or The Blind Beggar of Bethnal Green*, when he played Flipflap, an attendant on Harlequin, a part especially written into the harlequinade. On Boxing Day there was some dissatisfaction with the first piece on the programme, but Hazlitt reports that

> the pantomime, with Mr Grimaldi, soon brought all to rights, and the audience drank in oblivion of all their grievances with the first tones of their old friend Joe's voice, for which indeed he might be supposed to have a patent. The great man (we really think him the greatest man we saw at the theatre last night) will not 'die and leave the world no copy', as Shakespeare has it, for his son is as like him in person as two peas.[3]

The Clown's heir seemed to be firmly in the saddle. Grimaldi looked forward to an old age made glorious by his son's success in the roles which he himself had made famous and in new theatrical adventures. For a few years his hopes seemed to be justified, but a very different future was in store for his family.

*   *   *

Many great expectations were disappointed in the years after Waterloo. When Napoleon sailed for St Helena, the manufacturing towns of the industrial revolution were enjoying an unprecedented boom, and many skilled workers were earning more than they, or any members of the working class, had ever earned before. Their rulers, too, shared in the prosperity of a changing England: while Yorkshire woolcombers made the record wages of five shillings a day, London ladies paid fifty guineas a dozen for their handkerchiefs or gave breakfast parties at £100 a time. The future must have seemed rosy in that first year of peace, but by 1817 there was mass unemployment in the industrial towns, the Irish poor were living on stalks and nettles, and 10,000 liveried servants were said to be out of work. Rioting spread throughout the country, and the number of bankrupts multiplied. Theatre business, too, began to dwindle: neither Sadler's Wells nor Covent Garden did the roaring trade of the war years, even with their pantomimes, and both theatres soon ran into financial difficulties. It was an attempt to carry through economies at the Wells which resulted in a breach with Joe Grimaldi. For probably the first time in thirty-six years, he was not in the company when the new season opened on Easter Monday 1817.

Sadler's Wells without Grimaldi! It seemed inconceivable, but there on the playbills, in smudgy black letters, was the news for all to see: the Clown of the Wells for 1817 was Mr Paulo. The usurper of Grimaldi's throne was a boy half his age, fresh from two successful years at Drury Lane: Paulo, the son of his old friends the Redigés, the rope-dancers, had returned to the Wells in 1816 as Clown to the Rope with a ten-year-old prodigy, Hyacinthe Longuemare. When Grimaldi took a fortnight's leave of absence that summer, Paulo stepped into his shoes and made such a success that Dibdin chose him — above other, long established clowns — as the star of the next season. But why did Grimaldi leave? Was his attraction waning? Did the managers of the Wells — now that Richard Hughes had died in the previous December — think that new talent was required to improve their box office receipts, and so picked a younger, more acrobatic buffoon?

There are several accounts of the affair. According to the *Memoirs* Grimaldi's articles had expired in 1816, and he applied, modestly enough, for an increase of salary from £12 to twelve guineas. To this the proprietors agreed, but they stipulated, to his amazement, that he should have henceforward only one benefit, instead of two, a season. Joe could not agree to this proposal, for he never cleared less than £150 and usually made over £200 on such occasions, and he wrote a letter of refusal to Dibdin. The letter, however, was never answered, and the next thing Grimaldi knew was that Paulo had been engaged in his place. Charles Dibdin tells a somewhat different story.[4] Although he does not mention the matter of benefits, he says that it was impossible to approve Grimaldi's request for regular leave during a critical part of the season, because it meant a severe drop in the box office takings. Yet it is clear that he must have lost faith in Grimaldi's commercial value, or he would have risked this loss to keep the greatest Clown of the day on the establishment; and he must have had a strong belief in young Paulo, if he believed that his talent would make up for any slump in business caused by Grimaldi's absence. It is likely that Dibdin and Grimaldi had been at loggerheads for some time, and whatever the cause of the quarrel it seems evident that the Wells had decided it was time for a change: they could not afford Grimaldi any longer. The news of this revolution at Islington caused great excitement, especially when it was heard that James Barnes, the Pantaloon (see Appendix B) was also leaving the theatre. Ruin and bankruptcy were predicted for the management, and in the neighbourhood of Grimaldi's house placards were posted by supporters of the rival Clown, with such inscriptions as 'Joey for ever !', 'No Paulo !' or 'No Grimaldi !' It was widely rumoured among the more cynical members of the profession that Grimaldi had posted them up himself, but this he solemnly denied.

When the theatre opened its doors on 14th April Grimaldi was there, not on the stage but in the boxes. He had come, burning with resentment, to see how the usurper was received and to safeguard his own interests: for he had heard that Dibdin meant to address the house, in the event of any demonstrations, and he was ready to contradict him in a counter-speech. There he sat, nursing his grievance above, while his old comrades played upon the stage below, and the news of his arrival caused excited gossip in the dressing-rooms. Would there be a riot? Would manager and Clown make a scene? Grimaldi, however, was spared the need for any speechmaking, and the evening seems to have passed without much disturbance, for, according to his own account, the public showed its disapproval of the management by staying away, and the theatre was less than half full. As there was clearly going to be no demonstration by the customers or the management, he left in high glee before Paulo, Hartland and May (the new Pantaloon) got into their stride, and went back to Covent Garden to play in *Robinson Crusoe*.

Although the incident was a blow to Grimaldi's pride, and excited his fears of insecurity and illness, his self-esteem was restored by the many offers he received from provincial managers when they heard that he was at liberty. The Wells, he decided, would discover that it needed him more than he needed the Wells, and he would soon be asked to return. In the meantime, he took his son on a triumphal tour of Regency England: that summer they appeared in Birmingham, Worcester, Liverpool, Preston, Hereford, Glasgow, Edinburgh, Berwick and other towns, receiving the homage of playgoers in every part of the country. Most of them saw Grimaldi for the first time and, though it should be remembered that he was then thirty-eight, and was approaching the end of his career, the arrival of the Clown from London must have been a red letter day. He acted with his son in a potted pantomime which he contrived for such occasions,

presented portable versions of a few of his most famous scenes —
on that tour of 1817 he appeared as Dame Cicely Suett, sang
'Typitywitchet', and danced the *Mother Goose* jig — and also
played Orson, Bob Acres and Scaramouch in *Don Juan*. From
this tour he earned nearly £1750 for forty-six nights, whereas if
he had stayed at the Wells he would have received less than half
that amount for four times as much work. He was the gainer
from the quarrel with Dibdin, in more ways than one.

It had been a particularly bad season at Islington, for although
Paulo had been well enough received after initial opposition he
was no substitute for Joe. In spite of being more agile and acrobatic, he lacked the kindling wit and radiant good humour of his
predecessor: as *The Times* said in comparing master and pupil at
a later date, Paulo was 'an amusing clown, but not a clown of
genius. What is set down for him, he does well; but, if left to his
own resources, he shows at once that his means are very slender.'
He was the most persistent of Grimaldi's rivals; he outlasted
Laurent, who returned to France, and Kirby, who went to
America; and he was still playing Clown at Drury Lane in 1832
(he died in 1835). Moreover, if Mr Willson Disher is correct, he
deserves a special place in the history of pantomime because he
adopted the tights and triple-tufted wigs of French performers on
the slack wire, in whose techniques he had been brought up by
the Little Devil, and helped to stabilize the costume of the Clown.
Certainly Grimaldi, who bore him no ill will, acknowledged that
he was a first-rate artist. Yet Paulo could not make up for Joe's
disappearance in the season of 1817, and the other attractions —
the Dog Drama and the Water — had ceased to draw. For the
first time in fifteen years, Sadler's Wells lost money.

There were other changes in the London stage that summer.
On 23rd June, John Philip Kemble chose to make his last appearance at Covent Garden in the role of Coriolanus, the heroic enemy
of the mob, and the Londoners who had howled him down and
stormed his house eight years before now roared and cheered and
stamped in bidding him a spectacular farewell. With respect and
affection the company paid homage that night to the old tragedian,
and begged for mementoes of the sad event. Among those
privileged was Grimaldi's sister-in-law, Louisa Bristow, who
'obtained the handkerchief he had used that evening while
uttering his farewell, which she playfully promised to keep with

more true faith than Desdemona did the first gift of the Moor'. Four days later there was a public dinner at the Freemasons' Tavern in Kemble's honour, and among the celebrities who attended, to watch the presentation of a vase, was Joe Grimaldi. As he sat down at table with Kean, Incledon, Bannister and other famous guests, the triumphant symbol of those mummeries that Kemble had so much despised, he may well have recalled his old fears and angers at Drury Lane and Covent Garden. All was forgiven and forgotten long ago. Yet Grimaldi had not heard the last of the Kembles.

* * *

The Covent Garden pantomime that year — *Harlequin Gulliver: or The Flying Island* — was among his most successful, and was played sixty-three times that season; but the new Easter piece of 1818 met a very different fate. *The Marquis de Carabas: or Puss in Boots* was staged on 30th March, with a strong cast which included Liston, Emery, Tokely, Simmons, and Norman, while Joe himself played the Fairy Grimalkin, or Puss in Boots. Up to the end of the first act the piece went well, and Grimaldi's cat-work was greeted with loud applause. 'His mewing,' said a critic, 'was more entertaining, we had almost said more like nature, than his human voice, for Grimalkin was a speaking part in the piece. He also imitated the sneezing of a cat with ludicrous exactness'. But in the course of the story Grimalkin persuaded the Ogre to demonstrate his magic by turning himself into a mouse, which he then swallowed, and this act of cruelty outraged the moral susceptibilities of the audience. They began to shout and hiss, and demonstrations continued long after the piece ended. When Liston came forward to announce its repetition, they would not give him a hearing, and demanded its withdrawal; after half an hour, in which they began to pull up the seats, throw things at the lights, and tear a hole in the green curtain, John Fawcett at last appeared and agreed to their demands. The unfortunate *Puss in Boots* was shelved.

For Grimaldi this reception was in sharp contrast to the previous Monday, when he had returned to Sadler's Wells in triumph. Charles Dibdin had been defeated, and the proprietors had drawn their own conclusions about the failure of the 1817 season. Paulo and Hartland remained in the company, but their names were printed in small type on the new, sedater bills, which had been re-designed in a style similar to those of the Theatres Royal. Guerint was the new Harlequin — Ellar had gone to Astley's; and Barnes returned as Pantaloon. Grimaldi's triumph, however, was tinged with tragedy: the crowds were so thick on the opening night that some people in the gallery were forced over the balustrade into the pit below, and one young man was trampled to death. A panic began, but a repetition of the terrible 'Accident' of 1808 was avoided by Grimaldi, who came out before the curtain, quelled the crowd's hysterics and kept them under control while the injured people were carried out into the yard. Then, when all was still, the pantomime — *The Elements: or Where is Harlequin?* — began, and Joe Grimaldi was back in his old form, back where he belonged, as the Clown of Sadler's Wells.

At the end of July he went off, as previously arranged, to fulfil his provincial engagements. He took with him, however, fresh responsibilities, for he now owned an eighth of the theatre.

Earlier in the year Grimaldi learned that, if he applied to the proprietors of the Wells, he would be encouraged to return almost upon his own terms, but he was too proud to make the first move. It was not until Mrs Hughes asked him to come back to the Wells that he agreed, on the condition that he was admitted as a part-proprietor. By this request, he hoped to guarantee for himself and his family some financial security, by earning a share of the profits in a theatre whose fortunes he had helped to found, but he was none the less surprised when the proprietors agreed to admit a Clown as their partner. Maria's brother, Richard Hughes, sold him an eighth of the theatre's forty shares, and the proprietors agreed that he could pay the purchase money in instalments. Grimaldi's partners were now Mrs Hughes, the chief proprietor, who owned fourteen shares; Mrs Jones, the daughter of Reeve the composer, with seven shares; Barfoot, a business man, and Charles Dibdin, who both had seven shares in the theatre. The amount which Joe paid is unknown. Fifteen years before, when the theatre was still enjoying a very modest success, the Dibdin brothers paid William Siddons £1400 for his share, and it seems probable that in 1818 the cost would be considerably higher, although the value was soon to be considerably lower. An eighth share used to bring in about £600 or £800 a year in the Wells's wartime heyday, but Grimaldi had bought too late. He soon had reason to regret his venture into management.

Grimaldi needed the respite from work and worry which, he believed, his eighth share of the Wells would bring, for his feverish energy was ebbing away and his clowning was becoming quieter and less active; but when the theatre reopened in 1819 there was not less, but more work for him to do. Charles Dibdin left the Wells at the beginning of the season after a quarrel with his colleagues, and Grimaldi gave up his projected summer tour of the provinces in order to supervise the stage management. He himself appeared during the season in *The Great Devil*, the piece which had indirectly introduced him to his wife eighteen years before, and on 31st May he produced *The Fates: or Harlequin's Holiday*, in which his old friend Jack Bologna returned to the Wells after ten years' absence, with Louisa Bristow as his wife. On that night, with all its additional work and responsibility, Grimaldi also appeared in another première at Covent Garden — a new revival of *Mother Goose*, with Tom Ellar as Harlequin, which included scenes from some of his best known pantomimes. This recurrent strain helped to undermine his already weakening health, and throughout the year he was more frequently afflicted by cramps and rheumatic pains. A role such as Orson put him on the rack: as soon as the act-drop fell on the first scene, he would stagger off the stage, sink into a chair, and cry aloud in pain, while his frame was convulsed with violent muscular spasms. The body of the Clown was beginning to take its revenge for thirty years of overwork.

If Joe had retired from the stage for a year or two, and lived quietly in the country with his family, he might have recovered his health and prolonged his working life, but in the circumstances such a retreat was unthinkable. Although the proprietors once again had a profit to share at the end of the 1819 Sadler's Wells season, Grimaldi missed the income of his provincial tour. There was too much to do, and too little money in the bank; and, as his strength declined, he became more susceptible to the melancholia provoked by the heavy death-roll among his friends and enemies. Aaron Graham, the man who was responsible for his departure from Drury Lane, died on Christmas Eve, 1818; and in September 1819 little Samuel Simmons fell down an area in Hanover Square and died immediately, two days before he was to appear with Joe in a *Mother Goose* revival. The deaths of clowns, in particular, filled Grimaldi with gloom: old Johannot, one of the stars of his boyhood, died in poverty and obscurity, and his old master and rival Dubois also passed from the scene about this time, forgotten by the crowd.

Grimaldi's weakness had already been reflected in the 1818 Covent Garden pantomime of *Harlequin Munchausen: or The Fountains of Love*, when it was noted in the press that 'Grimaldi, though as comic, is not as active as he used to be'; and *The Times* observed coldly that 'we have been so accustomed to see him luxuriate in his vocation, to display such superfluity of good humour amidst its hardships and exploits, that we fear we are hardly competent judges of his last performance'. None the less, it was a popular show: John Keats saw it twice and declared it to be excellent. Grimaldi's exhaustion may have been reason for the revolution the following Christmas, when, in *Harlequin and Don Quixote: or Sancho Panza in his Glory* there was neither Pantaloon nor Clown. Barnes, who now appeared at Covent Garden for the first time, played Longo-naso, Grimaldi was Sancho Panza, and although Harlequin and Columbine appeared, the piece was more of an extravaganza than a pantomime, and included dialogue in a comparatively consistent plot. If Farley and Fawcett were trying to break new ground, the audience would have none of it. As *The Times* observed: 'It is difficult to turn the current of established notions on any subject, and it was felt that even the laws of pantomime are not to be deviated from with impunity.' The innovations were vigorously and noisily opposed, in particular the removal of the Clown, and the piece was only saved from damnation by Grimaldi's personal success in the part of the Squire. A few days later, however, Sancho was changed into Joey, a transformation which was given prominent billing by the management and a cordial reception by the press. 'With all our goodwill to Mr Grimaldi,' Hazlitt wrote, 'we have a greater affection for Sancho Panza, and do not want to see him metamorphosed into anything but himself.'[5] Business was still bad, but it was worse at Drury Lane, where Southby was now installed as the Clown, with Jack Bologna as Harlequin, and a 15-year-old singer, Eliza Povey, as the Principal Boy of the 'opening' in *Jack and the Beanstalk: or Harlequin and the Ogre*.

In other respects, however, Drury Lane had the advantage, for the old prosperity of Covent Garden was declining. Elliston, at the Lane, had Kean, Munden, Mrs Glover, Fanny Kelly, and Eliza

Vestris in his company, but at Covent Garden there were notable absentees — Liston was ill, Young and Eliza O'Neill had left, Kitty Stephens was on leave, and Charles Kemble, who had long been at loggerheads with Henry Harris, finally withdrew after a violent quarrel. Business was so bad that Macready and other leading players voluntarily agreed to postpone the payment of their salaries until Christmas, when the pantomime, it was expected, would make all right. But fortunately they did not have to wait for *Harlequin and Don Quixote* to balance the theatre's books: at Henry Harris's urgent request, Macready courageously took up Kean's famous part of Richard III and made a great success in the part. The following Saturday the treasury was reopened, and the ghost walked again.

A month after the pantomimes opened, the mad old King of England died at last, on 29th January 1820. (The three weeks of compulsory closure had a disastrous effect upon the theatres' exchequers.) The Regency was over — and so, too, was the golden age of pantomime, and the ascendancy of Covent Garden.

It is a curious fact that it was only now that Grimaldi's name was distinguished upon the Covent Garden bills by bigger type from his colleagues of the harlequinade. Perhaps it was the controversy over Sancho Panza which prompted the change; perhaps the management was anxious to make the most of its assets in a bad year; but, whatever the reason, the new Easter piece gave the Clown, for the first time, the honour of star billing — thirteen years after *Mother Goose*. It was unusual to stage a new pantomime at Easter, but *Harlequin and Don Quixote* had been unsuccessful and the theatre hoped to make up for its failure with *Harlequin and Cinderella: or The Little Glass Slipper*. During the show, Clown lost his arm in some violent horse-play, but a few minutes later an arm sprang up from a stage-trap and hopped about as if in derision. He chased this tantalizing member all over the stage in a frenzy, and when he at last caught it he threw the arm furiously on the ground and began to stamp on it. As he did so, however, he let out a scream of agony — he had forgotten that it was his *own* arm. Is it too fanciful to see in this buffoonery a symbol of Grimaldi's own ill-treatment of his body, which now racked him continually with intimations of the day of reckoning? Moreover, he was beginning to lose his grip over the audience — or so it seemed, for he was roundly hissed for his strip-tease in the Baroness's bedroom when she 'exhibited the mysteries of her dress rather too plainly': taste was changing, and the Clown was failing to catch up with the new prudery seeping in from the provinces. It was a sign of the times that Covent Garden closed down early after 'one of the most disastrous campaigns it has ever experienced'.

*   *   *

At Sadler's Wells, too, a new era began in the first year of George IV's reign. For the first time the theatre was rented out to an actor-manager, John Howard Payne (author of *Home Sweet Home*), from whom the proprietors hoped to earn steady dividends with less risk. Grimaldi's responsibilities, however, were not diminished, for he not only played in pantomimes and melodramas but also arranged a good deal of the stage business. He took particular care in the production of his son who, after some years away from the theatre, appeared in *The Yellow Dwarf: or Harlequin of the Golden Mines*. This pantomime included a preview of the new King's Coronation — 'a series of Moving Figures, in appropriate Costume ... obtained from the most authentic Sources and arranged with the greatest Attention, so as to give an accurate general idea of the customary forms of that Splendid and Imposing Ceremony.' In spite of such attractions, however, it was an unsuccessful season, and the proprietors of Sadler's Wells bore an additional burden. In March the Exeter theatre was destroyed by fire, and as it was only half-insured a loss of some £3000 fell on the Hughes family, a loss from which Grimaldi, in spite of all his hard work that season, also suffered. After the seasons of 1818 and 1819, in fact, his share in the Wells was of little value to him, and instead of bringing him in a comfortable annual income for the rest of his days, as he had hoped, he found that he had mortgaged himself to little purpose.

On 2nd October Grimaldi presented, for Howard Payne's benefit, an anthology of some of his most successful scenes in *Scraps: or Fun for the Gallery!*, when every customer in the boxes and pit received a free portrait of Grimaldi (after Wageman). Once again he set the house roaring with his 'Typitywitchet'; once again he danced with Jack Bologna the *pas de deux* from *Mother Goose*; he relived, on that autumn night, the glories of his former state as the Clown of Sadler's Wells. It was his last appearance that season. It was also, although he did not suspect the truth, his last season at the theatre.

Seventeen

All the pantomimes are good in which Mr Grimaldi plays the clown.—WILLIAM HAZLITT (1820)

IN THE WEEK OF JOE GRIMALDI'S LAST APPEARANCE at Sadler's Wells, his old employer at Covent Garden, Thomas Harris, died in his sleep at Wimbledon; and with him, so it seemed, died the peace and prosperity of Covent Garden. Some months later John Philip Kemble returned to London from his retirement in Lausanne, in order to transfer his share of Covent Garden — already in difficulties — to his brother Charles, a move which, according to Macready, 'was destined to darken the fortunes of this once flourishing theatre, to break up a company of actors and actresses that presented a phalanx of talent unequalled, perhaps, in the history of the stage, and ultimately to reduce this splendid property to a state of irredeemable insolvency.'[1] Within a few years, 'Drury Lane was the fashion, and Covent Garden was literally a desert', but by that time one of its main props, Joe Grimaldi, had been removed.

In spite of increasingly frequent illness, however, Joe appeared in three more pantomimes at Covent Garden, with undiminished success and effect. The first of these, in the 1820–1 season, was *Harlequin and Friar Bacon: or The Brazen Head*, based on the old story used by Robert Greene in his play *Friar Bacon and Friar Bungay*, in which Joe played Miles, the comic servant, and his son took the role of Lover in the harlequinade. Among the scenes was a satire on what was described as 'the rage for quick travelling. A "safety coach" in "five hours from Brighton" is ruined by the competition of a "steam coach" in "one hour"; the passengers, by a sudden explosion, are strewed about the stage, to the infinite diversion of the gallery, whose taste for practical jokes retains its full vigour.' The gallery did *not* enjoy the less grisly buffoonery in which Grimaldi, drinking from Aldgate Pump, inhaled gas instead of water and was blown up to Falstaffian size; but he gained great applause by his dumb show of the dagger-scene from *Macbeth*, performed with complete solemnity in his Clown's dress, by his horseplay at an Irish fair, and by appearing as a chimney-sweeper who invades the boudoir of a lady of quality and covers her white chairs, dressing-table, carpet and even her bed with his all-embracing soot. Theodore Hook observed that 'the strength of Grimaldi, the Garrick of Clowns, seems, like that of wine, to increase with age: his absurdities are admirable,' and George IV, paying his first visit to Covent Garden for many years, found Joe so funny that he burst his stays with laughter.

By Easter, however, Grimaldi's strength was exhausted, and although he initiated a new role in the Easter piece of *Undine: or The Spirit of the Waters*, he had to hand it over within a week to his son, who played it for the rest of the season. It is, perhaps, fortunate that Joe had quarrelled with the new tenant of Sadler's Wells, Egerton, for he would have had no physical reserves for the 1821 season: for the first time in forty years, with the exception of 1817, he had no connection with the Islington theatre, and his understudy Hartland, who had been overshadowed for so many years, at last had his opportunity to be the Clown of the Wells. Grimaldi was well enough that autumn to fulfil several provincial engagements, and he took *Friar Bacon* with him to Birmingham and Dublin, where Henry Harris of Covent Garden was in management, but the rigours of Georgian travel accelerated his decline, and he fell ill again in Ireland. Recovering in time for the 1821–2 pantomime — *Harlequin and Mother Bunch: or The Yellow Dwarf*, which was a big success — he had to take to his bed again in the following July, while playing at the Coburg (the present Old Vic), where young Joe was appearing as a second Clown; but he still refused to accept defeat, and within a few weeks of his convalescence he was on the stage again at Cheltenham, where he earned £150 in twelve nights. Grimaldi would not acknowledge the possibility of retirement: he was, after all, only 43, and he could not yet afford to give up clowning; and, when he returned to Covent Garden for the season of 1822–3, he was in better pocket, and better health. In the new pantomime, *Harlequin and the Ogress: or The Sleeping Beauty of the Wood*, he showed no signs of decline, and indeed won eloquent tributes to his work:

Mr Grimaldi is the most intellectual and irresistible of clowns, and he never displayed his talents to more brilliant advantage than in the pantomime of Harlequin and the Sleeping Beauty. He was all grin and good humour, and has the singular faculty of appearing younger every year. Time seems to pass harmlessly

by him, except to increase the rich lubricity of his face. . . .
What a sentiment there is in his action! What interesting
pathos in his countenance, when he fails in some innocent
jocularity . . . what an encyclopaedia of wit is his face! What
a magazine of merriment!

There was so little sign of illness, such comic strength in his
performance, that in January his contract was renewed for another
three years. This was, indeed, one of his most successful pantomimes.

Harlequin and the Ogress had already run for fifty-four performances when on 31st March Grimaldi took part in the Easter
piece, a melodrama called *The Vision of the Sun: or The Orphan
of Peru,* in the role of Tycobroc, slave to the Enchanter of Uxi.
To his dismay he found that he could scarcely struggle through
the piece, and this time he had no reserves of energy or will-
power to draw upon. His joints were stiff, his muscles slack, and
his old energies had drained away in a thousand fights and tom-
fooleries: the pantomime had exhausted all his store. Every effort
he made upon the stage, among these tuppence-coloured Peruvians
in their finery, was paid for by agonizing spasms, and Farley had
to put men in the wings as he came off, for 'his sinews were
gathered up into huge knots by the cramps that followed his
exertions, which could be reduced only by violent rubbings, and
even that frequently failed to produce the desired effect'.[2] For
days Grimaldi fought against his own exhaustion: he had always
recovered before, and he was determined to do it again; there was
too much at stake to surrender. Then, for a week, he went back
into the less exacting business of the pantomime, and it was in
his livery of Clown that Joe Grimaldi made his last appearance at
Covent Garden, on the night of Saturday, 3rd May 1823.

Somehow he forced himself to stay upon the stage until the
concluding scene, and then as the curtain fell for the last time
between him and the noisy, happy audience, he was carried off
to his dressing-room. There, in his Clown's motley, Grimaldi lay
gasping for breath, in exhaustion, pain and shame, while his
friends gathered round with words of comfort and advice.
Whatever they said, he knew at that moment — he must have
known — that it was finished. He could fight no longer. After a
time, he wiped off the fixed, red laughter of his grinning mouth,
with the powder and the paint; he put aside the famous tufted wig
and the ballet shoes; he hung his suit of frills and flaps in its usual

place with his usual care . . . and he knew that he would never take it down again. Whatever his later hopes, Grimaldi on that Saturday night made his farewell to Joey in his heart of hearts.

*   *   *

On Monday, young Joe took over the role of Tycobroc, and a special announcement was made of his father's illness. Mr J.S. Grimaldi, said the bill, 'humbly hopes for that kind indulgence which is never withheld on such emergencies', but the emergency continued indefinitely and he played the role until the end of the season. In August his father believed that he had recovered, and appeared at Cheltenham and Birmingham without apparent injury, but these were positively his last professional engagements.[3] On returning to Cheltenham, where he had agreed to play Orson, his most exhausting role, to the Valentine of his old patron Colonel Berkeley, he was taken seriously ill once more. For a month he was confined to his bed, and when at last he was allowed to get up, he found that he would not be able to play Orson; that he would never again be Scaramouch or Acres; that his days of Clowning were finally at an end. He was a cripple, and a cripple he apparently remained for the rest of his life.

Whatever caused this final blow to Grimaldi's health — it may well have been infantile paralysis — it marked not only the end of his stage career but also the end of his private happiness and prosperity. It was a terrible test of the Clown's courage and kindliness to leave the theatre at the very height of his fame, before he was 45; but from this time forward destiny, not content with crippling his body, heaped him with afflictions of the mind.

When the new Covent Garden season opened on 1st October, both father and son were announced as members of the company, for Grimaldi, in a last desperate hope for health, was being driven from one doctor to another in a search for someone who would give him back the use of his legs, 'that witty pair', as Thomas Hood remembered them:

> *Lord! how they leap'd in lamplight air!*
> *Caper'd — and bounced — and strode away: —*
> *That years should tame the legs — alack!*
> *I've seen spring through an Almanack!*[4]

Above. Grimaldi's farewell at Drury Lane (1828). *From the British Theatre Museum*
Below. Left: Grimaldi's farewell at Sadler's Wells (1828): Hock in 'The Sixes',
a print by H. Brown. Right: Grimaldi's farewell at Drury Lane: the barber's shop
scene from *The Magic Fire*, a print by H. Brown

Illustrations to Grimaldi's *Memoirs*
Above, by George Cruikshank. Left: Joe, dashing between theatres, is recognized by the crowds. Right: in action, with Harlequin, Columbine and Pantaloon.
Below, by F. W. Pailthorpe. Left: Joe finds the bailiffs at home. Right: he is held up by footpads.

In the end Grimaldi had to accept the bitter truth, the truth he had known that last despairing, pain-racked night at Covent Garden. But there was one consolation: he urged Kemble and Fawcett to give his son the opportunity of succeeding him that Christmas, and after long consultation they decided to take the risk. Not until ten days before Christmas was the news ventilated in the press, when hundreds of his admirers saw this brief paragraph in *The Times*:

Mr Grimaldi, the clown at Covent-garden Theatre, is afflicted with an inward complaint, supposed to have been brought on by over-exertion when performing the character of clown last season. It is said to be doubtful whether he will be able to perform this season.

There was no word of this heavy change on the bills, where the first announcement of the new pantomime appeared, belatedly, on 9th December; but the news soon spread among the people of London that the long reign of their King of Clowns was over.

*   *   *

Throughout that December the crippled Clown lavished advice and tuition upon his erratic and impatient son, now eager to escape from the tutelage of his father; and during the day he often limped into the theatre, to watch the preparations for the pantomime and gossip to his friends about his beloved boy's chances. It was a sombre Christmas for the Grimaldis that year, the first that Joe was not due at the theatre for a dress-rehearsal, but it was brightened by their hopes that young Joe would prove himself a true chip of the old block. At last Christmas was over, and Boxing Day arrived; and for the first time, perhaps, Grimaldi watched the first night of a Covent Garden pantomime from the audience. The theatre itself had changed since his last appearance in May: the stage doors had been removed, and two boxes built on their site; mahogany backs had been fitted to seats in the circle and the pit; and the interior of the auditorium had been re-decorated. For Grimaldi, everything had changed: everything had stopped. Yet the future had some meaning, if he could live to see young Joe acclaimed, in his turn, as the King of Clowns.

On that December night in 1823, in *Harlequin and Poor Robin*:

201

or The House That Jack Built, Grimaldi's dream seemed to be coming true, for young Joe made a great success as the Clown and was applauded with a warmth that brought tears to his father's eyes. This success was reflected in the newspaper reviews, which Grimaldi read with eager delight during the next few days, for they took the occasion to pay tribute to his own genius in commending the talent of his son. The report of *The Times* must have given him particular pleasure: the pantomime, said the critic,

> is a complete hit, rather contrary to expectation, without Mr Grimaldi; but we hope, nevertheless, that Mr Grimaldi's secession is not to be considered final. Grimaldi belongs to Covent-garden theatre as completely as St Paul's belongs to Ludgate-hill; and has probably drawn more money to it in his time, than any man upon the boards.

But, said *The Times*,

> Young Grimaldi is decidedly better than we had anticipated. He is not like his father: for Grimaldi, père, has the soul of a comic actor. Apart from all twisting and tumbling, there was so much intelligence about everything he did. It was as good as the performance (and not unlike it) of Elliston, or Liston. . . . Without being equal to his father just yet, Mr Grimaldi, junior, however, shows a great deal of cleverness: and his attempt may be considered as decidedly a successful one. He has great activity and some humour. Tolerably light of finger, and uncommonly light of foot, he avoids, and with very good judgment, any servile imitations, and gets on by a rather juvenile capacity, than by that sleepy style of humour which Mr Grimaldi senior latterly relied upon. Upon the whole he is at least, as good a clown as any now upon the stage; and if he takes pains, and avoids breaking his neck, we see no reason why he should not be as great a man as his progenitor.

'He has great activity and some humour' — there lay one main difference between the father and the son. As Hood wrote:

> *Tho' Joseph, junior, acts not ill,*
> *'There's no Fool like the old Fool' still!*

But young Joe had captured the town's attention at his first attempt, and justified all his father's loving care and pride, without being labelled as a mere imitator of the older Clown. It was some compensation to Grimaldi to hear the compliments from everyone in the theatre upon the triumph of Joey the Second, and to watch him courted and flattered as the 'coming man'.

A few months later, however, young Grimaldi left home and plunged into a career of wild dissipation and debauchery, which rapidly led to the extinction of all his father's hopes and of his own wasted life. This 'worthy scion of the old stock', as he was hailed in 1823, turned his back upon his father and mother at a time when they were most in need of his help and affection. The next time he came to the door of his old home, young Joe was in a straitjacket. For Joey the Second drank himself into a mental breakdown, and died soon after his thirtieth birthday.

*   *   ✻

It all started, so Grimaldi believed, when he was recovering from his last illness in Cheltenham in the summer of 1823. Until then young Joe's conduct had been beyond reproach, in his father's eyes at least, and they had been on intimate and friendly terms during their long provincial tours. To outsiders the younger Grimaldi may have seemed a spoiled son, who held his father in some contempt and strained at the bonds of family love and adulation; but at Cheltenham his father discovered that while he was on his sickbed young Joe had been leading a riotous night life in the local taverns, and soon after he was allowed out of bed again he was obliged to bail his son out of Cheltenham jail. A drunken brawl had started in the streets one night, and in a struggle with the constables the boy received a crack on the skull from a truncheon, an accident to which his devoted father ascribed his later vagaries, for from this time his nature was transformed. 'Instead of the kind and affectionate son he had previously been, he became a wild and furious savage; he was frequently attacked with dreadful fits of epilepsy, and continually committed actions which nothing but madness could prompt.'[5] The handsome young man, sweet-voiced, good-tempered, highly-praised, turned into a drunken ruffian whom only the less scrupulous managers would employ, and — towards the end of his brief career — he 'so shocked and disgusted even those who were merely brought into contact with him at the theatre for a few hours in a night, that it was found impossible to continue his engagements'. Young Grimaldi, in fact, became a citizen of that underworld into which Kean and Cooke made only brief excursions, and his boon companion — who, perhaps, was more to blame than the Cheltenham constable for his plight — was Henry Kemble, the black sheep of that famous family.

Kemble, who was thirteen years older than his protégé, was the unsuccessful son of an unsuccessful father, Stephen Kemble, and nephew of Sarah, Charles, and John Philip. He seemed to take a pleasure in degrading the family name, and — it is likely — inspired the same appetite in Grimaldi's son. Nothing went right for Henry Kemble. He was educated at Winchester and Trinity by his doting father, but against Stephen's wishes he left Oxford to go on the stage, and later married a young actress in his father's company, from whom he soon separated. When Stephen Kemble took over Drury Lane in the 1818–9 season, he carried nepotism to excess and gave his son many parts for which he was quite unqualified: the performance of Romeo with which the season ended was an especially spectacular failure. Thereafter he sank into obscurity and debauchery, brawling with managers (he once shot another actor in the wrist), insulting the audience, drinking himself into a stupor, saddled with a great name that he could never hope to justify. Before he was forty, it is said, Henry Kemble's hair was snowy-white, and he died, destroyed by his own excesses, at the age of forty-six. In the meantime he had helped to destroy J.S.Grimaldi. They probably met for the first time in the summer of 1822, when the two Clowns appeared at the Coburg. Henry Kemble worked there for a fortnight, until he was dismissed by the management for his behaviour. Young Grimaldi was then only 19. Was he seduced by the older man, or was there already in his brain the seed of madness? Was a constable's blow the real cause of the boy's callous and amoral conduct? Or had the melancholic, furious energy of his father and grandfather turned in upon himself, in self-destruction? The tragedy is that, whereas Kemble was a mediocre waster, young Grimaldi was an artist of high promise; his talent was ripening and maturing quickly in the sun of success. Thus, in 1825, a critic in the *London Magazine* noted that

Grimaldi junior is daily growing up into his father; (where is his father?) his voice is thickening into that ancestral and sonorous *batter*, his limbs with more of strength, spread in the same attitudes; his eye lacks none of its parental lustre and wickedness, and this indescribable turn for mischief and humour is *genuine Grimaldi-ism!*

Yet perhaps that was part of the trouble. Young Joe grew up under the shadow of old Joe, and whatever he did was compared with his father's achievement; for his triumphs Grimaldi took the credit, but his failures were his own. (Already, in the 1821-2 pantomime, he had been warned about 'certain gross vulgarities'.) He had only to occupy the throne which his father had made ready; it was the consummation of all his training; and to old Grimaldi it was the realization of his destiny; but perhaps young Joe could not live up to these expectations, and, surfeited with success and comfort, plunged for the excitements of the gutter.

*   *   *

Grimaldi had little capital, in spite of the big sums he had earned for so many years, and what he had was quickly spent; but he was saved from hardships — from the hunger and suffering which so many of his colleagues endured in their premature old age — by his connections with Sadler's Wells. The picture of his poverty in retirement is commonly overdrawn, and by comparison with his old friends he was a man of property. Although his share seldom brought in any money, some seasons *were* profitable, and moreover he was given a job in the stage management in 1825. After the experiments of sub-letting, the proprietors decided to run the theatre themselves again for that season, Tom Dibdin was engaged as acting-manager, and Grimaldi was appointed as a kind of supervisory assistant — his functions are not clear from the available evidence — at a salary of £4 a week. This season, in which J.S.Grimaldi was, intermittently, the Clown, brought many changes to the old theatre at Islington. The Hughes family house, in which Grimaldi's first wife was wooed and won, became part of the playhouse's offices; wine-rooms were opened, from eleven in the morning until eleven at night; half-price was introduced for the first time, at 8.30; and the theatre was kept open for most of the year, instead of being restricted to a summer season. The potential public for the Wells had increased enormously during the last twenty years, for the great wen of London, swelling out into the countryside in every direction, had surrounded the once rural theatre with straggling estates and streets of houses. In spite of the changes, the Wells incurred heavy losses in 1825, but in July, 1826 horse-racing was introduced and business picked up again. It was a sign of the times that Sadler's Wells could only balance its books by setting up a racecourse in its grounds: but — as yet — the managers were not obliged to bring the horses inside.

Grimaldi's duties were not onerous, but they were enough to keep him occupied and in touch with the theatre that was his second home. He sat in at the pantomime rehearsals, gave advice to the new Clowns, made models for the tricks and transformations and, when he had the opportunity, compared notes with his old colleagues at the other theatres. Sometimes he sang for an actor's benefit, and in 1827 it was even planned that he should make regular appearances at the Wells again, for the bills announced in bold black lettering that 'Mr Grimaldi will, occasionally, appear'. The result was as one might have expected. 'As a *dernier* resource,' an unofficial critic wrote, 'poor old Joey Grimaldi was dragged from a sick bed, with a view to prop the falling fortunes of this former scene of his early fame: but alas! all would not do — for Joey . . . broke down under the accumulated pressure of *mental* and *bodily* infirmity.'[6] For Grimaldi this failure was still hard to accept. At Christmas, 1826, he wrote that he was 'quite ashamed of looking at himself in a Glass this season of the year without his original painted Mug', and his inactivity was all the more frustrating when there were so many weaknesses in the current pantomimes that he felt he could eliminate. To his old friend and Pantaloon, Norman, he wrote that January to say that 'The Pantomimes at Both Theatres are the best for these 3 seasons but they both want the something which is business. There is positively nothing for anybody to do.' If only he could see that painted Mug in the Glass again. . . .

There were many minor consolations. He enjoyed the company of his friends at the Myddelton's Head, drinking in the evenings; and sometimes he would drive up the hill to the Belvedere, a few steps away from the house where he took his first wife on their wedding day. Fame, too, was pleasant in retreat: his picture appeared in the print shops and theatrical Phantasmagoria, his name was used to christen racehorses and stage-coaches, his opinion was sought by the young pantomimists of the minor theatres,[7] and he was modelled in the waxworks (although Mrs Farley of *The Old Curiosity Shop*, to conciliate the young ladies, transformed him into 'Mr Lindley Murray as he appeared when engaged in the composition of his English Grammar'.) Above all, Grimaldi, whatever his tendency to melancholia, had always the power, until the last few years of his life, to put a brave face upon his misfortunes, though he no longer had the assistance of his Clown's paint to do it.

Eighteen

*O my heart grieves! Well, there must be an end to every-
thing mortal, and, as poor Palmer said (his last words):
'There is another and a better world.' I wonder if I shall
be able to 'clown' it THERE! Well,* adsum.—GRIMALDI
(December, 1836)

IT is most respectfully announced that

MR. GRIMALDI

From severe and incessant Indisposition, which has
oppressed him upward of Four Years, and continues
without any hope of Relaxation, finds himself compelled to quit a Profession, in which almost from
infancy he has been honoured with as great a share
of Patronage and Indulgence as ever fell to the Lot
of any Candidate for Public Favour; nor can he quit
a Theatre where his Labours commenced, and were
for so many years sanctioned, without attempting the
Honour of Personally Expressing his Gratitude ...
and however inadequate he may prove to paint the
Sincerity of his Feelings, it is his intention to offer an
Address of Thanks to his Friends and Patrons, and
conclude his Services with the painful duty of bidding
them

FAREWELL

In response to this announcement, blazoned in smudgy theatre-
bills throughout the city, hundreds of Londoners made their way
towards Sadler's Wells Theatre on the afternoon of St Patrick's
Day 1828. At the age of 49, Joe Grimaldi was saying goodbye to
his public; eight years after his last season on the Islington stage
he was preparing a formal renunciation of his power; and the
crowds that gathered by the New River, under the long line of
poplar trees, had come to say farewell to their crippled king. As
befits a King of Clowns, however, the sad news was announced

on the bills in a style very different from the studied humility of the official advertisement — in Grimaldi's own notorious doggerel:

> *To greet his Friends, ere he retires*
> *To rural Scenes and Village Squires,*
> Grim *takes a Night to say Adieu,*
> *And thank his Patrons* tried *and* true,
> *To find relief from many woes*
> *He seeks retirement and repose.*

> *To those who would give all their* Ribs *such a treat,*
> *They'll find plenty of Tickets at* 8, *Exmouth Street;*
> *At a quarter-past Six commence breaking the ice,*
> *And (as usual) between* Eight *and* Nine *take* HALF-PRICE.

There was no room for half-price on the night, for by midday more people were assembled in the yard of the Wells than the theatre could hold — about 2000. The doors opened at 5.30, and the people surged in with one struggling, shouting rush, filling the gallery and the pit; and when the curtains drew apart an hour later the house was packed with restless, eager customers in every part. For once, everyone was on time.

The old Clown himself was scarcely able to reach the theatre. He spent the day in bed, and a friend who called at the house in Exmouth Street found him in great distress. All he could say was 'I'll play tonight if it cost me my life', before he burst into tears. By a great effort of will, however, he roused himself, overcame his weakness, and arrived punctually at the Wells for his last performance, in the company of his doctor. Tom Dibdin explained the state of his health to the audience, who greeted the speech with a noisy warm-hearted sympathy that set Grimaldi off in a flood of tears; and then it was time to begin. It was in the rôle of a drunken sailor, Hock, that he acted for the last time on the stage of Sadler's Wells, in Tom Dibdin's melodramatic piece *The Sixes: or The Fiends*, and although this was an unexacting part, he performed it with the greatest difficulty, hindered as he was not only by physical affliction, but by his sense of the finality of the event. There was another cause for grief: his son, whom he had not seen for many months, appeared with him in the bill, and in the duet which the two Grimaldis sang together the old man was almost unmanned by sorrow. At last, however, the piece was over, and amidst roaring cheers, whistles and shouts of homage, the great Clown hobbled back to his old dressing-room, helped by a dozen willing hands.

To round off the entertainment came that 'matchless fling, so loved of yore', the comic *pas de deux* from *Mother Goose* — danced, on this night of nights, by Tom Ellar and J.S.Grimaldi. As Ware's music died away, the noise of the house hushed into expectant silence; the time had come for the Farewell Address. Slowly, painfully, quietly, Grimaldi walked on to the stage for the last time. He was dressed in black, with a white waistcoat and gloves. As he advanced towards the footlights, the other performers silently ranged themselves behind him, and he addressed the audience in a voice that was often rough with emotion.[1] When he had finished, with tears streaming down his cheeks, the company moved towards him, and amid deafening applause the back scene was drawn off to reveal the manager's *pièce de résistance* — a set of coloured lights arranged in the words GRIMALDI'S FAREWELL. After bowing and waving to the audience, Grimaldi was led off into the green room, and there he wept aloud 'with an intensity of suffering that it was painful to witness and impossible to alleviate'. He was in so disturbed and hysterical a state that he could not carry out his promise to distribute his farewell wardrobe as souvenirs among his friends, and after a few hurried goodbyes he was lifted into a coach and driven home to Exmouth Street.

The next day his house was besieged by scores of people who had been unable to get a place the night before, and he was urged to take another benefit night at the King's Theatre. Grimaldi, however, refused — 'I can't scream *there*,' he said, 'because I'm no opera singer'[2] — for although his benefit at the Wells had brought him £230, as well as some £85 in anonymous contributions, he was reluctant to go through another ordeal at Covent Garden. But under the persuasions of Fanny Kelly, who had urged him to take the benefit at Islington, he went along a week afterwards to ask Charles Kemble if he could have the theatre for a farewell benefit — if possible, at a low price. It was a modest request, and Kemble promised that he would put the matter up to his co-proprietors at their weekly meeting. 'If the theatre were solely mine,' the manager said, 'I should say "Take it — 'tis yours, and without charge at all"; but unfortunately our theatre is in Chancery, and nothing can be done without the consent of others.'[3]

Grimaldi waited at home for the promised news, but the appointed day passed without any word from Kemble. Three weeks later he asked the manager, in a discreetly humble reminder, if a decision about his benefit had yet been reached. By return he received a letter, not from Charles Kemble but from the theatre's treasurer:

> *Dear Sir,*
>
> I am directed by the proprietors of this theatre to acquaint you in reply to your application relative to a benefit, that they much regret that the present situation of the theatre with regard to Chancery proceedings will prevent the possibility of their accommodating your wishes.

This was the considered reply of the proprietors of Covent Garden to a man who had for years been the prime attraction of their theatre, who had 'probably drawn more money to it in his time, than any man upon the boards'.

It fell to Stephen Price, their American rival at Drury Lane, to give Grimaldi the unsolicited hospitality of his theatre for a fare-well benefit. This enterprising manager — described as 'Star Giver General to the United States' — brought many London actors to theatres in Philadelphia, Boston and Baltimore, at a time when 'the mania for theatrical emigration to America was at its height'. It was a matter of note that Price 'obviously thinks little about a voyage on the ocean. He takes to the Atlantic like one of its own leviathans, and refreshes New York with English of the latest pronunciation of any man alive. He is a sort of general trader in human stock, and has now grown into a monopoly of the rejected, the ambitious and the avaricious in the northern hemis-phere.' Macready was one of the many actors who had hard words for him, describing him as 'a reckless speculator . . . boastful and overbearing, not popular even with his own countrymen . . . in short, he was not a gentleman'. But it is pleasant to record that, in a season which cost Price heavy losses, he had the good heart to give Grimaldi his theatre for the night.

For Charles Kemble there seems to be no excuse, even if Grimaldi's own account of the matter is distorted by natural resentment. If he had wished, it is clear, Grimaldi could have had the benefit to which he was entitled, Chancery or no Chancery, but he was not interested: the Clown had ceased to be an asset, and had less claim to the theatre than the Western Philanthropic Institution for the Relief of the Necessitous and Deserving Poor, which took Drury Lane for a benefit in May. Before he left the room, Grimaldi told Kemble what he thought of his conduct: London was left to draw its own conclusions at the sight of Covent Garden's Clown making his farewell at the Theatre Royal, Drury Lane. The incident rankled in Joe's mind for years to come, and in the following April he wrote to Richard Norman: 'Oh my poor Old Master Mr Harris, God Bless him, had he still been in possession I should not have asked such a favour a second time. ...'

The Drury Lane event was to be more spectacular than the farewell at Islington, and among Fanny Kelly's arrangements she persuaded Tom Hood to write an address for Grimaldi. Joe called at Hood's house to plead that it should be brief, not only because he was a 'bad study', but also because he could not trust his strength to carry him through a long speech. Hood was shocked at his appearance:

the lustre of his bright eyes was gone — his eloquent face was passive and looked thrown out of work — and his frame was bowed down by no feigned decrepitude. ... Of his suffering he spoke with a sad but resigned tone, expressed deep regret at quitting a profession he delighted in, and partly attributed the sudden breaking down of his health to the superior size of one particular stage which required of him a jump extra in getting off. That additional bound, like the bittock at the end of a Scotch mile, had, he thought, overtasked his strength.

Whatever the cause, he was now, Hood noted, a total wreck.

The only day which Price could offer was the last night but one of the season — 28th June 1828[4] — but it was to Joe's advantage that Covent Garden had closed a week before, for most of its staff were in the audience. Miss Kelly herself played Columbine in *Harlequin Hoax*, the Dibdin skit on pantomime in which she had made a success in 1814, and she brought many of her Lyceum company with her. It was in the middle of this burlesque that Grimaldi appeared for the last time in his Clown's dress. He played in a barber's shop scene from the pantomime of *The Magic Fire*, which required a minimum of physical effort. A chair was brought out and set near the footlights, and then, as the short familiar figure in motley limped out towards it across the stage, he was greeted with a tremendous roar of applause and cheering from the great audience which packed the Theatre Royal. They were paying homage to the man and to the Clown. He stood up, his knees trembling, and every feature of his face convulsed under the red insignia of his trade; his friends, standing anxiously in the wings, were moved to tears, and Harley had to be restrained from running on to the stage. It was the young Grimaldi, who was taking part in the performance, who held him back. He knew that his father had summoned up all his energies for one last effort, and was determined to do it on his own, whatever the cost. Clown, sitting in his chair, let his irresistible laugh scream out once more across the pit; once more he rolled his eyes up at the gallery; once more he sang 'Hot Codlins', and all the house joined in that absurd rhyming chorus with a violent heartiness that could have carried to Covent Garden, demanding an encore that he had no power to give. Soon the brief scene was over, and Grimaldi limped off into the wings. Now Joey the Second appeared in a scene from *Harlequin in his Element*; a third Clown, Southby, appeared in a scene from the current Drury Lane pantomime, *Harlequin and Cock Robin: or The Babes in the Wood*, with Barnes as the Pantaloon; a fourth Clown, Tom Ridgway, appeared with his brother as Pantaloon, and his father, one of Grimaldi's old comrades at the Wells, as Harlequin; and the two young Clowns of Drury Lane, Master Wieland and Master Chikini (the Babes of the Wood) danced a comic *pas de deux*. The theatre was full of Clowns and Harlequins that night, but the greatest of them all was changing into his own clothes for the very last time. It was in a formal black suit, as at Sadler's Wells, that he hobbled out again before the audience, with Hood's farewell address clenched firmly in his hand. These, however, were the words he spoke: the stylish composition, published as his farewell, was forgotten.[5]

Ladies and Gentlemen, I appear before you for the last time. I need not assure you of the sad regret with which I say it; but sickness and infirmity have come upon me, and I can no longer wear the motley! Four years ago I jumped my last jump, filched my last custard, and ate my last sausage. I cannot describe the pleasure I felt on once more assuming my cap and bells tonight — that dress in which I have so often been made happy in your applause; and as I stripped them off, I fancied that they seemed to cleave to me. I am not so rich a man as I was when I was basking in your favour formerly, for then I had always a fowl in one pocket and sauce for it in the other. [Laughter and applause from the audience.] I thank you for the benevolence which has brought you here to assist your old and faithful servant in his premature decline. Eight-and-forty years have not yet passed over my head, and I am sinking fast. I now stand worse on my legs than I used to do on my head. But I suppose I am paying the penalty of the cause I pursued all my life; my desire and anxiety to merit your favour has excited me to more exertion than my constitution would bear, and, like vaulting ambition, I have overleaped myself. Ladies and Gentleman, I must hasten to bid you farewell; but the pain I feel in doing so is assuaged by seeing before me a disproof of the old adage, that favourites have no friends. Ladies and Gentlemen, may you and yours ever enjoy the blessings of health is the fervent prayer of Joseph Grimaldi — *Farewell! farewell!*

The audience rose and cheered him, waving their hats, stamping their feet, calling out his name; and once more he called out 'Farewell — and', with choked voice, 'God bless you!' For a few minutes he stood there bewildered and silent, swaying to and fro as if hypnotized, as if he could not bear to leave the stage, overcome by the splendours and miseries of the evening. Harley now forced his way through the crowd in the wings, and with young Grimaldi's help half-led and half-carried the Clown into a quiet room backstage. Here, for a few minutes, Grimaldi rested; while he drank two glasses of Madeira, he gave Harley his new wig and the address he still held in his hand, as 'a remembrance for his kindness to poor old Joe!' Then he had to face another ordeal: the members of the company, actors, singers and dancers, came to say their goodbyes, and they were followed by carpenters, dressers, and scenemen of both theatres, who wanted to pay their respects to the great man in this moment of farewell. It was a long, quiet file of people who came through the room to shake the old man's hand, as he sat there in a chair, with tears streaming down his face, moved now beyond all restraint by the enthusiasm of the crowd and the affection of his comrades. At last it was time to break away, but when he came out into the street, a crowd had gathered to cheer him on his way; and outside the house in Exmouth Street, there were more people to greet him. There they stayed, shouting for Grimaldi, until he came out again and made a farewell bow from the door.

The door shut. The crowd dispersed. The street emptied. And there was silence ... silence in which Joseph Grimaldi, lying awake in his bed, relived that evening's glory and pain, and cried again to think of the world that he had left behind, to think of the son who did not come home, to think of the uncertain years ahead.

*   *   *

Stephen Price had not given Drury Lane free for the benefit, so Grimaldi had to pay the night's charges of £210, but even so he made a considerable profit; and this was supplemented by private gifts, most of them anonymous, which amounted to more than the benefit itself. In all, he received £580, and this, with the Sadler's Wells profits, provided a sizable next-egg for the next few years. Even so, his future was precarious, and Joe decided — prompted again, perhaps, by Miss Kelly — to apply for assistance from the Drury Lane Theatrical Fund, to which he had belonged for some thirty years. His appeal was swiftly answered with an annual grant of £100, and a quarter's instalment was paid in advance by the secretary in person. This annuity helped to keep him from the fate of a man like Carlo Delpini, who died that year in lonely poverty in a room off the Strand, after years of sickness and begging for charity; while he kept his job at the Wells, Joe's income was as much as £4 a week for several years and he had put away a few hundreds from his heyday.

There were soon new claims upon his capital, however, for not long after his benefit his son had another mental breakdown and arrived at the house in Exmouth Street in a state of near-madness. On this occasion his parents could not give young Joe shelter, because of his mother's illness, but Grimaldi had him taken to his own lodgings and met the bills for his treatment and nursing until he was well enough to return to the stage. J.S.Grimaldi was back at Covent Garden when the 1828–9 season opened, in some of his father's old parts, but he disappeared from the bills in February and was dismissed from the company. Sadler's Wells, too, sent him packing, when the proprietors' respect for the father could no longer be allowed to outweigh their disgust for the son. He starred as Clown in the Whit Monday pantomime at the Wells — *Harlequin and the Three Wishes: or, Puck and the Puddings.* This was 'compiled and arranged' by his father from 'twelve of the most favourite of those pantomimes which for the last twenty years have ranked highest in public estimation,' said *The Times*, 'and in which he has attained the celebrity so justly his due.' For his son's benefit, 'no pains have been spared by him to cull the choicest flavours from that vast bed of comic incident in which he so long revelled as the hero.' But his son did not revel in it for long: his name vanished from the bills, and he never returned to the Wells. In the Christmas of 1829 he appeared as the Clown of Drury Lane, while Paulo took his place at Covent Garden, but he was soon under notice. Thereafter Joey the Second was never seen again at either of the patent theatres, and he sank deeper into the mire. Meanwhile, in 1829 his father moved to a smaller house, not far from his old home — 23 Garnault Place; and in 1832 the Grimaldis went to Woolwich. (The two apparently different addresses of 31 George Street and 6 Prospect Row were the same house.) Joe lived briefly nearby in Bowling Green Row before moving back in 1835 to Pentonville.

So the tragi-comedy went on, darkening the years of Grimaldi's retirement, the years in which he had dreamed of watching his son's triumphs on the London stage. At one period young Joe went into a debtors' prison to escape his creditors, an experience which cost his father £40 of his dwindling savings; at another time a theatre manager whom he had attacked threatened to jail him for assault and battery. According to *The Times*, reporting in March 1831 that he had been 'liberated in the Insolvent Court', the younger Grimaldi was 'not infrequently arrested'. Throughout all his misadventures his father never turned his back on him, in spite of all the humiliations and miseries that the boy had cost him. When in the autumn of 1831 young Joe came home once more to ask for shelter, his mother, who had been intermittently ill for several years and 'had suffered greatly from his misdeeds, outrageous conduct and gross and violent abuse',[6] wanted to shut the door in his face, to save her husband any further misery — and expense. But Grimaldi once again took his son in and supported him on his tiny salary. This was a brief period of reform and reconciliation, in which father and son resumed their old intimacy. Letters survive in which Joe humbly applies for free tickets to theatres for J.S. and himself ('I know it is a great favour to ask, but as I cannot *now* put my hand in my pocket I have taken this liberty, which, if complied with will add an additional obligation...'); and he wrote to old friends and acquaintances still in power, beseeching them to give young Joe another chance. In September 1832, for instance, he wrote revealingly to the author-manager Alfred Bunn:

> From the many Dealings we have had together, and, I may say, all to our mutual advantage, has induced me to write a few lines to solicit your Interest on behalf of my son Mr J.S. Grimaldi who is at present disengaged — his line and style of acting is well known, but it may be as well to state them — Comic and Serious Pantomime — Melodramatic business — Combats &c — and any other exertion wherein his service may be required — Salary is not so much the object as a permanent situation — Should he be so fortunate as to succeed I have many Pantomime Models which you may select from, which shall be entirely at your disposal.

This devoted father could not take Bunn's 'no' for an answer. He wrote again the following month, renewing his plea and increasing the emotional blackmail.

> I am confident you would find him a valuable acquisition in every department...An Article perhaps for three or five years might still (*by your kind interference*) not be objected to, commencing at £3 per week — Should an opportunity present itself I hope and trust you will interest yourself in his behalf for the sake of *Old Joe* and *Auld-lang-syne*.

In the same letter Grimaldi thanked Bunn, in almost obsequious terms, for 'the good opinion you still have of me and of my poor humble abilities'.

> It is certainly a great consolation to know in my solace that I am as much respected and esteemed in my retirement as when in my public Character...Your kind offer to me to superintend the forthcoming Pantomime (*however gratifying to my feelings*) I shall never forget, but must decline — I could no more sit in an Arm-Chair to instruct a Pantomime than I am capable of jumping out of a Garret Window without injury to myself.

All that Grimaldi could offer by way of help was (with J.S. still

in mind) a 'good opening', which Bunn was invited to 'inspect'.
He could, said Joe, 'upon a pinch assist you with a comic Scene or
two of business if required'. Moreover,

> I have as many Models and tricks as would furnish six or
> seven Pantomimes of which you may select what is necessary
> for your *Xmas Novelty*...This I can promise without *fee* or
> *reward*, provided an arrangement can be made for my
> son.

This paternal lobbying was a labour of love usually doomed to
disappointment, for J.S.Grimaldi's character had rapidly become
notorious and he had acquired the reputation of being unemploy-
able. His father's efforts were not helped by incidents of the
following kind, reported in the *Morning Herald* in breathless prose
(left unedited here for reasons of historical curiosity).

> On Friday evening, he went, rather intoxicated, to the house
> of a young lady, and informed her that he had occasion to go
> out, and she, being remarkably attached to him, persuaded him
> not to go, and flew to the door, in order to prevent him leaving,
> when he struck her a blow in the eye, and left her, which she
> took so much to heart that she went into the kitchen and drank
> a large draught of vitriol, upon which she was immediately
> taken to hospital, where she now lies in a most precarious state,
> and without the slightest hope of recovery. On the following
> night (Saturday) as he was playing in *Paul Jones*, the intelligence
> reached him, which preyed so much on his mind as to cause his
> death.

This announcement was premature, as the *Globe* pointed out, for
both Mr Grimaldi junior and his lady friend. The *Morning Herald*,
however, repeated its assertion that young Joe was dead; whereupon the *Globe* rebuked it once again.

> The *Herald* has been grossly imposed upon with this infor-
> mation. Mr Grimaldi is not dead, but at the house of his father
> ...His illness is brain fever, but he was this morning considered
> much better. A female of a certain class, styled by our con-
> temporary 'a young lady', who had poisoned herself in a fit of
> irritation at some dispute with Mr Grimaldi junior, is now
> much better, although not quite out of danger.

There was more than a touch of the Signor in J.S.Grimaldi, at
least in his attitude to women. Was he, perhaps, the heir of the
Signor's syphilis?

In November 1832 J.S.Grimaldi was offered a job at the Queen's Theatre in Tottenham Street until Christmas, when he was engaged as Clown for the Coburg pantomime. It seemed too good to be true. But some weeks later at the Queen's the young man was appearing as Scaramouch in *Don Juan*, when he hurt himself in going through a trap. Although he did not complain at the time, he later told the stage manager's wife, Mrs Elliott, that he had a pain in his side, asked her to feel the place, but could not bear the pressure of her hand. After he returned to his lodgings he was seized with violent vomiting, which continued throughout the night, and as he showed no sign of improvement his landlady sent word to his father in the morning. Grimaldi sent his own doctors, but he himself could not leave the cottage at Woolwich, where Mary was ill in bed. His son, who became delirious, had to be held down, and in between his bouts of violence he babbled snatches from his old parts — parts which his father had taught him with such loving patience and high pride. Twisting and turning and vomiting on the bed, he was Scaramouch again, or Orson, or the Clown; until, some hours later, Joey the Second was dead. It was 11th December 1832, a month after his thirtieth birthday, at 24 Pitt Street.[7]

When a friend came to Woolwich to break the news, Joe hobbled down from Mary's bedroom to let in the visitor. At the tidings of his son's death,

in one instant every feeling of decreptitude or bodily weakness left him: his limbs recovered their original vigour; all his lassitude and debility vanished; a difficulty of breathing, under which he had long laboured, disappeared, and starting from his seat, he rushed to his wife's chamber, tearing, without the slightest difficulty, up a flight of stairs, which, a quarter of an hour before, it had taken him ten minutes to climb. He hurried to her bed-side, told her that her son was dead, heard her first passionate exclamation of grief, and falling into a chair, was once again an enfeebled and crippled old man.[8]

What was it that *The Times* had said? 'If he takes pains, and avoids breaking his neck, we see no reason why he should not be as great a man as his progenitor.' But that was nine years ago, and long before his death Joey the Second had betrayed himself and his high promise — in the eyes of everyone but his father. Now Grimaldi could hope no longer. 'I have more than done my duty by him,' he wrote to Norman — but it was small comfort in the end.

*   *   *

From the news of their son's death, neither Joe nor Mary ever fully recovered. Joe wrote to Norman:

> She has had a Paralytic attack which has deprived her of the use of Limbs and Speech and is confined to her bed, and is assisted out of Bed and in Bed by 3 persons — her Speech has partially recovered but the Limbs I fear never will . . .

For the next two years, while he himself endured recurrent bouts of illness, Joe helped to nurse his wife through a long ordeal of suffering. Old friends and colleagues came out to Woolwich to see him, when their work permitted, and one actor took such an opportunity when the death of a member of the royal family closed down the theatres. In the course of conversation with Grimaldi he mentioned this fact, saying:

> 'Calamity has closed the theatres, and I am rejoicing in a holiday upon this day of death.' Grimaldi fell back in his chair, and pointed to something covered up at the further end of the room; his power of articulation was temporarily gone and his gestures were frantic. His friend removed the cloth at which he pointed, and found the bust of young Grimaldi. The bereaved father was at length relieved by tears, and exclaiming, 'It is indeed a day of death, for it is the anniversary of the demise of my poor boy,' gave way to the agony of grief: he was conveyed to his chamber, and did not quit it for several days. A similar accident awakening his sensibility a few months prior to his death superinduced a fit of apoplexy...[9]

From his retirement he watched the ranks of his friends and colleagues being thinned by mortality. Barrymore, Munden, Elliston, Charles Dibdin, John O'Keeffe, and Edmund Kean — all died with a year or two; and the glittering figures of Regency pantomime passed away in illness and poverty. Bob Bradbury died in rags in 1831, at 54, and four years later Paulo left his family destitute at the age of 48. James Barnes retired in 1834, and lived on the charity of such friends as Tom Ellar, who soon followed him into bitter poverty, singing in the London pubs and squares to earn a few coppers (see Appendix B); and Jack Bologna, who had settled in Glasgow as a teacher of dancing, had to take a job as a conjuror's black-faced stooge (Ebony, servant to Anderson, the Wizard of the North). It was a bitter end to the harlequinade, and Grimaldi was the most prosperous of them all, despite his sufferings. He had £450 invested at his death in 1837.

At last Mary Grimaldi herself passed away in 1834–5, leaving Joe alone at Woolwich, and with her passing he found the cottage in Bowling Green Row unbearable. He moved to another address in George Street, and sold off some of their household goods and theatrical properties to raise money, asking Tom Ellar and Richard Norman, two of his most faithful friends, if they would like to buy a bookcase for £8, a firescreen for £15, or a lamp for a guinea. 'My Manuscripts, Tricks and Music,' he wrote to Norman, with heavy underlinings, 'will all be yours, some day!' To Ellar he wrote one of those rhyming letters in which he delighted, and which reveal the true Grimaldi so much more clearly than his more formal epistolary style. He was trying to sell the Harlequin, among other things, 'a case with two fiddles' — (although Ellar was in much worse circumstances).

> *My Dear Friend Tom, Answer this I pray*
> *Do you mean to have my Instrument, say Yea or Nay.*
> *For if I do not hear from you without more delay*
> *In a short space of time I shall send it away.*
> *So Dear Friend Tom, without more Ceremony,*
> *Come and take the Music and bring me the Money.*
> *I have something left still, for your judgment and approve-all*
> *Which I wish to dispose off, before my remove-all,*
> *A Case with Two Fiddles, of exquisite sound*
> *You shall have the Case and Fiddles for the sum of £5.*
> *So Dear Friend Tom ever yours till I die,*
> *The once Merry Momus, Poor Joe Grimaldi.*
> *I shall quit Woolwich soon, for another situation,*
> *And glad enough I shall be, to return from Transportation.*
> *Once more enjoy Society, the Song, the Glee and Laugh,*
> *Tell droll Storys, think of present Times — Not forget the past,*
> *Be merry and wise, for Time approaches fast*
> *For Death will, you know, have the Odd Trick at last.*

Within a few months he arranged to return to his old haunts at Sadler's Wells, and — with the help of the faithful Hughes family — he took a house in Pentonville, at 33 Southampton Street, next door to Mrs Mary Arthur, who had been a servant of the Hugheses for many years. With a housekeeper, Susannah Hill, to look after him, Grimaldi settled down in what was to prove his last London home. (Renumbered and renamed, it survived until 1960 as 22 Calshot Street, with a blue plaque in its latter years.) Sometimes he managed to hobble along under the poplars that still lined the New River and take a drink at the Myddelton's Head; he would watch the new Clowns such as Tom Matthews and Jefferini, and hear the latest gossip from Barnes and Ellar; and nearly every evening he would take a Scotch ale, or a little gin and water, at his local pub, the Marquis of Cornwallis, a few yards away at the corner of Southampton Street. (Like the house, this has now been demolished.) When Joe lost the power of his legs, and was no longer able to make such excursions, the landlord, William Cook, used to carry him to and fro on his back, so that the old Clown could still enjoy a drink and talk in the evenings. His routine was quiet and regular, with plenty to eat and drink: breakfast at eight, lunch at twelve, dinner at half-past two, tea at six and 'Say-go' at ten — that was how he described his life in a letter to a friend. Now that he was back in Pentonville, it was easier for theatre folk to visit him at home, but he still pined for company; and although he mainly depended on the Theatrical Fund for his living, he was still generous to his old comrades in the theatre. A few days before Christmas he wrote to one of these, apologizing for his inability to appear at a benefit:

I am sorry I shall not be able to oblige you this year even by making an appearance for an hour. I am very ill — so ill indeed that I can scarcely hold the pen in my hand to write this to you. I am rheumatised — goutised — puffised — and generally done up. No more for poor Joey the larks and games, the sausages and baggy breeks, the Little Old Woman and Hot Codlins. Eheu! My foot is swathed in bandages, my body is wrapped in flannel, and my heart is bandaged in calico. I am always in pain ... I enclose the sum of Three Guineas towards your benefit. Come and see me and talk of old times when life was young and no one was happier than your old and true chum,

Joe Grimaldi

P.S.—Come on Christmas Eve if you can.

In another letter, written in a similar mood of despair, he says:

My dear Friend, I am very ill — my days of staging are nearly over. I am afflicted with rheumatism so severely as to be scarcely able to lift this pen. Do come and see me. My poor Wife being dead I am all alone — but not kicking — unfortunately. I feel truly miserable: I am sure my end is approaching. O for the days when I was delighting Audiences at Old Drury and the Wells! I will do all I can to assist your poor Friend, but come and see your old Friend and have an hour's chat with him. Come on Sunday, I shall have no one here but an old housekeeper. Come dear Friend and cheer me up. *Your honest and true Friend,*

Joey Grimaldi.

Yet there were many times when he still faced the future with all his old cheerfulness and courage. He gave away some of his tricks to Alfred Bunn, who called one day at Southampton Street, and destroyed many of his manuscripts, but he still dreamed of staging a pantomime again at the Wells: he had an 'opening' of his own which, he wrote in March 1837, 'I intend shortly to make use of myself.' Moreover, he had decided to write his reminiscences, and for many months he ranged back over his years of Clowning, ransacking his memory for anecdotes and dates, dictating his past to an amanuensis sent in by Richard Hughes and making his own autobiographical notes when he was able to hold a pen. He completed this on his birthday in 1836, with these words (according to the *Memoirs*):

In my solitary hours — and in spite of all the kindness of my friends I have many of them — my thoughts often dwell upon the past: and there is one circumstance which always affords me unmitigated satisfaction: it is simply that I cannot recollect one single instance in which I have intentionally wronged man, woman or child, and this gives me great satisfaction and comfort.

This is the 18th of December 1836. I was born on the 18th of December 1779, and consequently have completed my 57th year.

Life is a game we are bound to play —
The wise enjoy it, fools grow sick of it;
Losers, we find, have the stakes to pay,
That winners may laugh, for that's the trick of it.
                                        J. GRIMALDI.

                    *   *   *

In the January of 1837 Grimaldi paid a visit to the Wells to see the pantomime, Nelson Lee's *Fee-Fo-Fum!!!; or Harlequin Te-To-Tum!!!*, in which Jefferini was the Clown. Word of his arrival was soon passed round backstage, and although Joe sat at the rear of a box, keeping as far out of sight as he could, he was soon recognized by the audience. In the course of a duet between Jefferini and Jim Crow (one of the early nigger minstrels) came the verse:

> *Prythee tell me, Master Crow,*
> *Why you look so full of glee?*

And Jim Crow replied:
> *Why? cos our old friend Joe*
> *I'm delighted here to see.*

He pointed to the box where Grimaldi was sitting, and the audience began to clap when the Clown cried from the stage:

> *Now he's here, to welcome him,*
> *With a hearty three-times-three!*

Led by the company on the stage, the people of Sadler's Wells gave three resounding cheers for their old favourite, standing up in their seats and calling for a speech. After some persuasion, Grimaldi came forward to the front of the box, leaning on a friend's shoulder for support, and through his tears made his last address to an audience.

'You may judge the feelings of one who has travelled through the world of pantomime, and reached the declining years of life without losing one jot of his enthusiasm,' he said, and concluded with these words. 'Years have passed since I had the honour of addressing you and in all probability for the last time. Had I been prepared for this, I should have endeavoured to acquit myself more creditably. I came here but to oblige the manager, and to look once more on scenes which I' — here he paused, choking with emotion, and hastily throwing out his arms towards the house in a gesture of affection he cried 'God bless you all! God bless you all!'

Such was his enthusiasm for the world of pantomime that in the spring he came to watch the rehearsals of a revival of *Mother Goose*, in which Jefferini took his old role of Squire Bugle. This was staged on Whit Monday, 15th May, and was billed 'as originally, with all its comic effects, being under the superintendence of the Veteran Grimaldi.' It seemed, indeed, that the Veteran was taking a new lease of life, and some of his melancholia was dissipated. Since he had finished his memoirs the previous December, his health had 'considerably improved, although his bodily energies and physical powers remained in the same state of hopeless prostration', and 'he looked forward to the publication of his manuscript with an anxiety which it is impossible to describe'.[10] But this apparent improvement was a false dawn. A fortnight after his last production at the Wells, on the evening of 31st May, Grimaldi complained to Mrs Hill of a tightness in the chest, and he lacked his usual hearty appetite. About half-past ten the housekeeper went down the road to the Marquis of Cornwallis, as was her custom, helped Joe on to the landlord's back, and saw him safely home. After saying goodbye to his loyal carrier, with a 'God bless you, my boy, I shall be ready for you tomorrow night!', Grimaldi was helped up to bed. In the middle of the night Mrs Hill heard an unusual noise in his room, as if he were snoring, but when she looked in all was quiet and the night-light was still burning on the table. Next morning, when she entered her master's room, she found that his body was cold. She rushed out of the house to fetch a surgeon, Mr Fennell, who came at once, ran up to the bedroom, and announced that Mr Grimaldi was dead. An inquest was held at the Marquis of Cornwallis that day, and the verdict was 'Died by the visitation of God'.

The news of his death occupied only a few lines in the daily press, and Joe's funeral, at midday on the following Monday, was 'strictly private and extremely plain'. Two coaches carried the handful of mourners round the corner to St James's, Pentonville. At the graveside were Maria's brother, Richard, loyal to the last;

Dixon, another proprietor of the Wells; Dayus, treasurer of the Wells and an old friend; Richard Lawrence, with whom Joe had once run to the Haymarket with a stopwatch, now treasurer of the Surrey; Dicky Wells, the landlord of the Myddelton's Head; the steadfast Pantaloon, Richard Norman; and Mr Arthur, Joe's neighbour in Southampton Street. They were watched, according to *The Times*, by 'a vast number of very respectable persons'. The yellow press periodicals of the day paid their respects in their own inimitable way. 'It is to be regretted,' said one obituary notice, 'that so great a public favourite should have been in private life not equally estimable, as, it is said, he had but few qualities that could attach to him real friends.' *Figaro in London* made a venomous and coarse attack upon the dead man, bringing forward rumours of his drinking habits which his friends were quick to repudiate in print:

> We don't know why so much fuss has been made about the death of this certainly very clever mountebank. His own habits had rendered him dead to the public for many years, during which, but for those habits, he might have been continuing his calling with profit to himself and a certain species of satisfaction to the public. But as by his own intemperance he has long deprived us of any pleasure we might have derived from seeing him perform, we cannot make out how he is any more lost to us now than he has been for the last ten years. ....
> He could certainly cram more sausages down his throat, and make uglier faces than any man alive, but as he had for so long rendered himself unfit to do anything of this kind in public, we cannot look upon his death as a national calamity.[11]

Was that all? Even after death, Grimaldi still had his enemies; but his friends were numbered in thousands, and he was mourned throughout the country, in prose, in verse and in silence, by those to whom he was more than a mere face-maker and sausage-guzzler.

> *The curtain falls — life's last sad scene is o'er,*
> *Poor Joe Grimaldi falls to rise no more,*
> *And till th' awakening trumpet's note shall flow*
> *No further change can Motley undergo.*
> *Ye countless thousands, who for forty years*

Bestowed your laughter, now bestow your tears,
Nor strive your honest feelings to suppress
For one who laboured for your happiness,
And in the service, 'stead of golden gain,
Earned ten long years of unremitted pain.

That was one elegy, in *Bell's Weekly Messenger*. The author of another bad piece of commemorative verse wrote:

When Christmas comes, and with it, boys from school,
Tell them, ye sires, of this transcendent fool,
Whose wit, in every gesture, plainly spoke,
Whose lips, tho' silent, yet conveyed a joke,
And show combined (as in his case you can)
A matchless Clown, and meritorious Man.

Perhaps the best of all farewells was written by Thomas Hood, some years before Grimaldi's death (see Appendix D). It included this verse:

Thou didst not preach to make us wise —
Thou hadst no finger in our schooling —
Thou didst not 'lure us to the skies' —
Thy simple, simple trade was — Fooling:
And yet, Heav'n knows! we could — we can
Much 'better spare a better man!'

'If to be loved by a whole nation in his lifetime and to live in all men's fancies a hundred years after is a true sign of greatness,' as Maurice Willson Disher wrote in 1925, 'then Joseph Grimaldi has a right to be reckoned among our famous men.'[13] Today his name survives, from the forgotten fools before the world of cinema and television, as the legendary master of 'a vast and inextinguishable laughter', the greatest of British pantomimists, a symbol of holiday theatre and permanent anarchy, a lord of misrule (in English style) declaring, in the words of 'Typity-witchet', that 'the only way's to laugh'. Two hundred years after his birth some pilgrims still come to the little graveyard in Pentonville where he was buried in the summer of 1837, not far from 'poor dear Maria', his first wife, half a mile from their first home together.[13] The church is now closed; the churchyard is turfed over; and only a few gravestones remain, stacked against a wall. But here, in honourable isolation beside the church — in what may be its sixth resting place — is a simple, repointed memorial to the King of Clowns, with a rose-tree growing beside it.

Sacred
to the Memory of
Mr Joseph Grimaldi
Who departed This Life
May 31st, 1837
Aged 58 Years.

Notes

CHAPTER ONE *Prelude*

1. See Appendix D.
2. From a description by Thomas Hood in 1828, as he remembered Grimaldi in his heyday.
3. R.H.Horne, *London Journal*, 12th August 1871.
4. *The Life of Joseph Grimaldi*, by H. D. Miles, 194.
5. See Appendix C.
6. Here is a typical example of this error, from an American book on the circus: 'The Joey — so called because Joseph Grimaldi, the archetype, was thus immortalized in a study by novelist Charles Dickens — is an athlete. He performs on horseback or the tight wire and works in his buffooning with the wide sphere of non-clown acts which take place about him. Poodles Hannaford, the Irish bareback artist . . . is perhaps the purest type of Joey since Grimaldi, who also worked the tanbark.' *The Big Top*, by Fred Bradna, p. 178.
7. This catalogue may be found in the Finsbury Library collection of Grimaldiana: it is by Henry Stevens, in 1874.

CHAPTER TWO

1. The original register contains the entry, under the baptisings of 28th December, of 'Joseph Grimaldi, of Joseph and Rebecca'.
2. It was a feat to survive so long: in the first year of young Joe's life, between December 1778 and December 1779, 8,640 males were christened and 10,208 buried within the bills of mortality, of whom by far the greater part were less than two years old.
3. The family shop seems, from the evidence of the Holborn records, to have been not in Newton Street (as the *Memoirs* say), but in Parker's Lane, where Zachariah Brooker owned a house and yard.
4. 'The distinction between wife and mistress was not sharply defined. Men and women often lived together for years whose friends scarcely knew whether they were married or not.'—A. F. Fremantle, *England in the Nineteenth Century* 1801-5, I, 70. The Signor, at the time of the birth, lived at 125 High Holborn. Rebecca Brooker was billed, at the outset of her career, as 'Miss Brooker', and later as 'Mrs Brooker'; in 1795/6, at Drury Lane, the 'Miss' was changed to 'Mrs' after three performances. Neither Grimaldi nor Brooker is mentioned in the Stanhope Street rate books.
5. In a later redecoration of the theatre, the motto was replaced by the equally appropriate 'Mirth, admit me of thy crew'.
6. *European Magazine*, July 1801.
7. See Appendix D.
8. *Sophie in London* 1786, by Sophie von la Roche, translated by Clare Williams (1933).
9. The *Memoirs* say that Joe made his début at Drury Lane in November 1781, at the age of twenty-three months — he believed that he was born in 1779 — and in Sheridan's pantomime of *Robinson Crusoe* he is said to have played the rôle of Little Clown, while his father appeared as 'the Shipwrecked Mariner' and his success was so great that 'he was instantly placed on the establishment,

accorded a magnificent weekly salary of fifteen shillings, and every succeeding year was brought forward in some new and prominent part'. The facts, however, are otherwise. Far from rising steadily to celebrity, he only emerged from obscurity some fifteen years later. Moreover, *Robinson Crusoe* — staged for the first time on 29th January 1781 — was not presented in November; Signor Grimaldi's rôle in it was not a Shipwrecked Mariner, but Pantaloon; and there is no evidence that Joe was in the pantomime at this period, or that it contained the character of 'Little Clown'. According to the *Memoirs*, young Joe as a child used to paint his face 'in exact imitation of his father's' in *Robinson Crusoe*, but in one of Cruikshank's famous illustrations, the Signor is represented with the clown's make-up which his son invented and with a wig apparently belonging to Pantaloon.

10. Mr C. H. Donelan suggests, in a letter to the author, that it might have been Putney School, which was for some eighty years 'the largest and best known boarding school in the village'.

11. This was the kind of antic which little boys were expected, in that hardier age, to endure as part of their training; it was a feat of which the old Signor may still have been capable, and it may well have happened to Joe himself; but it did *not* happen at Sadler's Wells, for the elder Grimaldi never appeared at that theatre after Joe was born — except for Placido's benefit performance. (16th September, 1782.)

12. Mr Willson Disher, in *Clowns and Pantomimes* (89/90), quotes a passage from a newspaper of 1777: 'The Painter and Ballet Master have had a terrible quarrel. Signor de Grimaldi drew his fiddle-stick upon Monsieur de Louther-bourg — upon which the last, with a brush of red oaker, gave a diagonal line across Pantaloon's face, which looked as if he had cut his head into two parts — the Frenchman retired and left the Italian with his mouth open, as we have often seen him in a Pantomime. As they are both sprung from great families, it is expected this affair will not end so comically.'

CHAPTER THREE

1. Quoted in *Literary and Miscellaneous Memoirs*, by Joseph Cradock (1828).
2. *Ibid.*
3. *Sketches and Impressions, Musical, Theatrical and Social (1799–1885): from the after-dinner talk of Thomas Goodwin*, by R. Osgood Mason (1887).
4. See Appendix A.
5. The National Portrait Gallery is one of the institutions which gives 1779 as the year of Grimaldi's birth.
6. *The Life and Times of Frederick Reynolds* (1826), **2**, 230.
7. *Reminiscences*, **2**, 152–3.
8. *Memoirs of the Life of John Philip Kemble* (1825), **1**, 389.
9. *The Life of Joseph Grimaldi*, by H. D. Miles, 17.
10. *New Monthly Magazine*, July 1839.
11. See *The Casket of Literature*, 1837–8.
12. In April 1768 she was dancing in 'A French Dance' at Drury Lane; Raymond's *Life of Elliston* (**2**, 453) refers to 'Grimaldi and his wife' as 'chief dancers' in 1765, when they earned £1 a night.
13. *Annals of the Liverpool Stage*, R. J. Broadbent (1908), 38–9.
14. 'Two new-laid eggs, half a pint of verjuice, two ounces each of camphorated

oil and spirits of turpentine: to be well rubbed in, two or three times a day. Also vinegar and gin in equal quantities, with twice the quantity of water. The part affected to be kept well wetted.'

15. *Reminiscences*, Henry Angelo (1830), **2**, 152–3.
16. *Ibid.*
17. *The Casket of Literature*, 1837–8.
18. *The Memoirs of J. D. Comedian*, John Decastro (1824).
19. *Ibid.*
20. *Reminiscences*, Henry Angelo, **2**, 36. Roderigo's death scene in a Haymarket *Othello* of 1793 reminded one critic of 'the death of the Clown in "Harlequin Skeleton" '.
21. *The Times*, 22nd August 1866.
22. It is best known as the Surrey, the name which Tom Dibdin gave to a new building on that site in 1816: in the 1920s it became a cinema, and was eventually pulled down in 1934.
23. The veteran pantomimist William West described himself on the occasion of his benefit in 1834 as having been 'two years Pupil, seven years Apprentice, and three years Principal Assistant to the late Signor Grimaldi'.
24. *Mandarina, or The Refusal of Harlequin* was, it seems, something of a novelty in being a kind of Georgian revue performed by children: it included scenes from a popular pantomime *Harlequin's Choice*, the tent scene of *Richard III*, musical parodies of Edwin's popular comic songs, and ended in a Chinese wedding and a spectacular procession.
25. See Charles Dibdin's *The Royal Circus Epitomized* (1784) and *The Professional Life of Mr Dibdin, written by himself* (1803).
26. *The Children of Thespis*, first published 1786.
27. *The Letters of David Garrick*, edited by David M. Little and George M. Kahrl (1963), **2**, 741–2.
28. *Memoirs.*

CHAPTER FOUR

1. Grimaldi's father died on 14th March 1788, and was buried on 23rd March at the Spa Fields Chapel in Exmouth Street, Islington. Jacob Decastro reports that he died in his lodgings in Theatre Court, Lambeth. Lambeth rate books indicate that 'his last home was in Stangate Street (rented at £16 p.a.)'.
2. Grimaldi gave Sheridan, improbably, the credit, although John Philip Kemble took over as stage manager in 1788.
3. *Memoirs.*
4. *Memoirs.*
5. Mary Williamson made her début at Drury Lane in 1779, on the Signor's benefit night, in the same year that she was married. By 1786 she is found appearing under her married name in theatre bills. From 1796 onwards, she frequently appeared at Astley's, where her husband was billed — in 1796 — as ballet-master, principal comic dancer, Harlequin, pantomime composer, and a pupil of 'the late celebrated Signor Grimaldi'. It seems likely that he later appeared under the name of Lassells.
6. Wheeler's manuscript letter on the history of Sadler's Wells, written in the workhouse and preserved in the Percival Collection in the British Library, provides an entertaining sidelight on the theatre's internal politics.
7. *The Wandering Patentee*, **3**, 20–1.

8. *Londinium Redivivum*, J. P. Malcolm (1803), **3**, 235–6. According to Charles Dibdin the younger, Malcolm sat in the pit at the Wells every night for many seasons.
9. *The History of Clerkenwell*, William J. Pinks (1881), 422.
10. In 1755 this was known as the Queen of Hungary's Head; by 1766 it was the King of Prussia's Head; some years later the name was changed to the Myddelton's Head; in 1831 the Sir Hugh Myddelton's Tavern was built on the site; it was destroyed in 1891.
11. Mr Maurice Willson Disher is the authority for this statement.
12. *Londinium Redivivum*, **3**, 235.
13. *The Indian Jugglers.*
14. The Placides and Redigé, it seems, quarrelled with Wroughton over his managerial policy, and threatened to withdraw for a time to Astley's. At the time (1784) the Wells was presenting a Surprising Hare, a Singing Duck, and Scaglioni's Dancing Dogs, and to these attractions the ambitious Wroughton wished to add a Learned Pig — a recruit to whom the rope-dancers strongly objected. Another cause of dispute, according to theatrical gossip, was the intimate relationship between Mr Wroughton and La Belle Espagnole. The Placides apparently kept a copyright in the name of 'the little Devil', because a performer of that name worked with them in America at a time when Paul Redigé was, according to the evidence available, still on the Islington stage: in America Placide played Pierrot and his wife was Columbine.
15. His obscurity is suggested in a contemporary press notice: 'We remember two or three years back a young son of Grimaldi's who frequently entertained us in the likeness of a Monkey; but the Fairy of the Wells can do more, and gives us a Song and Recitative in such correctness and execution, that (as far as the accompaniments of clapping and applauding would permit us to judge) every other specimen of infantile acting is left far behind.'

CHAPTER FIVE

1. Unpublished diaries in the British Museum.
2. Quoted in Tom Dibdin's *Reminiscences*, **I**, 201.
3. The *Memoirs* say that he had to 'dress for Clown' at the Wells, but he did not play that rôle until six years later.
4. According to the *Memoirs*, by 1794 his salary had been raised from three shillings to four pounds a week, but as it also declares that in this year his Drury Lane salary was trebled — which did not happen until 1801 — this date, like most of the dates in the *Memoirs*, must be treated with caution. It is also doubtful whether it was in 1794 that he and Mrs Brooker left their lodgings in Great Wild Street for a six-roomed house with a garden in the new suburb of Pentonville: even if they let part of the house — to Mr and Mrs Lewis of the Wells — it is unlikely that they could have afforded such a way of life until some years later. (Readers of *Bleak House* may remember Mr Guppy's proposal to Esther Summerson: 'My own abode is lodgings at Penton Place, Pentonville. It is lowly, but airy, open at the back, and considered one of the 'ealthiest outlets.')
5. *The Prelude*, Book 7.

CHAPTER SIX

1. See *Theatrical Biography*, 1805; Richard Wheeler's manuscript memoirs; *The Dramatic Mirror*, Thomas Gilliland, 1808; and Charles Dibdin's autobiography for the character of Richard Hughes.

2. The following account is based upon chapters two and three of the *Memoirs*.
3. Was it, perhaps, the platform which Signor Concetto Coco threw across the stage with his teeth: and afterwards supported it, with a small table, two chairs, and from three to six people — all by his teeth alone? Signor Coco and the Sicilians were one of the special attractions that season: another was Mr Askins, who — the bills announced — 'will exert himself to produce, in several points of view, the astonishing Supernatural EFFECT OF HIS TWO VOICES.'
4. The character of the street has changed, but the house still stands — as either No. 44 or (according to L.C.C. records) No. 46.
5. The date of the marriage is incorrectly given as 1798 in the *Memoirs*, and incorrectly amended to 1800 by Charles Whitehead.

CHAPTER SEVEN

1. The following story is told of Carlo Delpini: 'When he was old, the Prince of Wales urged Sheridan to get his name placed on the books of the Theatrical Fund, as he was growing weak and must soon retire. Sheridan pointed out that a clown who had never spoken a word upon the stage could not be considered eligible, and to render him so a few words were introduced for him to speak. He was to cry in the pantomime, as Harlequin and Columbine were about to embrace, 'Pluck them asunder'. For weeks Delphini (*sic*) went about speaking these three words, and nearly everyone in the Drury Lane company had been called upon in turn to hear him 'recite his part', which he did with every possible variation in accent and intonation, receiving from everyone advice, which, by way of fun, they purposely rendered as conflicting as possible. But when before the audience his memory failed him, and though voices from every side eagerly gave him the word, he seemed deaf to them, until, at last, with a most prodigious agonizing effort to recall them, he suddenly exploded with 'Masson dire plock et', while actors and audience on and off the stage roared with laughter. But, "Nevare you mind," said Delphini, as he came off, "dose may laugh dat lose. I have won and sal laugh to mine own self, by Gar! I 'av gain de Pension, ha! ha!, and I care noting at all for nobody".' *Old Drury Lane Christmas Annual*, 1886–7: 'Old Drury's Famous Clowns,' by A. H. Wall.
2. *Era*, 28th March 1896. William Robson, writing in 1854, described him as 'a greater actor than any one at present upon the stage'.
3. *New Monthly Magazine*, July 1839.
4. *Reminiscences of Michael Kelly* (1826).
5. *Memoirs of the Life of John Philip Kemble*, **2**, 126.
6. *Ibid*, **2**, 233.
7. *Memoirs of Charles Dibdin the younger*, 48.
8. *Ibid*.
9. *Memoirs*. These give the date of her death as 1799, incorrectly.
10. At some later date he moved to 8, Braynes Row, renamed Exmouth Street c. 1818–19, now Exmouth Market. The house has been destroyed.

CHAPTER EIGHT

1. *Memoirs*.
2. *The Life of Mr Joseph Grimaldi*, 63.
3. *Memoirs*.

4. *Memoirs of Joseph Munden*, T. S. Munden (1846), 77.
5. There is no other evidence for the story but the *Memoirs*, which gives the date as 1802, but 1801 seems more likely.
6. *The Life of Joseph Grimaldi*, 176.
7. *The Prelude*, op. cit.
8. The *Memoirs* date the accident as 14th August 1802 (when *The Great Devil* was not on the programme) and the year has been accepted by later editors; but it was only three months later that Mary gave birth to a son, and the *Memoirs* thus tacitly give the lie to J. S. Grimaldi's legitimacy, which there is no reason to doubt.
9. They included Charlotte, known as a singer and dancer as Mrs Bryan ('a first-class soubrette,' said Charles James Mathews of her in 1822).
10. The *Memoirs* give this as *Blue Beard*, which was not produced in the opening week of either the 1801 or 1802 seasons.
11. *The Life of Joseph Grimaldi*, 86.
12. *Memoirs*.
13. *Memoirs of Charles Dibdin the younger*, 48. It may have been in *Harlequin Phaeton, The Wizard's Wake: or Harlequin's Regeneration, Goody Two Shoes: or The Golden Head*, or *Harlequin Greenlander*. Grimaldi attracted more attention, however, by his dance with 'Nobody, Somebody and Everybody'; by singing 'The Sailor's Portrait' in a topical peace-offering, *Speed the Plough: or The Return of Peace*; and by fighting Jack Bologna's St George in two special combats, as St Alexander.

CHAPTER NINE

1. *Monthly Mirror*, 1807.
2. Many actors belonged to the Duke of Cumberland's Sharp Shooters, run by Barber Beaumont, which had a monthly mess at the Bedford Hotel in Covent Garden, and 'anniversaries' at Chalk Farm and Montpellier Gardens. 'George F. Cooke, Charles Incledon, Hill, Bologna and Spencer the harlequins, and little Simmons were among the most distinguished members,' says Henry Angelo. (*Reminiscences*, 2, 540.)
3. Grimaldi also appeared as the Old Man of the Mountains in *Gorthmund the Cruel*, who killed Christians, Jews and Turks alike because — in the well-known words of Joe's father — he had 'No religion at all': when his castle was besieged by Coeur de Lion and Saladin, he jumped into a cauldron of fire and expired in agony.
4. See *The Great Charlie*, by Robert Payne (1952), for an evocation of Pan as the godfather of Chaplin.
5. *Memoirs*.
6. *The Reminiscences of Thomas Dibdin* (1826), I, 298.

CHAPTER TEN

1. *The Reminiscences of Thomas Dibdin*, I, 298.
2. *Ibid.* I, 399.
3. *Ibid.* I, 397–8.
4. In 1830 Deburau staged it in Paris. *Ma Mère l'Oie, ou Arlequin et L'Oeuf d'Or*, described as a Pantomime-Arlequinade-Féerie, 'dans le genre anglais, avec changements à vue, travestissements, métamorphoses . . .', proved to be very successful. In New York, however, an early production at about that time met

a different fate. It opened at the Bowery Theatre at the end of February 1832, with E. J.Parsloe — member of a famous and ill-starred pantomime clan — as the Clown: during the voyage, he fell down the companion way and hurt himself severely, and on the fourth night of the pantomime's run — discouraged by its bad reception and suffering from his injuries and from mental anxiety — he broke down in the middle of the scene and had to be helped off the stage. He died the next morning. Gay, the Harlequin in this production, tried to earn his living as a dancing-master in Boston, but this proved unsuccessful and he went West — so the story goes — with nothing but his harlequin suit to wear. This gave him a reputation as a great medicine man with a tribe of Indians by whom he was captured, and he lived in their wigwams for over a year until he escaped — to end his days as a theatrical costumier in Liverpool. (See *Gentleman's Magazine*, January 1890: 'Pantomime in the United States', by W. J. Lawrence.)

Mother Goose, however, had a decisive influence upon the American pantomime: it was, W. J. Lawrence wrote, 'the model of most of the American pantomimes, with their succinct "openings" and long trick harlequinades. . . . In America, pantomime, as with Grimaldi, is an unpretentious semi-pastoral ballet-pantomime played almost entirely in dumb-show, with a harlequinade sequel. . .' The very first American production, according to Professor William Brasmer, was as early as 1810 — in Philadelphia.

5. *Theatrical Journal*, 24th December 1862; 'Outline of the Life of William Bestow, Esq.,' 208–9.
6. *Memoirs of an Unfortunate Son of Thespis* (1818), 208.
7. *Memoirs of the Life of John Philip Kemble*, 2, 430.
8. *Daily Telegraph*, 25th December, 1877.
9. *Memoirs.*
10. *Memoirs of J. S. Munden*, 127.

CHAPTER ELEVEN
1. *Monthly Mirror.*
2. This may have been in 1810, for in 1809 (4th May) Joe did appear at Fawcett's benefit, as Kanko in *La Perouse*.
3. According to a contemporary playbill Grimaldi's first appearance in Birmingham at the Theatre Royal was on 30th November, 1810, when he appeared for Miss Bristow's benefit. *Aris's Birmingham Gazette* announced on 3rd December that 'Mr Grimaldi being announced to perform in London to-morrow evening, obliged him to set off post as soon as the performance ends tonight.'
4. *Memoirs.*
5. *Memoirs of the Life of John Philip Kemble*, 2, 459.
6. There is no record of a visit to Liverpool before 1817, and his appearance at the Theatre Royal was then described as the first: his earliest recorded visit to Manchester was on 15th March, 1813.

CHAPTER TWELVE
1. *Memoirs.*
2. *Covent Garden Journal.*

CHAPTER THIRTEEN
1. *The Age of Elegance*, 368.
2. *Candles and Crinolines* (1926), 125. (1930 edition, in 'Travellers' Library.')

3. *The Age of Elegance*, 326.
4. *Comical Fellows*, 5.
5. W. J. Thom, quoted in *Clowns and Pantomimes*, 110.
6. *The Times.*
7. *London Journal*, 12th August 1871, R. H. Horne.
8. *Some Account of the English Stage* (1832), 8, 232.
9. *Dramatic Censor*, December 1811.
10. *Random Records*, George Colman, 1, 228.
11. See *Memoirs of Charles Mayne Young* (1871), 36–8.
12. The Clowns, too, used them as properties in the harlequinade, as one may see in a passage from Horace and James Smith's *Rejected Addresses* (in the pseudo-Coleridge 'Playhouse Musings'):

> 'Amid the freaks that modern fashion sanctions,
> It grieves me most to see live animals
> Brought on the stage. Grimaldi has his rabbit,
> Laurent his cat, and Bradbury his pig!
> Fie on such tricks!'

13. *Memoirs of Charles Dibdin the younger*, 113.

CHAPTER FOURTEEN

1. Quoted in *The Great Charlie*, Robert Payne, 178.
2. Quoted in *The Great Charlie*, 46.
3. Act A, *The Lady's Not For Burning*, Christopher Fry.
4. 'Interroge-toi quand tu ris.'
5. *A History of the English People in the Nineteenth Century*, 1 (1949 edition), 505.
6. *The Theatrical Recorder*, 1802, 'The Art of Acting', 66.
7. *Memoirs of Charles Dibdin the younger*, 47. Tate Wilkinson referred to Heaton as 'a very good actor in all the dry clowns, clodpoles, etc.'. Leman Rede's *Road to the Stage* (1835) prescribed red wigs for 'Country Boys'.
8. *The Eccentricities of John Edwin* (1794), 1, 284.
9. *Comical Fellows.*
10. *Memoirs of Charles Dibdin the Younger*, 48.
11. *The Old Play-Goer* (1854), 177.
12. *The Age of Elegance.*
13. *The Age of Elegance.*
14. *A History of the English People in the Nineteenth Century*, 1, 505.
15. *Authentic Memoirs of the Green Room.*
16. *Oxberry's Dramatic Biography*, 1, 1827.
17. Quoted *The Age of Elegance*, 262.
18. *New Monthly Magazine*, July 1839.
19. *The Times*, December 1823.
20. *New Monthly Magazine*, July 1839.
21. *Ibid.*
22. See poem by Thomas Hood, Appendix D.
23. *Oxberry's Dramatic Biography*, 1, 1827.
24. In *The Champion*, 29th December 1816.
25. *New Monthly Mangazine*, July 1839.

26. *Leigh Hunt's Dramatic Criticism*, 1808–31, 313.
27. *Ibid.*
28. *Oxberry's Dramatic Biography*, I, 1827.
29. 'My First and Last Pantomime', Dutton Cook.
30. *The Old Play-Goer*, 239.
31. 'My First and Last Pantomime,' Dutton Cook.
32. *Leigh Hunt's Dramatic Criticism*, 1808–1831, 110.
33. *Oxberry's Dramatic Biography*, I, 1827.
34. *Ibid.*
35. *Essays of Elia*, 'On the Acting of Munden'.
36. *A History of Caricature and Grotesque in Literature and Art* (1865), 144.
37. *Essays of Elia*, 'On the Acting of Munden'.
38. *Clowns and Pantomimes*, 29.
39. 'My First and Last Pantomime,' Dutton Cook.
40. See Appendix D.
41. *The New Monthly Magazine*, July 1839.
42. *Memoirs of Charles Dibdin the younger*, 42.
43. *The Old Play-Goer*, 236–7.
44. *Ibid*, 240–1.
45. Quoted in *The Great Charlie*, Robert Payne, 47.
46. In *De l'essence du rire*.
47. Quoted in *The Great Charlie*, Robert Payne, 35.
48. *The Old Play-Goer*, 239
49. *The Times*, 22nd August 1866.
50. *Era*, 28th March 1886.
51. Quoted *London Journal*, 12th August 1871.
52. *Collected Works*, ed. A. R. Waller and Arnold Glover (1903), 8, 236.
53. *Box, Pit and Gallery*, James L. Lynch, 301–2.

CHAPTER FIFTEEN

1. Quoted *The Great Charlie*, 71.
2. *The Old Play-Goer*, 238.
3. *Oxberry's Dramatic Biography*, I, 1827.
4. *Oxberry's Dramatic Biography*, 5, 161.
5. *Clowns and Pantomimes*, 100.
6. *The Casket of Literature*, 1837.
7. In Chambers' Repository of Instructive and Amusing Tracts, No. 67.
8. *Oxberry's Dramatic Biography*, I, 1827.
9. *The Life of Mr Joseph Grimaldi*.
10. *Once a Week*, 18th January 1868.
11. *The Lady's Own Paper*, 'Recollections by an Old Lady', by Margaret of Lancing. (Date unknown.)
12. *Ibid.*
13. *Ibid.*

14. *Memoirs.*
15. *Theatrical Journal*, 6th August, 1862.
16. *My Life and Recollections* (1865), Hon. Grantley F. Berkeley, and *Drama in Gloucestershire* (1908), T. Hallam-Clark.
17. *Memoirs.*
18. *Memoirs.*

CHAPTER SIXTEEN
1. *Collected Works* (1903), **8**, 526.
2. The *Memoirs* say that Master Joe's first appearance on any stage was at Sadler's Wells, on his father's second benefit, in 1814: he played Friday in *Robinson Crusoe*, and 'his intended appearance was kept a profound secret until within a week of the night on which he was to perform', The result was a box-office record for Grimaldi's benefits, and young Joe's 'exertions were both applauded by the public and commended in the newspapers'. I have found no confirmation of this story.
3. *Collected Works* (1903), **8**, 351.
4. *Memoirs*, 119.
5. *Collected Works* (1903), **8**, 398.

CHAPTER SEVENTEEN
1. *Macready's Reminiscences*, 170. (1876 edition.)
2. *Memoirs.*
3. Grimaldi wrote to Norman in 1827: 'The last time I ever played was at Birmingham in this Piece (*The Wishes: or Puck of the Puddings*). I got it up very Respectably, and at the request of many persons prolonged my engagement five Days longer than I intended it should.' The *Birmingham Reporter*, however, observed that he 'seems to be much the worse for wear'.
4. See Appendix D.
5. *Memoirs.*
6. *The Weekly Dramatic Register*, 2nd June 1827.
7. They included George Wieland, Jefferini, C. J. Smith, Southby, and the man commonly regarded as his heir, Tom Matthews, who owned a wig and a pair of shoes of 'my dear good old master ... and his painting brush he used to paint that glorious comic face'.

CHAPTER EIGHTEEN
1. This is the speech as reported in the newspapers that week: it differs in some particulars from the version printed in the *Memoirs*.
2. *New Monthly Magazine*, July 1839,
3. *Memoirs.*
4. This is the way in which Grimaldi was required, by the current convention, to solicit patronage. In a letter dated a week before the benefit, now in the Kay Robertson collection, he wrote: 'Sir, I presume to acquaint you, that on Friday next the 27th inst. my Farewell Benefit will take place at the Theatre Royal, Drury Lane, a Programme of which I beg leave to inclose. You Sir being the possessor of a Private Box at the above Theatre, I most respectfully venture to solicit it upon this occasion.'
5. See (1) above.

6. *Era*, 28th March 1896.

7. See *Conquest*, Frances Fleetwood (1953), 16–17.

8. *Memoirs*.

9. *New Monthly Magazine*, July 1839.

10. *Memoirs*.

11. *Figaro in London*, 10th June 1837.

12. *Clowns and Pantomimes*, 85. When he first played Clown, in 1800, there were 6 minor theatres: in 1837, there were nearly 60.

13. In his will Grimaldi left some £500 in investments: to three of his wife's sisters, Louisa Bristow (£75), Charlotte Bryan (£100), and Maria Greville (£50); to his neighbour Mrs Arthur (£100); to Dayus, the treasurer of the Wells, £22 — 'for his kind attention to me and my wife on all occasions'; to his old friends Richard Norman and James Banister, £25 each; to his house-keeper, Mrs Hill, £50 'for long and faithful service'. To Richard Hughes he left his share in Sadler's Wells, and to Charlotte Bryan he also bequeathed all his goods and chattels — apart from his 'plate and plated goods', which went to Mrs Elizabeth Gye, eldest daughter of Mrs Richard Hughes of Finchley, together with the two patchwork quilts worked by his first wife, 'poor dear Maria', and her sister Julia Bennett, the actress. His old friend Richard Lawrence proved the will. (Elizabeth Hughes married the younger Frederick Gye, 1810–78, whose father was co-proprietor with Richard Hughes of Vauxhall Gardens. Her grand-daughter Sylvia Gye still kept, in the 1950s, a snuff-box with Grimaldi's miniature and a piece of Grimaldi's silver plate.

The Grimaldi Family Tree

No EVIDENCE OF ANY KIND links the family of Joseph Grimaldi of Sadler's Wells with that of Prince Rainier of Monaco, beyond a name which had long been established not only in a number of Italian cities but in France, Spain and England by the time the great Clown was born. Yet it seems essential to record here that this name has been traced back over 1,200 years to Grimoaldus, great-uncle of Charlemagne. According to the English antiquary, Stacey Grimaldi, who corresponded with Joe Grimaldi on the question of his pedigree, Grimoaldus was ninth in descent from Pharamond, Merovingian king of the West Franks in 420; and the first Grimaldi to be Prince of Monaco in the tenth century was fifth in descent from Grimoaldus. The first Grimaldis known to have settled in England were three sons of this ancestor of Prince Rainier: their mother was daughter of Rollo, Duke of Normandy, and they were part of the Norman Conquest. Another branch of the family was planted in Britain in the late seventeenth century: the sixth Marquess commanded the Spanish troops in Genoa in 1685 when that city was captured by the troops of Louis XIV. His palace (and two other Grimaldi palaces) were destroyed; he was banished by the French invader; and he settled in England where, in 1705, he married a north country heiress. Stacey Grimaldi, Joe's contemporary, ranked himself as the ninth Marquess. There was a ducal Grimaldi house in Spain (two marquesses became, in effect, Prime Ministers in the eighteenth century); a princely house in France; in Genoa the family gave several Doges to the Republic; and Grimaldis owned property in Sicily, Naples and Lorraine. This information was published in 1895 in *The Descent of the Family of Grimaldi of Genoa and England.* The pedigree was begun by Stacey Grimaldi (1790–1863), the son of William Grimaldi, a miniature-painter of Albemarle Street whose sitters included Mrs Fitzherbert and the Duke of York. Stacey practised for forty years as a City solicitor, and was a Fellow of the Society of Antiquaries. The pedigree was continued by his son, the Rev. William Beaufort Grimaldi, who presented family scrapbooks about the Clown (though he was no relation) to the Shakespeare collection in Stratford-upon-Avon.

According to Grimaldi's *Memoirs*, his grandfather was once known in France and Italy as 'Iron Legs', a dancer who worked in the Paris fairs in the 1740s, in the *Grande Troupe Étrangère* directed by Restier and the widow La Vigne. When dancing at the Opèra Comique in *La Prix de Cythère*, one of Favart's *féeries*, 'Iron Legs' leaped so high that he broke one of the chandeliers above the stage doors, and a piece of glass struck the face of Mehemet Effendi, ambassador of the Sublime Porte. The enraged Turk ordered his servants to beat the dancer. Failing in that, he demanded a public apology, which served to give the leap a place in the annals of theatre history. The *Memoirs* quote a squib on the occasion:

> Hail, Iron Legs! immortal pair,
> Agile, firm knit, and peerless,
> That skim the earth, or vault in air,
> Aspiring high and fearless.
> Glory of Paris! outdoing compeers,
> Brave pair! may nothing hurt ye;
> Scatter at will our chandeliers,
> And tweak the nose of Turkey.
> And should a too presumptuous foe
> But dare these shores to land on,
> His well-kicked men shall quickly know
> We've Iron Legs to stand on.

'Iron Legs' created one of the most famous European pantomime troupes of the time, *Les Enfants Hollandais*, for which he wrote a number of scripts (published in the 1740s in France) and with which he toured Continental cities. Charles Whitehead, as editor of the *Memoirs*, asserted that 'Iron Legs' was the Signor himself. He was, in fact, Nicolini Grimaldi: the Christian names of Joe's father and grandfather were respectively, upon his own authority, Joseph and John Baptist. In a letter to Stacey Grimaldi of 6th May 1810 he declared that both were 'Natives of Italy, what part thereof I cannot say. And I have no Relative on my Father's side *that I know* of living in England. The time of my Father's coming to this Country I cannot exactly say but suppose it at least must be forty years.' By this letter he and Stacey established that there was no visible link between their families.

Nicolini Grimaldi is described in Campardon's history of the fairs as an English dancer. Was this, perhaps, the same Nicolini Grimaldi appearing in London at the Opera House in 1710, who was described by the *Tatler* (2nd January 1710) in the following passage: 'Every limb, and every finger, contributes to the part he acts, insomuch that a deaf man might go along with him in the sense of it. There is scarcely a beautiful posture in an old statue which he does not plant himself in, as the different combinations of the story give occasion for it. He performs the most ordinary actions in a manner suitable to the greatness of his character and shows the prince even in the giving of a letter, or despatching a message. Our best actors are somewhat at a loss to support themselves in proper gesture, as they move from any considerable distance to the front of the stage; but I have seen the person of whom I am now speaking, enter alone at the remotest part of it, and advance from it with such greatness of air and mien, as seemed to fill the stage, and, at the same time, commanded the attention of the audience with the majesty of his appearance.' There was, perhaps, a family likeness in that eloquence, if not majesty.

In the scrapbook preserved in the library of the Shakespeare Institute at Stratford-upon-Avon, it is suggested that Joe Grimaldi's *great*-grandfather was the Cavaliere Nicolini Grimaldi, who was born in Naples about 1667, first visited England in 1708, and was still alive in Venice in 1730. Joe's father, the same note suggests, was born in Genoa. A reference in the same scrapbook ascribes to the Signor's will (inaccurately) a statement that his father was 'of Malta', and that he himself was born in Italy but was called a 'Portuguese'.

As early as 1740 a Signor Grimaldi played Pantaloon in a Covent Garden pantomime, *Orpheus and Eurydice*, with John Rich as Harlequin. If this was not Joe's father, it may have been his grandfather. In the following decade one of the performers working in the London fairs — listed in *The London Stage, 1660–1800*, Part 4 — was 'Madam Grimaldi'. This was in 1752/3, five years before the Signor's first recorded appearance on the London stage. 'Madam Grimaldi' may have been the Signor's mother, Joe's grandmother, who was living in London at the end of the 1770s with the Signor and his wife. It is the Signor's mother, rather than his wife, who is probably the 'Signora Grimaldi' mentioned in a Drury Lane bill in 1768 for *The Witches: or, Harlequin Cherokee*.

It should also be noted that as early as 1737, according to a cutting hand-dated in the Kay Robertson collection, 'Signor Grimaldi's Most Agreeable Dentrifice Powder' was advertised by a London dentist in Middle Temple Lane as having been in use 'for years past', in combination with 'an Italian sponge prepared for that purpose'. (The dentrifice cost a shilling, the sponge sixpence.) The Signor was then 24. The powder is an almost certain indication that dentistry — like dancing — was an hereditary trade; although it was not one that Joe Grimaldi had the time or opportunity to pursue.

Soon after Joe's death in 1837 his executor, Richard Hughes, received a letter from Jane Taylor, claiming that she was Joe's sister and asking if he had remembered her in his will, for she was in extreme poverty. When Hughes replied that she had not been mentioned by Grimaldi in any way, no more was heard from her. Nothing more is known of Grimaldi's brothers and sisters, or of their descendants.

According to the Lupino tradition, young Joe lived with Marianne Lupino, and their daughter Florence took the family name and became an actress; but none of the claimants to direct descent from the Clown of Sadler's Wells has, so far as I know, produced any textual confirmation of their relationship.

APPENDIX B: BARNES AND ELLAR

OLD PANTALOON is a much more elusive and mysterious figure for the historian to chase through the labyrinth of Georgian pantomime than his servant Clown or his enemy Harlequin. When Signor Grimaldi and Delpini played the Old 'Un, he took pride of place in the harlequinade, but in the early reign of Joe Grimaldi Columbine's father or guardian was important merely as the butt or victim of the Clown, and even talented artists such as Richard Norman and Louis Bologna could not enlarge his power and glory. It seems likely that Pantaloon's costume became more or less stylized about the time that Clown's new dress was introduced, but the evidence is scanty. It is worth noting, however, that in the Covent Garden pantomime of 1801, *Harlequin Almanack*, Delpini 'bore away the palm for droll effect, by the laughable manner in which he dressed Pantaloon. Nothing could be more unlike himself, than he made the character: it must be confessed that the Italians have a stronger notion of the grotesque than plain John Bull. . . .' Whatever these innovations were, it is probable that Delpini was spurred on by the novelties of Harlequin and Clown in Drury Lane's *Harlequin Amulet* of the preceding year. But the best of all Pantaloons was James Barnes (1788–1838), who after his success in *The White Cat* — at the Lyceum in 1811 — continued to appear in this character for twenty-four years.

James Barnes was born in Enfield in 1788. Before he settled down to make a profession of old age — a state which he never reached in reality, for he died at 50 — he had experienced an unusually adventurous life. As a boy he was apprenticed to a shoemaker, but he ran away to enlist in the army. His height, however, was against him, and for a time he returned to his old trade, but he soon tired of cobbling, and made another attempt to be a soldier. Barnes made seven attempts in all to enlist, and at the seventh, after a short spell at sea, he was accepted for the 43rd Foot. Before he was twenty, however, he was back in civilian life, apparently uninjured. He found work in the travelling fairs, joined the famous showman Richardson, and by rapid stages reached the Drury Lane company, then playing at the Lyceum, in 1809. After the 1811 season at the Wells, Grimaldi took him to Covent Garden, where for some years he played 'secondary old men' and walk-ons in the legitimate repertory, until he developed his Pantaloonery at Christmas and Easter.

'If Joey Grimaldi was considered the king of clowns,' ran one obituary notice in 1838, 'surely Barnes must have been deemed the prince of pantaloons; many recollect his spare visage and small piercing pig eyes, and the unintelligible by-play chatter which garnished his humour. What playgoer does not remember his red-heeled shoes and frozen pigtail?' While still in harness, after Grimaldi's retirement, he earned the tribute that 'his Pantaloon has as decidedly the stamp of genius as . . . Grimaldi's Clown . . . his eager eyes, and real inborn love of mischief with the well kept up appearance and imbecility of age, as he hobbles about, the perfectly unconscious air with which he plunges into one dilemma after another, and his short chuckling laugh of exultation at the Clown's misfortunes, are as perfect specimens of true acting as anything that can be imagined. Every one must have noticed him, in the present Pantomime, put the bill under his feet to make him high enough to peep into the Show; it was by touches like these that he and Grimaldi used to make a Pantomime a really intellectual treat. . . .' Charles Dibdin testifies that Barnes's 'mode of playing that anomalous character, was as completely original as Grimaldi's Clown; and a Scene between Grimaldi and Barnes was the acme of pantomimical drollery'. He died destitute in 1838.

*　*　*

Tom Ellar (1780–1842), who completed the celebrated partnership of Clown, Pantaloon and Harlequin, was an unknown walk-on at the Circus in the year of *Mother Goose*, but by 1809 he was playing second Harlequin there and was then engaged as chief dancer at the Crow Street Theatre in Dublin. In 1813 he made his debut at Covent Garden as a junior Harlequin, and he did all the jumps for Jack Bologna after that veteran broke his collar-bone. In the minds of a later generation he was linked with Barnes and Grimaldi as the best of his kind. He is commemorated in an essay by E. L. Blanchard, who wrote (*The Life and Reminiscences of E. L. Blanchard*, **2**, 580–4) 'His walk was so peculiar — leaving the heel about an inch above the stage whenever he walked across — that he could always be easily recognized in any disguise he assumed. . . . As soon as he had changed he would finish his series of attitudes by spinning his head round with remarkable velocity, as if the masked face was only a whirling teetotum revolving on the centre of his frilled neck. This curious and rather unpleasant accomplishment he had learned from old Bologna, who originally adopted it to show the effect produced upon the brain by the bowl of arrack-punch he had ordered in a scene representing Vauxhall Gardens, and from which he only recovered by the columbine taking the bat and making him spin his head in the opposite direction.' A contemporary critic in 1817 described him as 'quicksilver in convulsions, or an electric eel in a St Vitus's fit.'

By 1831, however, he was being attacked by theatrical papers for his slowness and old age — 'he deserves indictment as a nuisance', said *Figaro in London*. It was not until 1836 that Blanchard, to whom Ellar had been a childhood idol, saw the Harlequin at close quarters. 'Ellar was then 56, and when he came to the prompter's box, where I was standing, looked a decrepit old man. He raised his mask to cool his face, as he came off the stage after his first trip with Columbine, and tears mingled with the beads of perspiration trickling down his cheeks. I noticed with surprise that his features were strangely discoloured, and that his skin had a bluish tint, which even stage cosmetics could not subdue. Afterwards I learned that the cast-off mistress of a chemist had a year previously administered to him, in one of her jealous moods, a mercurial poison which had thus changed his complextion, while emfeebling his frame. . . . During the run of the pantomime it was painful to note the physical exhaustion which followed even the slightest exertion of his powers. . . .'

In spite of his own hardships, he often lent money to his old friend James Barnes, and — according to Blanchard — on his deathbed Barnes said, pointing to Ellar: ' "There stands Tom Ellar, a man who has never deserted me. We have known each other since the year 1814. Many and many is the sovereign he has lent me when I did not know which way to turn. . . . He shall be the heir to all I have in the world — money, pictures, everything. God for ever bless you, my dear Tom; you have all been very kind to me, gentlemen, but Tom always stuck to me like a brother." Distant relatives, however, put in a claim; and, unable to go to law, Ellar received but a scanty bequest from the will.'

Thomas Marshall has left a moving picture of Ellar's last years: their encounter, which took place in 1839, was described by him some nine years later in *Lives of the Most Celebrated Actors and Actresses.*

Ellar told him: 'They seem to think my dancing days are over. . . . I have tried, sir, at every theatre, from Covent Garden to the Pavilion, but they all shake their heads. I was even discharged from the Standard (a place in Shoreditch, then half beer-shop, half show), because I raised from the stage a few halfpence, which were thrown to me from the gallery after I had danced one night.' He also used to frequent a pub in Shadwell, 'where I pick up a few halfpence by giving them a song or a dance, or a tune on my guitar — just as they may call for. But they are a low set, and often think they do quite enough if they ask me to take a drop of beer or gin for my pains. When they get drunk, too, they sometimes use me very roughly'.

Marshall rashly encouraged the wretched Ellar to write to Charles Dickens, asking him to write a biography: if it could be done for Joe Grimaldi, then it could be done for him. When Dickens understandably refused, Marshall reproached him for 'cold-blooded and heartless' conduct. However, he gave more practical assistance to the old Harlequin by getting him a small dole of £5 from the Covent Garden Theatrical Fund; unlike Grimaldi, he was not entitled to any regular allowance.

Ellar dragged out the rest of his days giving dancing lessons, and playing in taverns and public squares. On one occasion he was arrested, and Thackeray wrote:

> Our Harlequin Ellar, prince of many of our enchanted islands, was at Bow Street the other day in his dirty, faded, tattered motley — seized as a law breaker for acting at a penny theatre, after having well nigh starved in the streets, where nobody would listen to his guitar. No one gave him a shilling to bless him: not one of us who owe him so much.

Right at the end of his life, Ellar was engaged to play Harlequin again in a real theatre, the Adelphi; but a few days later, on 4th April, 1842, he died.

APPENDIX C

ALTHOUGH GRIMALDI completed his autobiographical notes to his own satisfaction in 1836, he soon came to realize that the bulky manuscript could not be published as it stood; and in March the following year he made a contract with a prolific journalist and playwright, Thomas Egerton Wilks, to 'rewrite, revise and correct' the memoirs. The book was to be called 'The Life and Adventures of Joseph Grimaldi', and was to be ready for publication on or before the first day of December 1837. Wilks and Grimaldi agreed to share the proceeds of its sale.[1] Two months after the agreement was signed Joe died, and Wilks had to finish the work on his own without being able to verify the material with its author. He 'applied himself to the task of condensing it throughout, and wholly expunging considerable portions, which, so far as the public were concerned, possessed neither interest nor amusement', and he also 'interspersed here and there the substance of such personal anecdotes as he had gleaned from the writer in desultory conversation'.[2] By September he had reduced the old Clown's notes to a manageable size, and he offered his manuscript to a publisher, Richard Bentley; and Bentley, who saw that there were possibilities in the work — though it was still too voluminous and was badly written — bought it and looked round for a better editor. His choice was a promising young journalist and novelist Charles Dickens, the successful author of *The Pickwick Papers* and *Oliver Twist* (which was still appearing in monthly instalments). On 29th November, Dickens signed a contract with Bentley to edit, enlarge or abridge Wilks's manuscript, into a book of no less than two volumes post octavo. Dickens was reluctant to tackle the book: 'it is very badly done, and so redolent of twaddle that I fear I cannot take it up on any conditions to which you would be disposed to accede'. These included an advance of £300 and no serial publication. Bentley, however, did 'accede', although two charges were made against the £300 (advanced on one half of the profits): production costs, and £85 'to be paid to the Executors of the late Mr Grimaldi for the material of the Memoirs dictated by Grimaldi and prepared by Mr Wilks'. The Clown's original manuscript — some four hundred closely written pages — may have remained in the possession of his executor, Richard Hughes, until its sale in 1878.

Dickens, who accepted the job as a piece of bread-and-butter hackwork, took little trouble with 'Mr Wilks's dreary twaddle', as he called it. The manuscript 'contained one or two stories told so badly, and so well worth better telling, that the hope of enlivening their dullness at the cost of very little labour constituted a sort of attraction for him.' These were such anecdotes as 'the burglary, the brother's return from sea under the extraordinary circumstances detailed, the adventure of the man with the two fingers on his left hand, the account of Mackintosh and his friends', all of which have been omitted by the present author. 'They were at that time told in the first person, as if by Grimaldi himself, although they had necessarily lost any original manner which his recital might have imparted to them', and Dickens put them into the third person. In the preface to the completed book, he explained that he had 'materially abridged' the manuscript, 'altering its form throughout, and making such other alterations as he conceived would improve the narration of the facts, without any departure from the facts themselves'. The account of Joe's first courtship, he explained, might seem unduly long, but it had undergone 'a double and most comprehensive process of abridgment. The old man was garrulous upon a subject on which the youth had felt so keenly; and as the feeling did him honour in both stages of life, the Editor has not had the heart to reduce it further.'

'Except the preface,' John Forster said, 'he did not write a line of this biography, such modifications or additions as he made having been dictated by him to his father; whom I found often in exalted enjoyment of the office of amanuensis.' This should not be taken to mean, as I myself have appeared to do, that John Dickens did the editing. Certainly, his son's hand is evident in the retelling of many anecdotes. Charles Dickens explained his approach in a letter to Dr J. A. Wilson, senior physician at St George's Hospital in London, who had treated Grimaldi and had written to the novelist offering his reminiscences of the Clown, an offer which arrived shortly before the book was sent out for review. Dickens wrote to Dr Wilson: 'I am very happy to find that I had not formed a wrong estimate of the poor fellow's character. I have merely been editing another account, and telling some of the stories in my own way, but I was much struck by the many traits of kindheartedness scattered through the book, and have given it that colouring throughout.' (*The Letters of Charles Dickens*, edited by Madeleine House and Graham Storey, 1965, **1**, 373.) To illustrate the book Bentley commissioned George Cruikshank, who had already worked in successful collaboration with Dickens on the *Sketches* and *Oliver Twist*. This great caricaturist had the advantage of acquaintance with Grimaldi, who had been the president of a drinking club — 'The Crib' — to which Cruikshank had belonged, and which met at the Myddelton's Head.

The product of all these talents was delivered to Bentley in good time, and in February 1838 it was published as *The Memoirs of Joseph Grimaldi*, edited by 'Boz', with twelve illustrations by George Cruikshank and a portrait, in two volumes, bound in pink cloth, at fourteen shillings. At first it went well, and Dickens wrote excitedly to Forster in the first week of publication that 'seventeen hundred "Grimaldis" have already been sold, and the demand increases daily'; but the demand soon dropped, as the high expectations which the book had aroused were disappointed by its reception amongst readers and in the press. Bentley, who had printed 3,000 copies, was later obliged to remainder nearly half. 'Possibly no other book,' wrote W.J. Lawrence, over-defensively, 'ever "came up smiling" under such a series of dastardly attacks; certainly none ever met with a greater variety of indiscriminative abuse. On the whole, Dickens's connection with it cannot be said to have improved its chances of longevity.' Yet there were good reasons for attacking the *Memoirs*, for the book was not only inaccurate but dull. In compressing and revising, the successive editors had squeezed much of the life out of the Clown's own story, and it seems a matter for lasting regret that Dickens did not make more of the opportunities that lay before him. At least one reviewer complained that he had apparently never seen the Clown in action. Dickens was, in fact, ten when Grimaldi retired; but he prepared a letter for *Bentley's Miscellany*, which was never published, claiming that he had been 'brought up from remote country parts' in 1819 or 1820 to see Joey, 'in whose honour I am informed I clapped my hands with great preciosity'. Moreover, he had seen Grimaldi act in 1823 (presumably in an appearance for some performer's benefit); but he was 'willing...to concede...that my recollections of his acting are, to my loss, but shadowy and imperfect. Which confession I now make publicly, and without mental qualification or reserve, to all whom it may concern.' Dickens also wrote, with defensive tartness, 'I have never heard it established as a sound proposition before, that to write a biography of a man (having genuine materials) or to edit his own notes it is essential that you should have known him.'

Even from such a man as Dickens, Joe Grimaldi was a victim of the snobbery that for so long clouded the recognition of pantomime. Why did a writer who professed 'a strong veneration for Clowns, and an intense anxiety to know what they did with themselves out of pantomime time, and off the stage' take no greater care of the reputation laid in his hands? 'As a child,' Dickens wrote in his 'Introductory Chapter' to the published *Memoirs*, 'we were accustomed to pester our relations and friends with questions out of number concerning these gentry — whether their appetite for sausages and such like wares was always the same, and if so, at whose expense they were maintained; whether they were ever taken up for pilfering other people's goods, or were forgiven by everybody because it was only done in fun; how it was they got such beautiful complexions, and where they lived; and whether they were born Clowns, or gradually turned into Clowns as they grew up.' When Dickens found that Wilks's manuscript was 'twaddle', he might have discovered some answers to these questions — had he sufficient curiosity — in the original testimony of Grimaldi himself; but he apparently preferred to botch his way through the second-hand version. Again, Dickens declared that 'Each successive Boxing-day finds us in the same state of high excitement and expectation. On that eventful day, when new pantomimes are played for the first time at the two great theatres, and at twenty or thirty of the little ones, we still gloat as formerly upon the bills which set forth tempting descriptions of the scenery in staring red and black letters, and still fall down upon our knees, with other men and boys, upon the pavement by shopdoors, to read them down to the very last line.' Yet in the *Memoirs* to which he affixed his name as editor there is no attempt to describe some of the most successful pantomimes ever produced, and he makes a merely perfunctory reference to Grimaldi's art and technique. Dickens goes on to say that 'when we first heard that Grimaldi had left some memoirs of his life behind him, we were in a perfect fever until we had perused the manuscript', and on receiving it 'we sat down at once and read every word of it'. Yet his fever apparently abated too quickly for him to consult Joe's original manuscript.

Dickens perhaps had neither the time nor the temperament to make a good editor of this story, but the 'Introductory Chapter' seems a dishonest piece of camouflage for shoddy workmanship; and although the book was later placed for Dickensians, as W.J. Lawrence says, 'within the Index Expurgatorius', it was not Dickens but Grimaldi who suffered the more from its publication, in its failure to suggest his theatrical genius. As Dr David Mayer says, 'the body of the text, assembled into a tidy Victorian moral tale, is an account of backstage and domestic life, greenroom gossip and intrigues, modest fortunes made and lost, the vicissitudes of provincial tours, crime in the vicinity of Sadler's Wells and cheerful anecdotes intended to demonstrate that Grimaldi's many personal misfortunes were balanced by moments as comic as any harlequinade'. (*Theatre Notebook*, **24**, 1.) It is one of the more depressing examples of conspicuous waste in Victorian publishing that England's greatest novelist and England's greatest Clown should have met in such a literary misalliance.

The *Memoirs* have, of course, had admirers, including D.G. Rossetti and Arthur Machen. The latter, in his preface to *Dreads and Drolls* (1926), wrote: 'I have no doubt that the Clown spoke the truth; but he had within him that love of mystery and wonder which...is the sure foundation, the only foundation of Art...This is a great gift: to be able so to tell the bare truth that it seems a magnificent lie.' One charge against Dickens for which there seems to be little justification, in my estimate, is that of plagiarism. Some of the stories in the *Memoirs* had already appeared in theatrical periodicals and reminiscences — in the memoirs of Jacob Decastro (1824), *Oxberry's Dramatic Biography* (1825/7) and the *Theatrical Inquisitor*. Henry Downes Miles, who pointed this out in his *Life of Joseph Grimaldi*, went so far as to declare that 'scarcely an anecdote' had not appeared in 'previously printed publications'. But this attack was clearly made in self-defence against the criticism that Miles himself had virtually plagiarized the *Memoirs* for his own *Life*. As Dr David Mayer said, in reviewing my edition of the *Memoirs*, 'there is some truth' in Miles's charge, but it is a matter that must await the long-delayed exhumation of the original Grimaldi MSS. Wilks may have inserted additional material; Dickens, less probably, may have done so; but there is a more plausible explanation — that Grimaldi had always liked (as we have been told) to talk about his past, when sufficiently mellowed, to friends, colleagues and fellow-drinkers. It seems scarcely surprising if, in writing his memoirs, he retold stories that journalists had heard and maybe published during the previous twenty years. Henry Downes Miles (1806–89) does not appear to be an impressive witness against Dickens. Best known as a translator of Eugene Sue's novels, he edited in later years *The Book of Field Sports*, *Miles's Modern Practical Farrier* and *The Licensed Victuallers Year Book*. In one respect only he had the advantage of Dickens: his *Life of Joseph Grimaldi* does supply, briefly but vividly, a verbal impression of the Clown at work, however indebted it may be to other authors.

Eight years after the first edition of the *Memoirs* some deficiencies of the previous editors were remedied by Charles Whitehead, who revised and annotated the book with the aid of new material collected by J.H. Burn. This new edition was published in 1846, with the original thirteen plates and a picture of Grimaldi in *Mother Goose* by De Wilde. Burn was an antiquarian of some repute: Whitehead, whom W.J. Lawrence described as an 'unfortunate genius', was a talented journalist in the same seedy, struggling world as Wilks, but in a higher class as a writer. He had originally been offered the job of writing stories around some humorous sketches by Seymour, but recommended Charles Dickens in his place and thus became foster-father of *The Pickwick Papers*. The annotation was incomplete and sometimes inaccurate, and no reference was apparently made to the original manuscript in order to clear up the many inconsistencies in the book; but, even so, the 1846 edition presented a text which was continually contradicted by the notes, exposing the unreliability of Dickens's version of Wilks's version of Grimaldi's reminiscences. Subsequent editions reproduced the 1838 text with or without the notes, and no attempt was made to reconcile the clash of evidence or to enlarge the scope of the Whitehead–Burn annotation until my own edition in 1968. (The first one-volume edition was published in 1853.)

1. This is taken from the account of the autobiography published in Henry Stevens's catalogue of 1874.
2. Introductory Chapter to the *Memoirs*.
3. The Dickensian, 1935.
4. Forster's *Life of Dickens*, I, 85 (1911 edition).
5. Introductory Chapter to the *Memoirs*.
6. *Ibid.*
7. *Ibid.*
8. Forster's Life of Dickens, I, 85. See also *Notes and Queries*, series 7, 2, 457.
9. *Notes and Queries*, series 7, 2, 34.
10. 'Grimaldiana', *Gentleman's Magazine*, February 1887.
11. Introductory Chapter to the *Memoirs*.
12. *Ibid.*
13. *Ibid.*

APPENDIX D
[A Garland for Grimaldi and the Wells]
1. BALLAD (*c.* 1780.)

Genius of Nonsense! lend thy friendly aid:
Kindly assist me, and thy fortune's made,
Instruct me in thy Mystery profound,
Things heterogene to jumble and confound;
Enraptur'd do I view thy Harlequin,
Thy Pantaloon who forces us to grin,
Thy Columbine, the envy of the Misses,
Thy Clown, at whom Nan laughs until she—;
If not too much engaged at Sadler's Wells,
Lend me awhile thy wondrous Cap and Bells,
Thy Arts ne'er fail to bring the needful Chink,
For folks can see, and laugh, who cannot think.

2. JAMES SMITH ('*Tributary Stanzas to Grimaldi, the Clown*'), c. 1813.

Facetious mime! thou enemy of gloom;
   Grandson of Momus, blithe and debonair,
Who aping Pan, with an inverted broom
   Canst brush away the cobwebs from the brows of care.
Our gallery gods immortalize thy songs,
   Thy Newgate thefts impart ecstatic pleasure;
Thou bidd'st a Jew's harp charm a Christian throng,
   A Gothic salt-box teem with Attic treasure.

When Harlequin, his charmer to regain,
   Courts her embraces in many a queer disguise,
The light of heels looks for his sword in vain—
   Thy furtive fingers snatch the magic prize.

The fabled egg from thee obtains its gold:
   Thou sett'st the mind from critic bondage loose,
Where male and female cacklers, young and old,
   Birds of a feather, hail the sacred goose.

Even pious souls, from Bunyan's durance free,
   At Sadler's Wells applaud thy agile wit,
Forget old care, while they remember thee—
   Laugh the heart's laugh, and haunt the jovial pit.

Long mayst thou guard the prize thy humour won;
   Long hold thy court in Pantomimic state;
And to the equipoise of English fun,
   Exalt the lowly and bring down the great.

3. D.J.M. ('Grimaldi.') c. 1815.

Well deem'd the chief of Thalia's school,
A thoro' Momus, yet no fool,
But such, tho' called, still I maintain
He's wise, who can thy part sustain.
All who behold must wish again,
To see thee mimic Cawdor's Thane:
Thy serious pantomimic skill,
When witness'd, every breast must fill
With pleasure, as thy wondrous art
In piercing all, like Cupid's dart;
Which, the great Kemble pleas'd to see,
Bestow'd that eulogy on thee:
That thou wert on the British stage,
First low comedian of the age;
Immortaliz'd, like his, thy name,
Enroll'd already, is thy fame,
May it increase, as years roll on,
And thou be crowned with laurels won.

4. ? 1823 (written as if by Grimaldi . . .)

Adieu to Mother Goose: adieu — adieu — adieu
   To spangles, tufted heads, and dancing limbs
Adieu to Pantaloon — to all — that drew
   O'er Christmas' 'shoulder a rich robe of whims!'

Ne'er shall old Bologna — old, alack! —
   Once he was young and diamonded all o'er,
Take his particular Joseph on his back
   And dance the matchless fling, so loved of yore.

Ne'er shall I build the wondrous verdant man,
    Tall, turnip-headed, carrot-fingered, lean;
Ne'er shall I, on the very newest plan,
    Cabbage a body; — old Joe Frankenstein.

Nor make a fire, nor eke compose a coach
    Of saucepans, trumpets, cheese and such sweet fare;
'Sorrow hath ta'en my number.' I encroach
    No more upon the chariot: — but the chair.

Gone is the stride, four steps, across the stage,
    Gone is the light vault o'er a turnpike gate!
Sloth put my legs into this tiresome cage
    And stops me for a toll — I find too late!

How Ware would quiver his mad bow about
    His rosin'd tightropes — when I flapp'd a dance.
How would I twitch the Pantaloon's good gout
    And help his fall — and all his fears enhance!

How children shriek'd to see me eat! How I
    Stole the broad laugh from aged sober folk!
Boys picked their plums out of my Christmas pie,
    And people took my vices for a joke.

Be wise (that's foolish) — troublesome! be rich —
    And oh, J.S., to every fancy stoop!
Carry a ponderous pocket at thy breech,
    And roll thy eyes, as thou wouldst roll a hoop.

Hand Columbine about with nimble hand,
    Covet thy neighbour's riches as thy own:
Dance on the water, swim upon the land,
    Let thy legs prove themselves bone of my bone.

Cuff Pantaloon, be sure — forget not this;
    As thou beat'st him, thou'rt poor, J.S., or funny!
And wear a deal of paint upon thy phiz,
    It doth boys good, and draws in gallery money.

Lastly, be jolly! be alive! be light!
    Twitch, flirt, and caper, tumble, fall and throw!
Grow up right ugly in thy father's sight!
    And be an 'absolute Joseph', like old Joe!

5. THOMAS HOOD

Joseph! they say thou'st left the stage,
To toddle down the hill of life,
And taste the flannell'd ease of age,
Apart from pantomimic strife —
Retired (for Young would call it so)
The world shut out — in Pleasant Row!

And hast thou really wash'd at last
From each white cheek the red half-moon
And all thy public Clownship cast,
To play the private Pantaloon!
All youth — all ages yet to be
Shall have a heavy miss of thee!

Thou didst not preach to make us wise —
Thou hadst no finger in our schooling —
Thou didst not 'lure us to the skies' —
Thy simple, simple trade was — Fooling:
And yet, Heav'n knows, we could — we can
Much 'better spare a better man!' . . .

But Joseph — everybody's Joe —
Is gone — and grieve I will and must!
As Hamlet did for Yorick, so
Will I for thee (tho' not yet dust),
And talk as he did when he miss'd
The kissing-crust that he had kiss'd.

Ah, where is now thy rolling head!
Thy winking, reeling, drunken eyes,
(As old Catullus would have said)
Thy oven-mouth, that swallow'd pies —
Enormous hunger — monstrous drowth! —
Thy pockets greedy as thy mouth!

Ah, where thy ears, so often cuff'd —
Thy funny, flapping, filching hands! —
Thy partridge body, always stuff'd
With waifs, and strays, and contrabands.
Thy foot — like Berkeley's Foote — for why?
'Twas often made to wipe an eye!

Ah, where thy legs — that witty pair!
For 'great wits jump' — and so did they!
Lord! how they leap'd in lamplight air!
Caper'd — and bounced — and strode away:
That years should tame the legs — alack!
I've seen spring through an Almanack!

But bounds will have their bounds — the shocks
Of Time will cramp the nimblest toes;
And those that frisked in silken clocks
May look to limp in fleecy hose —
One only (Champion of the ring)
Could ever make his Winter — Spring!

And gout, that owns no odds between
The toe of Czar and toe of Clown,
Will visit — but I did not mean
To moralise, though I am grown
Thus sad — thy going seem'd to beat
A muffled drum for Fun's retreat.

And, may be — 'tis no time to smother
A sigh, when two prime wags of London
Are gone — thou, Joseph, one — the other
A Joe: 'sic transit gloria Munden!'
A third departure some insist on—
Stage-apoplexy threatens Liston!...

Oh, how will thy departure cloud
The lamplight of the little breast!
The Christmas child will grieve aloud
To miss his broadest friend and best—
Poor urchin! what avails to him
The cold New Monthly's Ghost of Grimm?

For who like thee could ever stride!
Some dozen paces to the mile!
The motley, medley coach provide—
Or like Joe Frankenstein compile
The vegetable man complete!
A proper Covent Garden feat!

Oh, who like thee could ever drink,
Or eat — swill, swallow — bolt — and choke!
Nod, weep and hiccup — sneeze and wink?
Thy very yawn was quite a joke!
Tho' Joseph, junior, acts not ill,
'There's no Fool like the old Fool' still!

Joseph, farewell, dear funny Joe!
We met with mirth — we part in pain!
For many a long long year must go
Ere Fun can see thy like again—
For Nature does not keep great stores
Of perfect Clowns — that are not Boors!

Book list

This is a selection of sources in hard covers: other useful titles are cited in the Notes. Much of the detailed evidence in this biography is drawn not from books, but from newspapers and magazines.

ANGELO, HENRY. *Reminiscences.* 1830.

ARUNDELL, DENNIS. *The Story of Sadler's Wells.* 1965.

BAKER, HERSCHEL. *John Philip Kemble.* 1942.

BLANCHARD, E. L. *The Life and Reminiscences of E. L. Blanchard.* Edited by Clement Scott and Cecil Howard. 1891.

BOADEN, JAMES. *Memoirs of the Life of John Philip Kemble.* 1825.

BRYANT, SIR ARTHUR. *The Age of Elegance, 1812–1822.* 1950, 1952.

BUNN, ALFRED. *The Stage.* 1840.

DECASTRO, JOHN. *The Memoirs of J.D. Comedian.* 1824.

DIBDIN, CHARLES, THE ELDER. *The Professional Life of Mr Dibdin.* 1803.
     The Royal Circus Epitomized. 1784.

DIBDIN, CHARLES THE YOUNGER. *Memoirs.* Edited by George Speaight. 1956.

DIBDIN, THOMAS J. *Reminiscences.* 1827.

DISHER, MAURICE WILLSON. *Clowns and Pantomimes.* 1925.

FOOTE, HORACE. *A Companion to the Theatre.* 1829.

GILLILAND, THOMAS. *The Dramatic Mirror.* 1808.

GRIMALDI, STACEY AND W.B. *The Descent of the Family of Grimaldi of Genoa and England.* 1895.

HALLIDAY, ANDREW. *Comical Fellows* (1863) and *Mixed Sweets* (1867): part-author, with Mrs Henry Wood, Stirling Coyne, etc.

HAZLITT, WILLIAM. *Collected Works.* Edited by A.R. Waller and Arnold Glover. 1902.

HILLEBRAND, H. N. *Edmund Kean.* 1933.

HUNT, LEIGH. *Dramatic Criticism, 1808–1831.* Edited by L.H. and C.W. Houtchens. 1950.

KELLY, MICHAEL. *Reminiscences.* 1826.

MALCOLM, J. P. *Londinium Redivivum.* 1803.

MILES, HENRY DOWNES. *The Life of Joseph Grimaldi.* 1838.

MAYER, DAVID. *Harlequin in his Element. The English Pantomime 1806–1836.* 1969.

MUNDEN, T. S. *Memoirs of Joseph Shepherd Munden.* 1846.

MURRAY, D. L. *Candles and Crinolines.* 1926.

NICOLL, ALLARDYCE. *Masks, Mimes and Miracles.* 1931.

PARFAICT, C. and F. *Mémoires pour servir à l'histoire des spectacles de la foire.* 1743.

PASQUIN, ANTHONY. *The Children of Thespis.* 1786.
     The Eccentricities of John Edwin. 1791.

PINKS, WILLIAM J. *The History of Clerkenwell.* 1881.

RICHARDSON, J. *Recollections of the last half century.* 1856.

ROBSON, WILLIAM. *The Old Play-Goer.* 1854.

RYAN, RICHARD. *Dramatic Table Talk.* 1825.

SMITH, HORACE and JAMES. *Rejected Addresses.* 1812.

SMITH, JAMES. *Comic Miscellanies, in Prose and Verse.* 1841.

WELSFORD, ENID. *The Fool, his Social and Literary History.* 1935.

WEMYSS, F. C. *Theatrical Biography.* 1848.

WEWITZER, RALPH. *Green Room Gossip.*

WILKINSON, TATE. *Memoirs of his Own Life.* 1790.
     The Wandering Patentee. 1795.

WYNDHAM, H. SAXE. *Annals of Covent Garden Theatre.* 1906.

YOUNG, JULIAN CHARLES. *A Memoir of Charles Mayne Young, Tragedian.* 1871.

Index